FICTIVE KINSHIP

FICTIVE KINSHIP

Family Reunification and the Meaning of Race and Nation in American Immigration

Catherine Lee

Russell Sage Foundation

The Russell Sage Foundation

The Russell Sage Foundation, one of the oldest of America's general purpose foundations, was established in 1907 by Mrs. Margaret Olivia Sage for "the improvement of social and living conditions in the United States." The Foundation seeks to fulfill this mandate by fostering the development and dissemination of knowledge about the country's political, social, and economic problems. While the Foundation endeavors to assure the accuracy and objectivity of each book it publishes, the conclusions and interpretations in Russell Sage Foundation publications are those of the authors and not of the Foundation, its Trustees, or its staff. Publication by Russell Sage, therefore, does not imply Foundation endorsement.

Library of Congress Cataloging-in-Publication Data

Lee, Catherine.
Fictive kinship : family reunification and the meaning of race and nation in American Immigration / Catherine Lee.
pages cm. — (National poverty series on poverty and public policy)
Includes bibliographical references and index.
ISBN 978-0-87154-494-0 (pbk. : alk. paper) — ISBN 978-1-61044-803-1 (ebook)
1. Family social work. 2. Family policy—United States. 3. Refugees—Family relationships—United States. 4. Racism—United States. 5. United States—Emigration and immigration. I. Title.
HV699.L43944 2013
325.73—dc23 2013008623

The paper used in this publication meets the minimum requirements of American National Standard for Information Sciences--Permanence of Paper for Printed Library Materials. ANSI Z39.48-1992.

RUSSELL SAGE FOUNDATION
112 East 64th Street, New York, New York 10065
10 9 8 7 6 5 4 3 2 1

For my father, Kee Sup Lee, and in loving memory of my mother, Ip Cha Lee

Contents

Tables

About the Author

Catherine Lee is an associate professor in the Department of Sociology, faculty associate at the Institute for Health, Healthcare Policy, and Aging Research and the Center for Race and Ethnicity, and a graduate faculty member of the Department of Women's and Gender Studies at Rutgers University.

Acknowledgments

As an immigrant and child of immigrants in American society, I have long experienced the far-reaching impact of U.S. immigration laws and policies. As a young child, I shared my parents' sadness in our family's separation while we waited to be reunited in our new homeland. I could not understand the political or social implications of immigration law that shaped our lives. As a young scholar, I never thought that this personal history would be an important source of insight for a sociological investigation.

Many incredibly intelligent, talented, and patient scholars nurtured in me a sociological imagination that allowed me to link this personal history to a larger political and social world. Beginning at UCLA, first as an undergraduate and then as a graduate student, I had the good fortune of meeting William Roy, who seeded my interest in sociology and inspired me to pursue a life as a scholar and teacher. He taught me to think critically and to ask deeper questions while still caring about the social world and the people who inhabit it. I learned tremendously from working with him as a student and continue to grow as a sociologist and as a human being because of our friendship.

Also at UCLA, the incomparable Gail Kligman gave unselfishly of her time and energy, guiding me through a project that laid the foundation for this book. Her commitment to intellectual integrity encouraged me to think better and work harder. In addition, Laura Gómez guided my interests in race and American law early in my sociological training and has been a wonderful cheerleader for the project. The late Lucie Cheng and Shirley Hune also shepherded my intellectual development.

I could not have completed this book without the aid of many people and institutions. I am particularly indebted to the reference librarians and archivists at the National Archives in Washington, D.C., College Park, Maryland, and San Bruno, California; the Library of Congress; the Bancroft Library at the University of California–Berkeley; the libraries at UCLA; the special collections at the University of Washington; the Oregon State Archives; the Oregon Historical Society; the Multnomah County Library; the Washington State Archives; the Washington Historical Society; the American Jewish Historical Society; and special collections at Princeton University. I especially want to thank Marian Smith at the National Archives in Washington, D.C. As the senior historian for U.S. Citizenship and Immigration Services, she provided numerous research guides and sources and patiently answered my many questions about the workings of immigration law.

At various stages of research and writing, I benefited from support by UCLA, the Sexuality Research Fellowship Program of the Social Sciences Research Council, the Center for Comparative Immigration Studies, the Robert Wood Johnson Scholars in Health Policy Research Program, the University of Michigan, and Columbia University. At Rutgers University, I received generous assistance from the Department of Sociology, the Institute for Health, the Center for Race and Ethnicity, the Institute for Women, the Women of Color Scholars Initiative at the Institute for Women's Leadership, the Faculty Advancement and Reimagination Grant, and the Office of Research and Sponsored Programs. At the Russell Sage Foundation, where I was fortunate enough to be a visiting scholar, librarians Claire Gabriel and Katie Winograd provided valuable research assistance. I am also very thankful for my editor at the foundation, Suzanne Nichols, whose unwavering belief in the book and commitment to seeing it published guided me over the finish line.

At Rutgers University, I have been lucky to have so many terrific colleagues who offered caring advice and heartfelt support. I want to thank Deborah Carr, Karen Cerulo, Phaedra Daipha, Zaire Dinzey-Flores, Judith Gerson, Allan Horwitz, Vikki Katz, Norah MacKendrick, Paul McLean, David Mechanic, Ann Mische, Julie Phillips, Pat Roos, Sarah Rosenfield, Tom Rudel, Kristen Springer, and Ben Zablocki. I also want to thank Virginia Yans for her enthusiasm, careful reading, and comments on portions of the manuscript. I especially want to thank Eviatar Zerubavel, who spent countless hours discussing the project with me, offering critical questions and warm encouragement in equal measures. In addition, I have deep gratitude for the insight and good laughs from my colleague and friend Joanna Kempner, who helped me to make sense of the project time and again. Seminar fellows for the program on "Gendered Genealogies" at the Institute for Women gave useful comments on portions of the manuscript. Also, I want to thank my former undergraduate student Stephanie Murray and current and former graduate students who contributed research assistance and read chapters of the manuscript, giving thoughtful comments—Crystal Bedley, Asia Friedman, and Victoria Gonzales. I am particularly grateful for my research assistant and graduate student Ji-Hye Shin, who is a fantastic historian in her own right and whose amazing research talents, critical eye, and keen understanding of

American immigration history provided me with immeasurably important assistance in writing this book.

Over many years I have benefited from conversations and comments on the manuscript and cheerful encouragement from numerous scholars, including Leah Brooks, Nancy Foner, Paul Frymer, Ira Katznelson, Chris Kendall, Nadia Kim, Anna Law, Jennifer Lee, Stephanie Limoncelli, Mara Loveman, Susan Markens, Gina Masequesmay, Doug Massey, Aviva Meerschwam, Michael Omi, Robyn Rodriguez, Bhaven Sampat, Johanna Shih, John Skrentny, Sarah Staszak, Ann Swidler, Daniel Tichenor, Ellen Wu, and anonymous reviewers of the book. In particular, Troy Duster, Joan Fujimura, and Keith Wailoo have been amazingly giving of their time. They are inspiring models of scholar mentors. I also want to thank David Reimers for his time and deep and vast knowledge of immigration history. In addition, I thank Mae Ngai who kindly shared unpublished documents related to the Chinese Confession Program with me. My writing group colleagues, Ann Morning, Alondra Nelson, and Wendy Roth, provided invaluable feedback as they read chapters of the manuscript. For four years, we rallied one another to finish our books. Our virtual meetings to discuss our works have been intellectually stimulating and motivating.

I also want to thank my oldest friends Tammie Abel, Nathalie Brand, Monica Recinos-Tung, and June Zaelit, who sustain me with laughs, love, and lots of good food. I love them like sisters. Bessie Lee provided a home base during my numerous research trips to Washington, D.C. and took care of me so that I could focus on my archival work. My friends Susan Markens, Julie Meerschwam, and Johanna Shih have made my life in New York City more fun and much less lonely than before I knew them.

My husband, Scott Murry, had faith in my abilities and this project when I did not. He patiently and tirelessly listened to the many ups and downs of writing the book, encouraging me to not give up. I appreciate even more the reminder that he and our son Oliver provided—sometimes a picnic in the park or an afternoon at the dinosaur museum is just as important as, if not more, than any book. They are the loves of my life.

I am also thankful to the rest of the Lee and Murry families, including Cassie Won, Erin Chow, John Chow, Joon Yung Yang, Candon Murry Farias, Patricia Murry, Theresa Murry, and Alan Murry, for their support, and to Juanita Cortera, whose love and dedication to my family gave me the time and space to focus on writing this book. I am particularly grateful for the love and encouragement of my siblings, Michelle, Misa, and Patrick. Kindly, they never questioned why I was in school for so long or why this book was not yet finished. Instead, they championed my efforts. I could not have been born into a family with more generous and loving siblings.

In writing this book, I read numerous accounts of families that made tremendous sacrifices to be reunited in this country. I already knew of these deep sacrifices personally. My father arrived in the United States from South Korea in January 1976 without his wife or children. For several years, my siblings and I were separated from either our father or mother, and our parents alternately raised us as single parents.

My parents' sacrifices for a chance at a better life in the United States are too numerous to list. However, a short story about bananas illustrates the seemingly prosaic ways in which they did without so that we could have a little more and the sacrifices made for family that are so crucial to understanding the fight over family reunification. Not long after my father left South Korea for the United States, on a cold, late winter day, I asked my mother for an expensive treat—bananas. She promised to buy some, and I dreamed all day of peeling one banana after another and eating to my heart's content. My mother returned with bananas that were not the perfect, bright yellow ones that I had imagined. Instead, they were mottled brown and past their prime. I was so upset that she had not brought home a big bunch of yellow bananas that I initially failed to see that she had bought just four—one for each of the kids and none for herself. When we joined my father in the United States, bananas were everywhere—plentiful and cheap. Years later my mother explained to me that during the time he was in the United States without us, he never once ate a banana. He could not enjoy bananas, knowing that his children could not eat them with him.

These stories of doing without are not uncommon among parents, and among immigrant parents especially. My parents worked from dawn to dusk running small convenience stores without much-deserved and needed vacations so that their children could have the opportunities in life that they never did. Working through fatigue and boredom, they never complained about the hardships. Instead they gave us unconditional love and unwavering support, encouraging us to dream big and instilling in us the confidence to achieve our goals. I owe an immeasurable debt to them that I can never repay. Of course, they always said that our success and happiness were the best form of repayment. My biggest regret is that I did not finish this book before my mother passed away in 2011. My mother was an avid reader who dreamed of being a writer as a young girl, and she would have been thrilled to see my name on the cover of this book. I can never fully express my love or gratitude for my parents. They made everything worth having possible. I dedicate this book to my father, Kee Sup Lee, and to the loving memory of my mother, Ip Cha Lee.

Note on Terminology

I am quite mindful of the significance and role of language in shaping debate and signifying meaning in political discourse, particularly on topics as heated as immigration. Immigrant activists have criticized the use of terms such as "illegal alien," "illegal immigrant," and "illegal immigration" as dehumanizing and racist. Some activists have advocated the use of "undocumented" in place of "illegal." I am sensitive to these concerns.

Unfortunately, a simple replacement with the word "undocumented" raises a number of problems. Most importantly, it is not fully accurate. For example, many immigrants enter the United States with legal documents but simply overstay their visas. Other immigrants may have documents, but they are false or forged. Also, an "undocumented" status is only meaningful in a historical era in which travelers are documented. The documentary requirements for would-be immigrants during the long period I cover in the book varied over time.

Where appropriate, I use the term "unauthorized" to refer to immigrants and immigration whose legal status would be questioned or denied by the state. However, I also use the phrases "illegal immigrant" and "illegal immigration" in places where such usage helps to connote the sentiment expressed by actors in the given example. Likewise I use the term "undocumented" where it is appropriate.

Finally, I argue for an ideational approach to understanding policymaking and thus believe wholeheartedly that concepts such as race and gender are socially constructed. These words, along with racial and ethnic terms, are not placed in quotes as a stylistic preference and for simplicity's sake.

Chapter 1

Introduction: "Family Reunification Has Been the Cornerstone of Our Immigration Policy"

In 1903, Rihei Onishi, an immigrant from Japan, began a rice farm in Pierce, Texas. He achieved enough economic success that by 1906 several dozen men from Japan had joined him in Texas, leasing land from him. In 1909, when Onishi went to Japan for a visit, six of his tenant farmers asked him to bring their fiancées and wives back to the United States. As "settled agriculturists," summoning their wives, Onishi's tenant farmers were allowed to bring over these women.[1] Their success in reuniting with their wives was fortunate, and perhaps unexpected, for their request was made following the Gentlemen's Agreement of 1907, which banned further immigration of Japanese laborers. It was also a period of growing anti-immigrant attitude and the passage of ever more exclusionary policies. Within a few short years, Congress would deny entry to Asian immigrants—first through passage of the Asiatic Barred Zone Act of 1917, which used a language of longitudes and latitudes to deny entry to anyone from Asia, then through the Immigration Act of 1924, which excluded anyone unqualified for citizenship. The Supreme Court declared Asians ineligible for citizenship in Takao Ozawa v. the United States (1922) and United States v. Bhagat Singh Thind (1923).[2] Despite increased hostility toward immigration, men like those on Onishi's land who were already here used available family provisions in the immigration policy to bring their spouses and children to the United States as well in an effort to settle more permanently.

Nearly one hundred years later, in 2006, the *New York Times* reported the fourteen-year effort of Isaac Owusu to be reunited with the four sons he left behind in Ghana. After becoming a citizen in 2002, Owusu petitioned to have his sons join him in the United States, a right afforded to him as a naturalized citizen. When given the opportunity to prove his familial claims by taking a DNA test, Owusu confidently swabbed the inside of his cheek. Test results quickly dashed his hopes for reuniting with his children when government officials notified him that the test could verify paternity for his oldest son only. With these test results, Owusu learned that his deceased wife had been unfaithful and that he was not the biological father of his three younger sons. The government permitted the admission of his oldest son, but the younger three were denied entry. The only recourse Owusu had was to petition for the younger boys' admission as his stepsons.

Genetic tests rendered null and false the affective ties of the familial bond between father and sons that the Owusu family had unequivocally known for nearly two decades.[3] Today there are broad legal provisions—the most expansive and inclusive in American immigration history—that permit family reunification for permanent residents, and particularly citizens like Owusu. There are nevertheless hurdles for exercising such rights, and in Owusu's case DNA test results failed to provide the definitive proof of familial ties necessary for his effort to reunite his family.

The experiences of Onishi's men and Isaac Owusu highlight the often unrecognized but essential role of family reunification in periods of both exclusion and expansion in American immigration policy, which has included informal and formal family reunification provisions. Over this long history, family reunification has been a critical method for making a claim for entry, formulating immigration policy, and regulating immigration in the United States. From the mid-1800s to today, the United States has had some semblance of family reunification as a part of its immigration policy. Prior to 1924, family reunification provisions were briefly in place for Chinese merchants and Japanese laborers. In addition, a family preference system existed within the national origins quota system enacted in 1924. In 1965 Congress replaced national origins policy with one favoring family reunification, and today about 70 percent of all visas for legal immigration are reserved for family reunification. In exercising these family unity provisions, Onishi's tenant farmers, Owusu, and others like them have sought to identify and prove themselves not only as legitimate families but also as legitimate members of the nation, worthy of inclusion in the national fabric.

This book examines the centrality and significance of family reunification—provisions aimed at preserving or supporting family unity during or following migration—to the development of American immigration policy and the construction of race and nation. Although today the importance of family reunification to immigration policy is not questioned, its history—beyond the contemporary relevance—is not fully recognized. What family means and how it should be preserved in immigration policy are crucial to the ways we celebrate our immigrant history, declare a national identity, and debate immigration reform. Such discussions go beyond the simple categories of spouses, children, parents, and siblings; eligibility rules for immigration sponsorship; and immigration policy's structure, function, and role in shaping society. The meaning of family and family reunification is central not only to the formulation of immigration policy but also to understanding the impact of immigration itself on the meaning of nation.

In numerous ways, politicians remind the public of this unique significance of family reunification. Thus, in 2007, arguing in favor of a proposed bill, the Secure Borders, Economic Opportunity, and Immigration Reform Act, the late Sen. Edward Kennedy (D-MA) explained: "The plan maintains that more than a majority of future immigration will be based on family ties. That couldn't be more important. Family reunification has been the cornerstone of our immigration policy for decades and under this proposal it still will be."[4] Senator Kennedy referred to the family provisions outlined in the legislation that he helped pass in 1965—the Hart-Celler Act—which ended national origins policy and made it much more possible for American citizens and resident aliens to sponsor family members. In calling family reunification a "cornerstone," Senator Kennedy did what so many other politicians and even immigration scholars have done: he heralded the legislative prioritizing of family reunification as a modern accomplishment in U.S. immigration policy to be celebrated as part of the triumvirate liberal political achievement of the 1960s that included the passage of the Civil Rights Act of 1964 and the Voting Rights Act of 1965.

There are certainly many reasons to believe that family reunification has been hugely consequential and important, especially in the last four decades. As table 1.1 shows, family-sponsored immigration has been a constant in American immigration history. For example, nearly 125,000 immediate relatives of U.S. citizens immigrated between 1925 and 1930, a period when family immigration represented over 7 percent of total immigration to the United States. Since passage of the 1965 Immigration and Nationality Act (the Hart-Celler Act), these preferences have been an important and perhaps *the* central pathway to legal immigration to the United States. In 1970 and in 1980, 25 percent and 40 percent of legal permanent immigration resulted from family reunification, respectively, and in the 1990s about 55 percent used the family preference for immigration. In the decade from 2001 to 2010, family reunification represented nearly two-thirds of total documented immigration to the United States. When family members of skilled immigrants and lottery winners are included, family reunification immigration represents an even larger percentage of total legal immigration.[5]

Family reunification has also altered the racial and ethnic make-up of the United States. For much of U.S. history, Europe was the dominant continental source of immigrants. Since 1965, however, the majority of family-sponsored immigrants have come from Asia and Latin America rather than Europe. Furthermore, for the first time since the United States began counting immigrants in 1819, immigrants from Africa outnumbered

Table 1.1 Family Immigration as a Percentage of Total Immigration to the United States, 1925 to 2011

Year	Immediate Relatives of U.S. Citizens		Family-Sponsored Preferences		Family Immigration Total	
1925 to 1930	124,609	(7.1%)	—		124,609	(7.1%)
1931 to 1940	91,670	(17.3)	—		91,670	(17.3)
1941 to 1950	185,604	(17.9)	—		185,604	(17.9)
1951 to 1960	284,929	(11.3)	—		284,929	(11.3)
1961 to 1968	289,667	(11.2)	—		289,667	(11.2)
1969 to 1970[a]	139,238	(19.0)	184,890	(25.3%)	324,128	(44.3)
1971 to 1980	1,175,449	(26.2)	1,330,325	(29.6)	2,505,774	(55.8)
1981 to 1990	1,996,741	(27.2)	2,128,872	(29.0)	4,125,613	(56.2)
1991 to 2000	2,709,030	(29.8)	2,257,218	(24.8)	4,966,248	(54.6)
2001 to 2010	4,684,583	(44.6)	2,076,038	(19.8)	6,760,621	(64.4)
2011	453,158	(42.7)	234,931	(22.1)	1,062,040	(64.8)

Source: Author's compilation based on "Immigrants Admitted Under the Quota System: 1925–1968" and "Immigrants Admitted Under the Preference System: 1966–1991," in Carter et al. (2006); U.S. Department of Homeland Security, *Yearbooks of Immigration Statistics: 1996–2011.*

[a]The Hart-Celler Act became effective June 20, 1968.

Europeans from 2008 to 2011.[6] As I discuss further in chapter 5, these new patterns result from chain migration: as authorized immigrants arrive on work-related visas, as refugees, or as sponsored family members, they can seed new immigration through family sponsorship; over time, for instance, an immigrant from Taiwan or Nigeria can sponsor a spouse or sibling, who in turn can sponsor additional family members. The eventual effect of chain migration through family sponsorship can be quite significant. For example, at the end of the Vietnam War about one million immigrants arrived from the Vietnam region, mostly as refugees. By 2011, only 34,157 immigrants from Vietnam arrived, but of this number, 19,491 immigrants were family-sponsored under the preference system and another 12,551 came as immediate family members of U.S. citizens (with quota-exempt status).[7] The seeding effect of family-sponsored immigration can multiply as immigrants who previously might not have been eligible for family reunification are given fully authorized status. Thus, for example, a pathway to permanent resident or citizenship status offered to the estimated 11.5 million unauthorized immigrants as part of a new reformed immigration policy could lead to the sponsorship of millions more family members.[8]

With these changes in immigration patterns, particularly the rise of

Asian and Latin American countries as major immigrant-sending countries, family reunification is shaping U.S. national identity and the meaning of race and ethnicity. Indeed, some immigration scholars argue that there has already been a shift in the "color line." They claim that for much of U.S. history and prior to 1965, the line of significance between racialized groups lay between whites and nonwhites. Immigrants who arrived sought whiteness as a way to integrate into a racialized society in which whiteness was associated with privilege and power. Irish immigrants' efforts to "achieve" whiteness and Asian immigrants' claims to naturalization rights as "white" or "Caucasian" are just two of many examples.[9] Since the immigration reform of 1965, as most new immigrants have arrived from Asia and Latin America the line of racialized significance arguably has come to lie increasingly between blacks and nonblacks. Newly arriving immigrants from Asia and Latin America, who may not expect to be counted as white, seek privilege in the racialized hierarchy in the United States by distancing themselves from blacks and blackness.[10] Increasing rates of intermarriage between new immigrants and native-born whites and the adoption of a multiracial identification by their children further blur the earlier white/nonwhite color line, helping to shift it to a new black/nonblack line.

Given all of these important developments following the Hart-Celler Act of 1965, it is easy to see the seeming centrality of family provisions in contemporary immigration and to understand the public pronouncements establishing family reunification as the cornerstone piece to immigration policy today as a uniquely modern, liberal legislation. Family reunification has been active for far longer than this most recent policy period, however, and unfortunately this nearsighted lens limits our understanding of the significance of family reunification in American immigration policy and its continuing role in shaping an American national identity. Although the rates of family reunification today may dwarf the use of such provisions in earlier periods, previous family unity preferences were nevertheless consequential for the immigrants who were able to use them to reunite with their families and settle here permanently. For some immigrant groups, these preferences spelled the difference between the formation of a dwindling bachelor society and a viable second generation with birthright American citizenship.

Widening the historical focus provides evidence of continuing family reunification provisions since the beginning of immigration control in the mid-1800s, including during periods of exclusionary policies. American immigration policy has steadfastly preserved some semblance of family reunification for over 130 years, even though such provisions may have sometimes appeared contradictory to the policy goals of immigrant exclusion, particularly efforts directed at racial control during the period of extreme xenophobia of the 1920s. Although contemporary immigration policies are officially ethnically and racially neutral, there were no such claims earlier. These racially exclusionary policies could have denied entry to racially undesirable family members, but instead they included family unity provisions. For example, Chinese merchants were permitted to bring over their wives and children with passage of the Chinese Exclusion Act of 1882.

In essence, family reunification provisions are counterintuitive and in conflict with the intent of immigration restriction and efforts to maintain the racial status quo during periods of exclusion. The potential reproductive features of immigrant families are always possible threats to preserving an existing racialized national identity. So why did federal immigration legislation include family unity provisions, even when the objective was immigrant exclusion? What did this seeming reverence for family mean for the construction of a national identity? What role has family and family reunification played in the development of American immigration policy?

To answer these questions *Fictive Kinship* examines meaning construction around family, race, and nation in immigration policy. In so doing, the book demonstrates that family reunification was a feature of immigration policy long before the passage of the 1965 act. Furthermore, the book explains that family reunification is not simply the physical uniting of immigrant family members. Family reunification is an expression of what constitutes a legitimate family, which families should be united, and whether such families should be allowed to join the nation. In short, family reunification has been part of what I call *family ideation*—a conceptualization of what family means, constitutes, and features in terms of its idealized characteristics, such as gender or sexual norms, class ideals, and racial or ethnic attributes.

Questions related to meaning construction get at the heart of how and why certain constructs resonate and help shape policy development. Relatedly, this book explores how the very foundation of family reunification—family—is a fictive construct, much like the entities that it is purportedly supposed to strengthen—the nation and the racial or ethnic collective unit. The word "fictive" may imply for some readers that the construct is false or not real and that there exists a truly natural or real familial construct. This is not the case. Instead, all forms of kin relations are partly putative. Kinship that is constituted in nation, race, and family relies on claims that seek to blur the boundaries between social and supposedly biological relationships. Political commitments and cultural traditions shape biological claims about Jewish origin, for example, or assertions of a multicultural or French Canada.[11] Thus, by using the word "fictive," I wish to highlight the particularly constructed, invented, and contested nature of concepts that tie or bind such connections.[12]

An analysis of family ideation uncovers and explains seemingly unexpected or puzzling outcomes, such as the passage of family reunification provisions during periods of exclusion as well as increasingly more punitive measures against families during immigration expansion. The association between immigration and family does not necessarily elicit a particular policy or political response. Thus, for example, public declarations of support for family do not automatically equate with actual policy endorsement for families, including support for their efforts to reunite or for their economic and social well-being. Instead, such hortatory language is partly discursive posturing to uphold the central values of American culture, which include family unity and strength, and it is also storytelling that stresses the importance of these values.[13] Increasingly in the contemporary era, these discursive moves are made in the context of efforts to limit or undo the progressive gains of the civil rights era, including the immigration reforms of the Hart-Celler Act. To better understand these developments, *Fictive Kinship* evaluates the meaning and significance of family and family reunification in the *making* of immigration policy rather than simply asking why a particular policy developed. I do not seek to provide a history of why each major immigration act was legislated—especially not the complex and important history of refugee and displaced persons legislation, although I do refer to some of these acts throughout the book.

Immigration stakeholders—including politicians, immigration officials, intellectuals, business leaders, religious and ethnic organizations, and immigrant group advocates—have invoked family and family reunification in efforts to make sense of the challenges wrought by immigration. Through family ideation, immigration stakeholders constructed racialized, gendered, and class meanings and attached them to immigrants and immigration policy. Their talk of family allowed them to evaluate whether or not immigrants were indeed "like one of the family" and could be integrated into the larger family of the nation.[14] In the process, they helped to create immigration policy that was both exclusionary and expansive, both generally and with respect to family reunification.

In rethinking the meaning and significance of family and family reunification, *Fictive Kinship* shifts the unit of analysis in immigration policy research toward family. Too often, studies of immigration policy focus on individuals or on particular ethnic or racial groups, partly because of the emphasis that policymakers and scholars put on a neoliberal model of migration in which an individual moves across borders, motivated by economic opportunities for higher wages and a better quality of life.[15] An interest in immigrant exclusion has also trained researchers' eyes on ethnic or racial groups as the unit of analysis.[16] This orientation is understandable given the history of racial and ethnic exclusion in the United

States.[17] However, as this book shows, American immigration policy has directed the migration of families as well, and that migration has not always directly or consistently mapped onto racial exclusion: some families of racially excludable groups have had the opportunity to enter the country. Furthermore, an understanding of the outcome of ethnic or racial exclusion in policy does not necessarily derive from an analysis of the ethnic or racial group. That is, understanding the processes of racial or ethnic exclusion requires an understanding of racism and race-making processes, not an analysis of the racial group itself.[18] The entry and settlement efforts of racial and ethnic groups have been regulated through families and in the process have helped to construct the very meaning of race or ethnicity.

Researchers have shown that regulating immigration is crucial to the construction of race and nation in the United States.[19] I argue that the meaning of family and immigrant groups and the ways in which immigration stakeholders conceptualize the nation vis-à-vis these constructs are critical for how change is effected and implemented. For example, discussion of immigrants in familial terms—as assimilable, or as being "like one of the family"—attaches meaning that makes policies of inclusion or exclusion possible. Thus, I argue that immigration stakeholders have invoked family and engaged in family ideation to construct immigration policy in an effort not only to control immigration but also to shape a racialized national identity. Talking about family—regardless of whether or not family reunification provisions are extended—has allowed both immigration advocates and exclusionists to promote their ideas about the meaning of race and nation in immigration policy. Immigration policy is not simply about the control of the size and diversity of the population but also about articulating a particular vision of nationhood or a national identity.[20]

FAMILY AND OTHER KINSHIPS

Why do immigration stakeholders focus on family? In general, immigration involves the breaching of boundaries, both physical and symbolic borders—that is, geographical boundaries and ideas about who should be included in the nation. New, foreign, and perhaps polluted elements are introduced into the national body through immigration. The extent to which these new elements are assimilable depends on how "like us" the new immigrants are. Can they be incorporated? Can they be "like one of the family"? How might new immigrants alter or even threaten our families? Can our families be protected? Family often serves as a surrogate for the nation in these questions. Immigration stakeholders actively and subconsciously think about, create, and act upon the meanings that result from efforts to answer these questions.

More specifically, immigration stakeholders focus on family, because families enable state-building activities, one of which is immigration control. Physically, families settle lands, reproduce the next generation, and perform the labor necessary for economic development and expansion. However, state-building extends beyond physical settlement. As much as the state serves families by allowing for reunification and settlement through its immigration policies, families in turn serve the state. Successful settlement and expansion often require the construction and maintenance of a national identity that ties the physical expanse of land to the symbolic meanings of origin, community, and a shared future—sometimes far beyond the immediate reach of a central government or a culturally hegemonic authority. Families do the crucial work of making these linkages, which embody the putative claims of the nation and implicate proper gender roles, sexual propriety, class ideals, and racial identity. In addition, families pass narratives about these connections from one generation to the next. In this sense—controlling immigration through family is a way of creating a national identity, exemplifying the argument that immigration control is both a state- and nation-building activity.

Immigration stakeholders, especially politicians, also invoke family in part because such talk confers legitimacy on the state's regulation of public and private relations. Susan Gal and Gail Kligman write that talk about reproduction is coded rhetoric about state actors' legitimacy. For example, in the aftermath of the breakup of the Soviet bloc, political leaders talked about reproduction, including abortion rights and access to contraception, as a way to make a rightful claim to govern.[21] Talk of family as the site of reproductive decisions and regulations becomes talk about political legitimacy.

What is it about family that makes meaning constructions possible? Most importantly, family provides a narrative structure—one with a plot or story line about members, their roles and functions, and their purpose. It is a ready-made narrative that has been told for hundreds of generations.[22] Of course, the specific details of the narrative are murkier than any one narrator may know or concede. Nevertheless, family's narrative structure provides a way for evaluating how we are related and what those relations connote. That is part of the power of a family narrative: its plot lines and significance are diverse, and their meanings are open to varying interpretations. Thus, for example, we may turn to family to understand how individual members provide protection or nurture. If, when, and how these tasks are accomplished are less relevant questions than the one about who makes up the family. From the earliest origin stories etched on cave walls to modern-day genetic analyses, which purport to identify both our ancestral past and degrees of contemporary relatedness, efforts to tell a story about family demonstrate the desire to understand the substance of relation and the attendant roles—as illustrated by the myriad of studies on family genealogies and even by DNA testing in search of ancestral roots.[23] As such, narratives about family are one kind of story we tell to explain who we are, how we are connected, and how we should move forward into the future.

Stories of relatedness or connection and claims about who among us is indeed "like one of the family" all help to confer both privileges and responsibilities. This is true not only in the most intimate parent-child relations but in the distant fraternal orderings of a given racial or ethnic group or a nation that ethno-racial leaders or nationalists may declare to be rightful stand-ins for the intimate family. For each of these forms of relations, we ask how we are tied to one another and what such attachments mean. This seeming interchangeability among family, race or ethnicity, and nation suggests that the three constructs are conceptually quite similar. It also explains why family's narrative structure can be so powerful in generating emotions around immigration control. Talk of regulating family reunification rises to larger issues about race and nation.

The strength and malleability of family's narrative structure in a policy arena—particularly immigration—reside in the fact that family, race, and nation all have similar structural forms as types of kinship, which helps to elide one construct for another. There is no universal rule about blood, law, or affection that defines these constructs to be the same. As the anthropologist David Schneider argues, kinship is a cultural system of meanings.[24] Nevertheless, drawing partly from his ideas, I suggest family, race, and nation can be explored as forms of kinship that have two important elements: "relationship" (ties or connection) and "natural substance" (blood or genes), both of which become foundations or codes for conduct.[25] The "natural substance" is part of the putative claims-making and an "invention," although nationalists or family members may tout it as somehow more real when it is genetic or biological, such as in Isaac Owusu's case.[26]

Efforts to evaluate these elements of kinship, such as DNA testing, are often part of an elaborate system aimed at shaping codes of conduct, which can dictate both action (such as determining the financial support of a parent for a child or determining fitness for enlistment in the military during times of war) and emotion (the sense of responsibility, duty, or pride undergirding the affective ties that may provide the rationale or justification for such actions). Thus, what kinship tells us—how we are related and what our relationships are made of (the "natural substance")—is no small matter. It helps to explain, for example, what makes people love, die, or kill for nations.

The nationalist appeal rests in part on the notion that the nation is "conceived as a deep, horizontal comradeship."[27] However, people also envision nations as "imagined communities" in which members can conceptualize links to one another across time and generations in addition to space. These preternatural linkages across time suggest that nations are not just horizontal orderings but are vertical as well. Origin stories and royal family genealogy trees also assume this vertical relatedness.

The gendered work that men and women perform makes it possible to link family and nation, both vertically and generationally: not only do men and women reproduce the next vertical link, but this gendered work can quite literally transform the family into the nation. This is most apparent in studies of reproductive policies and the state or in ethnic conflict and sexual violence. Thus, for example, in Nicolae Ceausescu's Romania, anti-abortion and pro-natal policies were intended to secure the continued birthing of the nation.[28] During ethnic conflicts in Bosnia and Croatia in the 1990s and in Rwanda in 1994, genocidal and ethnic cleansing programs encouraged the rape of women of the ethnic enemy group because the children they bore would help to blur ethno-national claims as well as familial lines.[29] These examples highlight the importance of the work that gendered bodies perform under patriarchal and racialized notions of sexuality, nationalism, and reproduction, which help to obfuscate the lines of division between family and nation.

I argue that the work performed by gendered bodies rests on several important features of family and nation that are crucial for understanding immigration control and family reunification. First, to the extent that the rules dictating reproduction at the level of the family can be extended to the nation as a whole, family is the fundamental social unit of the nation. As explained earlier, the continuance of the nation assumes the traditional and biological (albeit often mythical) continuation of some groups (often ethno-racial or religious) through the passing of generations via the family. Thus, rules that maintain a family's racial purity are similar to efforts by the nation to limit contamination by a foreign or immigrant group.[30] Second, social and biological production and reproduction of the nation are constituted and shaped by practices of patriarchy and patrilineality. This is true in part because, with the nation defined by women's sexuality, the confinement and protection of women's sexual virtue help to govern the boundaries of the nation.[31] This is understandable when we remember that political and intellectual elites often conceive the nation as feminine, as being embodied by women, while they construct the state in masculine terms.[32] Therefore, limiting the extension of women's bodies through their reproductive work is crucial for preserving the nation, as I argue in chapter 3. Third, the nation as the family writ large is the result of rules and regulations that define the boundaries between insiders and outsiders. The actual embodied project often entails the regulation of some groups' sexual practices and reproduction but not others'. Such regulations have the effect of constructing or reiterating notions of racialized differences.

To this extent, we can recognize how immigration serves as the racial fault line for nation-building.[33] That is, although immigration makes useful and often necessary labor contributions to the nation, immigrant "foreigners" threaten ideals about who ought to be legitimate representatives of the nation. The meaning of the nation has to be physically and symbolically reproduced, which is possible only through the physical bodies of gendered and racialized persons.

A FAMILY AND IDEATIONAL APPROACH TO UNDERSTANDING POLICYMAKING

Increasingly, scholars are calling for greater attention to how meaning is constructed and deployed in policymaking.[34] Of course, a focus on meaning and the role of ideas in understanding social change dates much further back.[35] It is a cultural emphasis in general and a cognitive approach more specifically.[36] The cultural emphasis recognizes the importance of culture as a kind of "tool kit," while the cognitive approach focuses on how a tool kit shapes action or how we make sense of it.[37] In positing the relevance of meaning construction in explaining policy development, I am not arguing against the insights offered by other perspectives. Rather, the ideational approach, I argue, works in conjunction with other theories of policy change, most notably works on agenda-setting, interest group politics, and historical institutionalism.

In agenda-setting, for example, Deborah Stone notes that both the particular characteristics of the actors involved (such as bureaucrats, interest groups, or professionals) and the specific nature of the problem or issue (whether it is old, new, or recurring) can advance or halt policy attention and action on a matter.[38] Agenda-setting can also focus, however, on the use of language and symbols and their ability to convey meanings of significance or urgency.[39] As Stone explains, this social construction defines the social problem. For example, phrases like "anchor baby" and images of a fractured border control system that include trampled fences help to evoke strong emotions, especially the fear that the current immigration system is broken and that unauthorized immigrants are taking advantage of and taxing American society.[40] Thus, from this perspective, I draw upon the importance of recognizing how meaning is conveyed through particular language and symbols.[41]

The interest group politics perspective, especially in studies of immigration, seeks to explain crucial shifts in policy change over time by arguing that political and social groups coalesce around common goals or interests. Thus, for example, the coalition of immigrant restrictionists in the mid-1800s, which included moral reformers, labor unions, race scientists, and Southern and Western politicians, succeeded in passing the Chinese

Exclusion Act.[42] Similarly, interest in the free flow of labor has motivated a coalition of business groups, agricultural employers, and West Coast politicians to push for expanded temporary labor migration policies, such as those for farmworkers.[43] I rely upon insight from this research to provide crucial context for immigration policymaking.

Historical institutionalist studies of immigration explain policy change by examining the institutional context of interests and power.[44] This institutionalist perspective increasingly acknowledges the importance of ideas and meaning construction. For example, the discrediting of racial eugenics and the contribution of the black civil rights movement created a legacy of both institutional and ideological conditions that shaped later immigration policy.[45] These institutionalist investigations highlight particular meaning construction (for example, the extent to which a minority group's endeavors that followed black civil rights efforts were similarly "like blacks" in the civil rights movement) or the social construction of targeted groups (such as Mexican immigrants identified as illegal and undeserving) and demonstrate how ideas constitute institutional organization, power, and interests.[46] Despite these strengths, these studies of immigration policy are still unable to explain the empirical and theoretical significance of family and family reunification, including the unexpected findings of family reunification provisions during periods of racial exclusion. Simply stated, these other studies and perspectives neither explain nor anticipate the importance of family in American immigration policy.

I propose an ideational approach to understand how immigration policy evolved over the years from the mid-1800s to the early 2000s. In looking at immigration stakeholders' family ideation, I examine the ways in which they spoke and wrote about family and its constitutive elements. By invoking family, immigration stakeholders have offered a story about who we are, how we are related, and what roles we play or functions we fulfill. Family is layered with values and assumptions and makes available the building blocks for meaning construction. Family's narrative structure with its readily accessible plot and kinship elements of ties and natural substance make the communication of complex ideas easier. The ready set of symbols, meanings, and reference points associated with family allows actors to use family as a metaphor or synecdoche for related kinship constructs such as race or nation.[47] Family can also serve as a frame for interpreting how such structures operate.[48]

There is a large and growing literature on narrative analysis and the importance of storytelling in understanding social and political change.[49] These studies show that narratives can play a forceful role in not only explaining but also enacting political change. Despite these strengths of narrative analysis, I do not employ it exclusively. Methodologically, it might have been easier to stick with one specific ideational approach—studying narratives, for instance, by tracing them across policy change and over time. However, as with all forms of political change, the story of immigration policymaking is a complicated one with actors who do not invoke cultural repertoires in a consistent manner. When immigration stakeholders talk about family and family reunification, they do not always follow a traditional narrative structure with a plot line that has a beginning, middle, and end. Sometimes they offer snippets of these stories, or they conjure evocative images through the use of family as metaphor. Other times they use family as a frame to interpret a particular issue. It does not make sense to privilege narratives over these latter examples. They all explain *how* family ideation occurs.

How actors talk about family—how they engage in family ideation—creates opportunities for change by introducing ideas. Immigration stakeholders talk about family as a form of strategy to convince through rhetoric, provide rationale for a stated position, and make sense of new or unfamiliar conditions for themselves and their audience. In advocating an ideational approach, I am not arguing that family ideation alone can explain a particular policy development. Context matters—particularly the institutional arrangements of power, interests, and resources that make storytelling and discursive action possible.[50] Family ideation is a neglected part of the social mechanism that explains policy development.

I have documented how family ideation shapes immigration policymaking by tracing the historical development of American immigration policy. Because I am interested in policymaking, I focus on actors and institutions that shaped or were in a position to affect immigration policy, including politicians, academics and other intellectuals, labor organizations, business groups, and immigrant or ethnic group advocates. Family reunification is a provision in official immigration policy. Thus, I conducted content analysis of the extensive formal debates and documents surrounding legislative efforts. However, ideational work also includes actors' efforts to make sense of the unfamiliar, which can be done in private dialogue or discussion. Therefore, I also carried out content analysis of archives of personal papers and official collections of the key players involved. I researched over two dozen archival collections and systematically researched legislative and other government documents related to all major immigration acts and legislative proposals from 1875 through 2007. A more detailed discussion of data and methods is available in the appendix.

OVERVIEW OF THE BOOK

What the family is, means, or does can be examined sociologically and addressed socially or politically. That is, as social scientists, we can study family as a lived social practice or family-related social policy such as welfare support for single mothers or subsidized health care for poor families, which can affect how people structure their families. Politicians can enact policies to address the practices of a family or to encourage it to act in some new way. Thus, the discourse surrounding policymaking and the policies themselves are forms of normative claims-making and positive law. That is, both discursive and legislative acts are attempts to regulate and sanction particular meanings of family.

In the second chapter, I outline what family means sociologically and for policy purposes. Drawing from studies of policymaking, nationalism, and race, feminist accounts of gender and state, and sociological and anthropological investigations of family, I discuss how family has been defined and researched. I then provide an overview of what family means for the purposes of immigration policy, discussing the provisions that dictate family reunification in current policy. I also offer statistics on the use of these provisions over time and their impact on the demographic trends of immigration to the United States. This chapter also provides useful references on topics related to family reunification that I do not pursue in depth in the book but that are nevertheless important to the history of American immigration policy. These studies include historical accounts of refugee or displaced persons and of immigrant families.

Chapters 3 through 5 examine the implementation of family reunification in immigration policy. Chapter 3 asks whether there was family reunification prior to the modern era and uncovers family provisions during a period of increasingly exclusionary policies. Even in the most draconian, anti-immigrant laws, provisions for family unity were made, or at least seeming reverence for the preservation of family was expressed. Thus, family reunification provisions were included in immigration policy from the first federal immigrant exclusion policy, the Page Act of 1875, to the Immigration Act (National Origins Act) of 1924. In evaluating whether new immigrants were assimilable and "like one of the family"—that is, whether they could be incorporated into the national body—immigration officials, politicians, intellectuals, and moral reformers regulated immigration by engaging in family ideation and attached meanings of assimilability, racial fitness, and gender and sexual propriety. In these discursive efforts, they stated a seeming reverence for family as they found ways to extend family unity provisions *and* enact exclusionary policies.

I demonstrate this by first comparing the initially varying treatment of Chinese and Japanese immigrants. While the Chinese Exclusion Act of 1882 banned Chinese laborers and effectively denied family reunification efforts for most Chinese immigrants already in the United States, Japanese immigrants in the United States could call for their family members to join them following the 1907 Gentlemen's Agreement. This contrast in treatment invoked different racial, gender, and class ideals of family. Exclusionists argued that the Chinese were sources of contamination that threatened the purity of the American family and the nation. In contrast, Japanese immigrants enjoyed ethnic differentiation rooted in part in Japan's geopolitical might. At first, immigration officials, politicians, and public commentators approved their more appropriate family arrangements. However, as Japanese immigration increased, and as Japanese women's fecundity raised concern, exclusionists claimed that the Japanese attempt to "colonize" the United States was also a threat. Thus, in efforts to regulate them, politicians, intellectuals, and others talked about family as a way to attach meanings of racial contamination in the bodies and reproductive work of Chinese and Japanese immigrants. Nonetheless, these discursive actions also provided a liminal space for some immigrants as immigration stakeholders lauded the importance of families, and in particular a man's right to home and hearth. Such rhetoric enabled immigrants who possessed appropriate class and gender characteristics, including some Chinese and Japanese immigrant men, to lay claim to family reunification. Family ideation created unexpected opportunities for family reunification.

In the second half of the chapter, I show how this liminal space opened as politicians expressed gendered ideals of family and patriarchal ideas of coverture—the Anglo-American legal tradition that placed a woman's legal status under that of her husband. I trace the history and role of coverture in determining women's status and in permitting family unity provisions for supposedly racially undesirable immigrants. I close the chapter by examining how governmental regulation of these gendered ideals of family in a given immigration policy (such as derivative status) can reinforce immigrants' existing gender relations that politicians and moral reformers have declared to be deviant. I demonstrate this by looking at Chinese immigrants' claims to derivative citizenship as the sons of native-born citizens in the early decades of the twentieth century and the government's efforts to purge these "fraudulent" families. In recounting these histories, the chapter demonstrates how family ideation shaped immigration policymaking, which included both exclusionary goals and preservation of gender and sexual norms in family unity provisions.

In chapter 4, I consider how new cultural and political realities generated by the end of World War II created opportunities to construct and attach new meanings to immigration and examine postwar reforms that included unity provisions for military families: the McCarran-Walter Act of 1952, which upheld national origins policy, and the Hart-Celler Act of 1965, which abolished national origins policy. For reformers and defenders of national origins policy, family ideation provided a way of talking about what a national identity worth promoting or preserving meant. For reformers, national origins policy was clearly racially discriminatory and had no place in a modern world where the United States was a democratic leader. Reformers' reframing of immigration and its beneficiaries as meritorious helped to shift the focus away from race and toward families. They began by extending family unity provisions to military service personnel. In turn, reformers found a way to recast American immigration as not only just and humane but also a clear moral response to growing pressure to address racial discrimination in the United States as demands for civil rights for African Americans and the battle against communism shaped the larger domestic and international political landscape. Like civil rights legislation to end racial segregation, immigration reform overturning national origins policy became a matter of national security and of importance for international politics. The piecemeal immigration reforms led to a concerted effort to overturn national origins policy, with reformers repeatedly claiming that family reunification as a central feature of American immigration policy would strengthen the U.S. image on the world stage.

Talk about family is not inherently liberalizing for policy. Exclusionists and defenders of national origins policy also idealized family in their efforts to uphold the discriminatory policy. In supporting the reunification of military personnel families, they limited the discussion of meritorious and legitimate beneficiaries of the unity provisions to the men and women who had sacrificed for the war effort. They also argued that uniting military families would preserve the racial status quo—that is, the ethnic and racial composition created and preserved by national origins policy. As political pressure for overturning national origins policy grew, exclusionists sought to limit reform and preserve the policy by arguing that families would be protected. Thus, both exclusionists and reformers talked about the importance of serving families.

In chapter 5, I examine changes in the meanings of family and family reunification after passage of the Hart-Celler Act made family reunification the official centerpiece of American immigration policy. Politicians and scholars laud the 1965 reform as a liberal political achievement and a symbol of a pluralist national ideal. Immigration stakeholders—from conservative politicians to liberal immigrant activist groups—nearly unanimously support the continued centrality of family unity in American immigration policy. However, this endorsement across the political divide and the public declarations of support for family unity do not always indicate a commitment to a liberal, culturally pluralist vision of the nation. What is the meaning of family after the end of national origins policy and the codification of family reunification in American immigration policy? Is family fully protected in American immigration policy?

I turn to family ideation to answer these questions. I first show that family appears to be a firmly entrenched, privileged category in American immigration policy. However, this does not guarantee full protection and support for diverse forms and experiences of families in the United States. I argue that the postreform era has been marked by a harsh contrast between official and public pronouncements of support for family unity and policies that leave families vulnerable. Particularly since welfare reform in the 1990s, immigrant families face greater scrutiny for seeking family-related benefits. Eligibility requirements and tests for gaining access to benefits have become increasingly difficult to meet. Family sponsors of relatives seeking to immigrate also have had to prove not only their own financial independence but also the ability of their relatives to avoid becoming a public charge. In addition, mixed-status immigrant families—families with members who are both authorized and not—have been exposed to family separation as unauthorized immigrants have faced greater prospects of deportation, particularly after September 11, 2001, and increased emphasis on security and border control. I argue that these various tests and surveillance measures are tied to the fears of immigration restrictionists not only over security but over the nation's implied vulnerability when families fraudulently gain entry and access to benefits. An analysis of restrictionists' family ideation suggests less of a commitment to a culturally pluralist ideal of family reunification and immigrant diversity and more of an effort to shape a meaning of race and immigration that limits the gains of the civil rights era.

I conclude the book by considering how the inherent conservatism of the narrative structure of family limits the political framing and the stories we tell about the importance and goals of immigration. Regardless of the political commitment to liberal reform, immigration policy that focuses on family and the evaluation of its elements of ties and natural substance constrains the meanings that actors can attach to the goals, functions, or roles of immigration. Despite—or perhaps in spite of—these limitations, immigration stakeholders engage in family ideation in an effort to lay a claim about what family, race, or nation should mean as they seek to forge an immigration policy. These are the complexities associated with how immigration control works and policy develops.

Chapter 2

"The Fabric of Our Civilization as We Know It": Family in Research and Policy

On the floor of the House of Representatives on April 11, 1924, Rep. Victor Berger from Wisconsin, the first Socialist Party member elected to the House, offered an amendment to a bill that would provide non-quota status to spouses, minor children, and parents of immigrant residents who stated their intention to become citizens. He boldly declared:

> The basis of our present civilization is the family. The tribe and the Nation are only enlarged families. If you destroy the family you destroy the fabric of our civilization as we know it. If you let an alien come in to make this country his home you ought to make it possible for him to bring in his wife and children, especially after he has declared his intention of becoming a citizen. The amendment is humane and necessary.[1]

In making his argument, Berger emphasized the centrality of family for a growing nation and the importance for a civilized nation of humanity in uniting family members. Even during debates on limiting immigration through a policy of national origins quotas, lawmakers such as Representative Berger articulated the importance of family unity and struck the theme of humanity, which became so crucial for reform efforts after World War II. Unfortunately for Berger and his supporters, the amendment was defeated, and it would take several more decades before permanent residents could unite their families beyond the quota system.[2]

Sixty-five years after Berger's speech in defense of family on the House floor, the Senate debated a bill that would have changed which family members were eligible for sponsorship. On the Senate floor, Sen. Kent Conrad (D-ND) spoke against the bill, stating: "Family immigration must continue to be the mainstay of this country's immigrant flow—our culture, our economy, and our national character have been shaped by the diverse and vital communities who make up the fabric of this country."[3] Senator Conrad reminded his colleagues that family immigration was the cornerstone of American immigration policy. Arguing that family was central to the nation's history and identity, he linked the uniquely American narrative of "a nation of immigrants" to the idea of diversity and national vitality and to the work done by families.

These examples highlight the varying ways in which family has been used to articulate what is at stake with respect to immigration. Family is both the focal point of immigration policy and the lens through which immigration policy can develop. That is, policymakers have made family the object of regulation in immigration policy in addition to discussing what family means or should mean as a way to frame the contours of the debates over immigration. These policy and discursive acts speak to the ability of family to represent and mean so many things to so many people and to serve different goals and ideas. Often implicitly, immigration stakeholders have relied on family to achieve cultural, social, and political goals, invoking it as a way to say as much about the larger social or political context as about family itself. This seemingly fungible quality is part of the story about the significance of family in the making of immigration policy.

In this chapter, I explore how policymakers and researchers have conceptualized family by examining what family has meant in research on families and migration and in immigration policy. In addition to discussing the major U.S. immigration policies and their impact on family reunification throughout the history of immigration control, I provide statistics on the use of family provisions for entry and their effect on the changing demographics of immigration. I conclude with a brief international look at family reunification provisions.

There is an obvious reason for why we link family and immigration in political discourse and public media. As mentioned in the previous chapter, family immigration now represents, in sheer numbers, the most significant group of immigrants.[4] This does not include immigrants entering as family members accompanying immigrants who entered with visas such as the employment H-1B visa. There are currently about three million temporary workers and their families in the United States on this and other work-related visas.[5] The policies affecting such immigrants are beyond the scope of this book. Nonetheless, their arrival and stay in the United States contribute to the growing importance of family reunification as a goal and method by which ever more immigrants enter, not only through family reunification provisions for citizens and permanent residents but also through worker visas. Reflecting how important familial ties are to contemporary immigration, Rubén Rumbaut calls immigration a "family affair."[6] However, immigration has been a family affair far longer than most immigration scholars may initially concede. As the opening vignette suggests, the relationship between family and immigration has been an important feature of the public's imagination since the early years of immigration exclusion and control. From the moment the United States began to regulate migration, it has done so with consideration for what family is, what family means, and what family should mean.

FAMILY DEFINED AND STUDIED

So then, what does family mean? There are definitions both implicit and explicit in official policies and their implementations, in scholarly accounts, and in political claims-making. Although I do not want to privilege any one of these definitions, I offer a working definition and suggest that we conceptualize the family as a *putative* kin relationship between two or more people who are bound by blood, law, or affection. The emphasis on "putative" is critical, because most ideological claims about family are based on heterosexual assumptions about parental relations and the ties that produce biological offspring. Familial arrangements that include gay and lesbian families and sometimes even adoptive families are pushed aside. Furthermore, as feminist and queer scholars have pointed out, these assumptions are class-biased and racialized, as I discuss later.

Beyond this definition, we can think about family in a myriad of different ways: as a set of lived experiences or social practices, as a target of policy, as a political invention, as an administrative construct, as a historical concept, as a normative claim, or as an abstract set of ideals. What family is or means in addition to what a family actually does or how it operates has been the topic of decades of serious scholarship. Even identifying the topic as "family," "the family," or "families" reflects a set of assumptions about its meaning for some scholars and family activists, with "the family" representing a traditional conceptualization and "family" and especially "families" describing more diverse ones.

Early work on family assumed a traditional, heteronormative ideal—a household headed by a breadwinning man married to a stay-at-home wife, with two or more children. Social scientists' heteronormative assumptions guided not only their research but their advocacy work as well. Social science scholars collaborated with family planning promoters to help create a eugenics movement that supported the propagation of "fitter families." The efforts of these collaborators to foster a stronger nation included "race betterment" programs instituted in part through immigration control, particularly in the decades leading up to and following the Immigration Act of 1924. Although the atrocities of World War II helped to discredit the eugenics movement, many government-sponsored eugenics programs and research on "fitter families" continued.[7]

Feminist scholars have helped to lay bare these heteronormative assumptions in family scholarship, policies, and cultural debates. For example, feminist scholars of the state write that such traditional, patriarchal notions of family have been central to not only the development of pronatalist policies and the welfare state but state formation itself. State policies directed at encouraging traditional family arrangements have helped the state to justify its expansion and role in both public and private spheres.[8]

In addition to these historical accounts of family and the state, researchers have identified diversity in familial form throughout history.[9] Stephanie Coontz argues that nostalgia for a past that never happened or that happened only very briefly (for example, in the idealized vision of the 1950s) shapes present-day claims about the family's crisis.[10] Throughout American history, conservative commentators have regularly lamented the decline of traditional family arrangements and the moral decay it supposedly represents, particularly as women's traditional roles have changed, urbanization has spread, and immigration has threatened an ethno-racial national identity.[11]

Scholars who study the diversity of families in practice have also provided critiques of traditional assumptions in family research and policies. Gender and sexuality scholars in particular have shown how individuals construct the meaning of family through the choices they make in familial arrangement. These scholars have debunked heteronormative claims while outlining changes in the meaning of family and a growing diversity in its forms and functions.[12] In particular, studies of same-sex families and adoptive families show different configurations of families.[13]

Comparative and international research has also offered diverse views on familial arrangements and meaning. For example, research on family in international context has uncovered increasing diversification of household structures in Europe. In particular, as migrants cross borders for temporary or extended stays, families take on varying shapes, including female-headed households or multiple generations under one roof.[14] Judith Stacey,[15] adopting an international perspective on marriage and family, draws on examples from around the world to show that because of globalization and modernization, there are more and more ways to organize family life that do not necessarily, for example, couple love and marriage with child-rearing.

Similarly, race and ethnicity scholars have critiqued traditional definitions of family that assume a middle-class white identity.[16] Other scholars who look at underexamined communities have also added diversity to family scholarship. For example, Richard Rodriguez investigates varying modes of kinship, taking an anti-essentialist position to examine the construction of "family" in Chicano/a culture.[17] Likewise, Mignon Moore challenges racial and heteronormative assumptions in family scholarship as she explores racial identity, motherhood, and family formation in her study of lesbian women of color. Race and ethnicity scholars have also explored how gendered and racialized claims about family serve various political, cultural, or ideological goals.[18] Patricia Hill Collins argues that the gendered rhetoric of an American family ideal helps to naturalize other social hierarchies such as race; she concludes that such rhetoric fosters a racialized national identity.[19] Her analysis of African American women's treatment as second-class citizens while still being declared "like one of the family" is particularly helpful for theorizing how symbolic discourse can shape racial meaning, national identity, and incorporation for immigrants whose efforts to join the nation hinge on their supposed assimilability and characterization as legitimate family members.

Immigration scholars have also questioned definitions of family and its function and role in society, particularly as they relate to the migration process. Like other family scholars, immigration researchers have criticized the traditional conceptualization of family and challenged migration models that emphasize male breadwinners who leave families in home countries.[20] Researchers have argued that such traditional definitions of family have a negative impact on immigrants and minorities, particularly when such ideas are the bases of policies that affect their integration.[21] For example, social scientists studying the ramifications of the American welfare reform legislated in 1996 demonstrate the highly consequential effect of policy that employs traditional family definitions. Not only do traditional or narrow concepts of family affect welfare eligibility and utilization, but they shape immigrant adaptation and incorporation. As discussed further in chapter 5, the 1996 welfare reform and immigration legislation instituted stricter control on immigrants' access to welfare benefits—including family sponsorship rules—which limited access to welfare provisions for many eligible immigrants, especially children.[22]

Particularly given sociologists' focus on immigrant adaptation and integration, their research offers significant insight into how immigrant families facilitate these processes.[23] Many of these studies show the effect of an immigration policy that increasingly has emphasized family reunification.[24] These studies show how immigrants use familial relations as an important source in the migratory chain or use familial strength to smooth the transition to their new host society.[25] In addition, they have shown how the meaning, structure, and role of families shape and are altered by the migration process.[26] For example, Russell King and his colleagues argue that migration influences the practice and meaning of family and household by destabilizing traditionally held notions.[27] As gendered relations, familial relations, and migration intersect, the migratory experience may disrupt or threaten traditional gender ideas and roles. Pierette Hondagneu-Sotelo's study of undocumented Mexican immigrants finds that men and women, following migration decisions based on familial negotiations, reconsider and restructure their gendered relations, particularly as women gain new independence, thereby shaping new familial arrangements and roles.[28]

Although these immigrant family studies highlight the important resources and resilience that immigrant families often bring to surviving and even thriving in their host countries, families are not unequivocally the sources of strength. For example, immigration and welfare reform studies have shown the vulnerability experienced by families—especially immigrant families of mixed legal status, that is, families in which children have birthright citizenship and one or both parents are unauthorized immigrants. In his study of mixed-status families, Hirokazu Yoshikawa[29] argues that parents' unauthorized status confers risk on their children, even those with birthright citizenship and all of the rights that such a status implies. He writes that unauthorized immigrant parents' marginal status significantly affects their children's health and cognitive and emotional development.

Even legal status may yield precarious standing for immigrant families as they face the challenges of integrating into a society that seeks to limit immigration and curb welfare provisions through various means-testing and time limits in the name of reform and that voices increasingly hostile rhetoric about the negative impact of immigration. Thus, in addition to unauthorized immigrants who face great challenges securing social provisions for their citizen children, legal immigrants—particularly women—encounter strong opposition as well.[30] In her study of pregnant Asian and Latina women immigrants' efforts to access prenatal health care, Lisa Sun-Hee Park found that the women were perceived as a threat: the impending birth of their children signaled a challenge to the existing racial and class balance. She writes that these women's pregnancies embodied a "walking target for the expression of a number of national anxieties regarding the quantity and quality of our citizenry."[31] Fearing the consequences of utilizing health care provisions such as prenatal care, many of the women Park interviewed chose not to seek them. As I show in the next chapter, women's fecundity often kindles racial and national fears about the changing face of the nation as the politics of reproduction interweaves with the politics of immigration control.

Family policy studies highlight the importance of understanding how family is defined in political debates and in the policies themselves. For example, Stephen Sugarman argues that public policies that target families have favored the idealized family of the 1950s in policy arenas such as tax law, assistance for families with children, public housing, and immigration.[32] This is true even as tolerance toward more diverse family types has grown—particularly in policy programs directed at poorer families, such as food stamp and public housing programs.

Despite the centrality of family in many policies, family is a woefully understudied topic in public policy and American politics. Political scientist Patricia Strach laments the state of the research while showing that family is not simply "private" or only part of "family policy," but also an important feature of American policymaking in general—in policies ranging from immigration to tax and agriculture.[33] Strach and other policy scholars try to understand how changing forms of family shape different conceptions of family in policy development. Steven Wisensale shows how shifting family and workplace arrangements led to the crafting of a family leave policy in the early 1990s.[34] Both Strach and Wisensale argue that there are important gaps in current policies because they do not address changing familial relations and structures. Of course, whether or how to address these gaps is not always obvious to policymakers or to the targeted groups.

FAMILY UNITY PROVISIONS

Prior to 1924, the United States did not have a comprehensive immigration policy apart from treaties, group-specific laws, and executive orders, such as the Burlingame Treaty of 1865, the Chinese Exclusion Act of 1882, and the Gentlemen's Agreement of 1907, which directed Chinese and Japanese immigration. Table 2.1 shows all of the major federal immigration acts from 1875 to 1996.

In addition, before national origins policy of the 1920s was enacted, there was no general family provision or preference system for other would-be immigrants. Prior to that legislation, gendered ideas of coverture and family unity permitted some immigrants to reunite with their spouses and children, which I discuss further in the next chapter. Table 2.2 lists the family preference provisions in major immigration acts, beginning with the Immigration Act of 1924. Although there were no specific family provisions prior to the 1924 act (except those that regulated Japanese immigration, as will be discussed in chapter 3), we have some sense of the importance of family reunification as the reason for immigration.

Table 2.3 shows who, if any, immigrants stated that they were coming to the United States for the years between 1908 and 1927. Except for a couple of years at the end of the First World War, at least two-thirds or more of immigrants stated that they were coming to join a relative. These rates are not different from contemporary family reunification rates, as discussed

Table 2.1 Major U.S. Immigration Acts

Legislation	Major Provisions
Page Act of 1875	Excluded Asian contract laborers and Asian women engaged in prostitution
Chinese Exclusion Act of 1882	Halted Chinese immigration for ten years and prohibited Chinese from becoming U.S. citizens; was extended for another ten years in 1892 and became permanent in 1902
Immigration (Johnson-Reed) Act of 1924	Established national origins quotas; reduced the number of immigrants from southern and eastern European countries and virtually terminated immigration from Asia
Immigration and Nationality (McCarran-Walter) Act of 1952	Continued the national origins quota system; established preference categories based on immigrants' skills and family relationships; spouses and children of U.S. citizens were admitted without limit
Immigration and Nationality (Hart-Celler) Act of 1965	Ended the national origins quota system; established a preference system with a focus on immigrants' skills and family ties to U.S. citizens or residents; no numerical limit was set for immediate relatives of U.S. citizens
Immigration Reform and Control Act (IRCA) of 1986	Instituted employer sanctions; initiated a legalization program for immigrants in the country without documentation
Immigration Act of 1990	Continued the previous acts' family preference provisions; expanded employment-based preferences with separate categories and instituted the diversity visa lottery program
Illegal Immigration Reform and Immigrant Responsibility Act (IIRIRA) of 1996	Improved border and interior enforcement; incorporated employment programs and employment eligibility issues, including employer sanctions; restricted state and federally funded alien benefit programs

Source: Author's compilation.

later. Thus, regardless of the availability of formal preferences for family reunification, familial relations motivated or facilitated many would-be migrants' entry into the United States early in the twentieth century.

Beginning with the Immigration Act of 1924, Congress codified the preference system. The law capped immigration at 150,000, to be deter-

Table 2.2 Preference Provisions in Major U.S. Immigration Acts

	1924 Immigration Act	1952 McCarran-Walter Act	1965 Hart-Celler Act[l]	1990 Immigration Act[r]	
Limit	150,000[a]	154,657	290,000[m]	700,000	675,000
Per-country limit	2 percent of the total population of foreign-born persons of each nationality recorded in the 1890 census, minimum of 100. After July 1, 1927: overall cap of 150,000 determined by national origins of the total U.S. population recorded in 1920, minimum of 100 (became effective July 1, 1929).	Set the annual quota for an area at one-sixth of 1 percent of the number of inhabitants in the United States in 1920 whose ancestry or national origin was attributable to that area, minimum of 100, ceiling of 2,000 for Asia–Pacific triangle countries.	20,000	7 percent of the total preference	
Family preferences limit			74 percent	465,000[s]	480,000
Nonquota/ not limited	Wives and unmarried children[b] of U.S. citizens, Western Hemisphere immigrants, religious or academic professionals,[c] and students at least fifteen years of age	Spouses and children of U.S. citizens	Immediate family members (spouses, children, and parents) of U.S. citizens[g]	Immediate family members (spouses, children, and parents) of U.S. citizens[g]	

Table 2.2 Continued

	1924 Immigration Act	1952 McCarran-Walter Act	1965 Hart-Celler Act[l]	1990 Immigration Act[r]	
Limit	150,000[a]	154,657	290,000[m]	700,000	675,000
First preference	Preferences within quotas*: 1. Unmarried children,[d] parents or wives of U.S. citizens twenty-one years of age or over 2. Skilled agricultural laborers and their wives and children under the age of sixteen[e]	Preference within quotas: highly skilled immigrants whose services were urgently needed in the United States and the spouses and children of such immigrants	Unmarried sons and daughters[n] of U.S. citizens	Unmarried sons and daughters[n] of U.S. citizens	
		50 percent[f]	20 percent (58,000)	23,400	23,400
Second preference	*(1) and (2) are not ranked; no more than 50 percent of the nationality quota	Parents of U.S. citizens[g]	Spouses and unmarried sons and daughters[o] of permanent resident aliens	Spouses and children of lawful permanent residents (2A)[t] and unmarried sons and daughters[n] of lawful permanent residents (2B)[u]	
		30 percent[h]	20 percent (58,000)	114,200	114,200
Third preference		Spouse and children of aliens lawfully admitted for permanent residence	Members of the professions of exceptional ability in sciences and arts and their spouses and children	Married sons and daughters[p] of U.S. citizens and their spouses and children	
		20 percent[i]	10 percent (29,000)	23,400	23,400

Fourth preference	Brothers, sisters, sons, and daughters[j] of U.S. citizens[g]	Married sons and daughters[p] of U.S. citizens and their spouses and children	Brothers and sisters of U.S. citizens[g] and their spouses and children	
	Up to 25 percent of the quota unused for first three preferences[k]	10 percent (29,000)	65,000	65,000
Fifth preference	Nonpreference within quotas: applicant not entitled to one of the above preferences	Brothers and sisters of U.S. citizens[g] and their spouses and children	Employment-Based Preference[v]	
		24 percent (69,600)	First preference: workers with special talents or skills (40,000)	
Sixth preference	—	Skilled or unskilled workers in occupations in which labor was in short supply and their spouses and children	Second preference: workers with advanced degrees or technical expertise (40,000)	

Table 2.2 Continued

	1924 Immigration Act	1952 McCarran-Walter Act	1965 Hart-Celler Act[l]	1990 Immigration Act[r]	
Limit	150,000[a]	154,657	290,000[m]	700,000	675,000
			10 percent (29,000)	Third preference: workers with needed job skills, professionals, and others (40,000)	
Seventh preference		—	Refugees[q]	Fourth preference: special immigrants and religious workers (10,000)	
			6 percent (10,200)	Fifth preference: investor immigrants (10,000)	
				Diversity Immigration[w]	
				40,000	55,000

Source: Compiled from Gimpel and Edwards 1999, Hutchison 1981, Keely 1975, Mitchell 1992, Tichenor 2002; see also 1952 and 1965 Immigration and Nationality Acts; U.S. Department of Homeland Security, *Yearbooks of Immigration Statistics 1997–2010* ; U.S. Department of Justice, Immigration and Naturalization Service, *Triennial Comprehensive Report on Immigration* (2002).

Note: A "child" is defined as an unmarried person under twenty-one years of age, unless otherwise noted.

[a]Initially 165,000. After July 1, 1927, the total quota was set at 150,000.

[b]Nonquota status was granted to the unmarried child under eighteen years of age. The Act of May 29, 1928 (45 Stat. 1009) changed the limiting age of an unmarried child from eighteen to twenty-one and added husbands of citizens provided that they were married before June 1, 1928. The Act of July 11, 1932 (47 Stat. 656) changed the date to July 1, 1932. Those who were married after that date were put under a preference category.

[c]Included accompanying wives and children under eighteen years of age.

[d]Under twenty-one years of age. They were moved up to the nonquota category by the 1928 act.

[e]According to section 6(a)(2) of the 1924 Immigration Act, this preference for skilled agricultural laborers "shall not apply to immigrants of any nationality the annual quota for which is less than 300." The preferences within quotas were not ranked; that is, family preference did not take precedence over skilled laborer preference. By the 1928 act, the age of children had increased from sixteen to eighteen. This act also gave preference to unmarried children under twenty-one years of age and wives of alien residents lawfully admitted for permanent residence.

[f]Plus any not required for second and third preferences.

[g]To sponsor parents or siblings, the petitioning U.S. citizen had to be age twenty-one or older.

[h]Plus any not required for first and third preferences. Unmarried sons and daughters, age twenty-one or older, of U.S. citizens were moved up from the fourth preference by the Act of September 22, 1959 (73 Stat. 644).

[i]Plus any not required for first and second preferences. Under the 1959 act, unmarried sons and daughters (over twenty-one years of age) of permanent residents were added here.

[j]Accompanying spouses and children were included in the preference by the 1959 act. Now "sons and daughters" referred to married sons and daughters, regardless of age. Unmarried sons and daughters over twenty-one years of age were moved up to the second preference.

[k]The 1959 act increased it to 50 percent.

[l]The 1980 Refugee Act slightly changed the preference provisions of the 1965 Immigration and Nationality Act. The limit was now set at 270,000 instead of 290,000 (a single worldwide ceiling set by the 1978 law). Refugees were admitted separately and were no longer admitted under the preference system; therefore, the 6 percent preference for refugees from 1965 was now added to the second preference, increasing it from 20 percent to 26 percent, and the family preference limit also increased by 6 percent, from 74 to 80 percent. Percentages for other preference categories remained the same. The preference provisions set by the 1980 Refugee Act continued to be used until the 1990 Immigration Act became effective.

[m]The 1965 Immigration and Nationality Act set a ceiling of 170,000 on Eastern Hemisphere immigration. It also limited Western Hemisphere immigration, effective July 1, 1968, to 120,000 annually, without per-country limits. The 1976 Immigration and Nationality Act amendments applied the 20,000 per-country limit to the Western Hemisphere. The Immigration and Nationality Act Amendments of 1978 set a single worldwide ceiling of 290,000, and the Refugee Act of 1980 set the worldwide ceiling at 270,000.

[n]Aged twenty-one or older.

[o]The second preference "unmarried sons and daughters" included both minor and adult children.

[p]Married sons and daughters were persons who had a recognized parent-child relationship and were married, regardless of age.

[q]The seventh preference category of the 1965 act reserved 6 percent of Eastern Hemisphere immigrant visas to refugees. With the ceiling for the Eastern Hemisphere visas initially set at 170,000, the number for the category was 10,200. It increased to 17,400 when the Immigration and Nationality Act Amendments of 1978 set a single worldwide ceiling of 290,000.

[r]A transitional limit of 700,000 was allocated between 1992 and 1994 until the 1990 Immigration Act came into effect in 1995.

[s]This number did not include 55,000 Immigration Reform and Control Act (IRCA) legalizations (8 percent). Between 1991 and 1994, 55,000 visas per year were allocated for the spouses and children of migrants who became legal residents under IRCA, with the 1990 Immigration Act extending the cutoff date to May 1988.

[t]2A: 77 percent of the second preference, of which 75 percent were issued without regard to the per-country limit.

[u]The second preference expanded by at least 62 percent after 1990.

[v]Total limit of 140,000: 120,000 plus 10,000 for religious workers and 10,000 for investors. Employment-based preferences included visas for spouses and children.

[w]Diversity immigration was determined by lottery. In 1995 the permanent diversity program came into effect, with 55,000 visas available annually. When Congress passed the Nicaraguan Adjustment and Central American Relief Act (NACARA) in 1997, it reduced diversity to 50,000.

Table 2.3 Immigrants Arriving in the United States to Join a Relative or Friend, 1908 to 1927

Fiscal Year	Relative	Friend	Not Arriving to Join Either	Total Immigrants
1908 to 1914	5,348,687 (79.7%)	956,130 (14.3%)	404,540 (6.0%)	6,709,357 (100%)
1915 to 1920	1,055,878 (65.9)	228,482 (14.3)	318,320 (19.8)	1,602,680 (100)
1921 to 1927	2,536,856 (77.4)	310,564 (9.5)	431,156 (13.1)	3,278,576 (100)

Source: Author's calculations based on 1908 to 1910: United States and Dillingham (1993), vol. 20, table 40 (data not recorded before 1908); 1911 to 1927: U.S. Department of Labor, Bureau of Immigration, *Annual Report of the Commissioner General of Immigration to the Secretary of Labor* "Table VII. Sex, Age, Literacy, Financial Condition, Etc., of Immigrant Aliens Admitted by Races or Peoples."

mined by the national origins of the total U.S. population recorded in the 1920 census.[35] This law dramatically reduced the number of immigrants from southern and eastern Europe. According to the quota calculations, while Great Britain received the most quota visas with 65,721, Italy garnered just 5,802 visas and Greece only 307.[36] These numbers were in stark contrast to the number of immigrants who landed from those same countries in the years prior to the new quota law. In 1921, 222,260 immigrant aliens were admitted from Italy and 28,502 from Greece, while 79,577 entered from England, Ireland, Scotland, and Wales combined. The law also barred entry to anyone who was not eligible for citizenship. This meant that Asians, whom the U.S. Supreme Court declared ineligible for citizenship in the landmark cases Takao Ozawa v. United States (1922) and United States v. Bhagat Singh Thind (1923), could not legally immigrate.[37] They were racially barred, regardless of their nationality or place of birth. Nevertheless, within this exclusionary framework, the act codified a preference for family. The act allowed racially eligible wives and children of U.S. citizens to enter without limit. More importantly, along with skilled immigrants, immediate family members (unmarried minor children, parents) of legal permanent immigrants gained preferred status—albeit within the quota system—by 1928.[38] Although these measures were not nearly as family-permissive as later provisions, they nevertheless facilitated immigration for many who would have been otherwise unable to gain entry on their own.

After decades of declining immigration, Congress passed a number of limited, piecemeal legislations to allow families separated by World War II to reunite (discussed in greater detail in chapter 4). Men who served in the military during the war benefited most from legislative efforts to recognize their wartime sacrifices. Immigration reformers pushed to repeal national origins policy in part through this rhetoric of payment for military service. However, the law Congress passed in 1952—over President

Harry Truman's veto—preserved national origins policy even as racial exclusion against Asians was formally ended. As table 2.2 shows, the 1952 Immigration Act emphasized the demand for skilled migrants, giving them the first preference: 50 percent of visas went to them, their spouses, and their children. All of these preferences were applied within the existing quotas policy. As in years past, spouses and children of U.S. citizens had unlimited visas; however, parents of adult U.S. citizens received 30 percent of the visas and the second preference.[39] There were also family provisions allowing legal permanent residents to reunite with their spouses and children, who received the third preference and 20 percent of the visas available. Brothers and sisters of U.S. citizens—the group often targeted in recent decades by lawmakers and immigration restrictionists seeking to curb immigration—first received their official family preference in the 1952 law. The law made 25 percent maximum of any unused visas for the first three preferences available for brothers, sisters, and adult sons and daughters of U.S. citizens.[40]

The Immigration Act of 1965 (the Hart-Cellar Act) ushered in the contemporary family reunification provisions, which have so dramatically altered the U.S. population. In addition to setting the immigration cap at 290,000 and implementing a limit on Western Hemisphere immigration, which previously did not exist, family reunification provisions dominated the list of preferences, as table 2.2 shows. The law provided unlimited provisions for immediate family members (spouses, minor children, and parents) of U.S. citizens.[41] In addition, for the first time since passage of racially exclusionary laws, immigrants were eligible, regardless of their national origin, race, or ethnicity, to bring over their spouses and minor children beyond the national origins quota system as national origins policy was overturned. The law's first preference went to unmarried adult sons and daughters of U.S. citizens. Spouses and unmarried sons and daughters of permanent resident aliens received the second preference, with 20 percent of visas. Balancing the goals of encouraging family reunification with the need for skilled or other laborers, the act included provisions for workers. Thus, the third preference was for members of the professions "of exceptional ability" in sciences and arts and their spouses and children, and the sixth preference was for skilled or unskilled workers in occupations where labor was in short supply and their spouses and children. Even in these worker preferences, the new immigration law outlined provisions for family reunification.

As discussed in chapter 5, efforts at legislative reform following the 1965 law, particularly those related to unauthorized immigration, were stymied until passage of the Immigration Reform and Control Act (IRCA) of 1986. Without altering the preference system instituted in the 1965 law, there were two crucial elements to the new law. In addition to employer

Table 2.4 Immigrants Admitted to the United States by Preference and Other Provisions, 1925 to 2010

Year	Natives of Eastern Hemisphere Countries[a]	Natives of Western Hemisphere Countries[b]	Immediate Relatives of U.S. Citizens	Others Under the Immigration Quota System	Family-Sponsored Preferences
1925 to 1930	903,119 (51.2%)	705,322 (40.0%)	124,609 (7.1%)	29,560 (1.7%)	—
1931 to 1940	308,341 (58.4%)	113,086 (21.4%)	91,670 (17.3%)	15,334 (2.9%)	—
1941 to 1950	583,707 (56.4%)	251,888 (24.3%)	185,604 (17.9%)	13,840 (1.3%)	—
1951 to 1960	1,098,970 (43.7%)	805,573 (32.0%)	284,929 (11.3%)	326,007 (13.0%)	—
1961 to 1968	927,285 (35.8%)	1,230,957 (47.5%)	289,667 (11.2%)	141,863 (5.5%)	—
1969 to 1970	—	—	139,238 (19.0%)	—	184,890 (25.3%)
1971 to 1980[f]	—	—	1,175,449 (26.2%)	—	1,330,325 (29.6%)
1981 to 1990	—	—	1,996,741 (27.2%)	—	2,128,872 (29.0%)
1991 to 2000[g]	—	—	2,709,030 (29.8%)	—	2,257,218 (24.8%)
2001 to 2010[h]	—	—	4,684,583 (44.6%)	—	2,076,038 (19.8%)

Source: Author's compilation based on "Immigrants Admitted Under the Quota System: 1925–1968" and "Immigrants Admitted Under the Preference System: 1966–1991," in Carter et al. (2006); U.S. Department of Homeland Security, *Yearbooks of Immigration Statistics: 1996–2011.*

[a]Between 1925 and 1929, the annual quota on natives of Eastern Hemisphere countries was 164,667, based on the 2 percent rule. For the years 1930 to 1965, a "national origins" formula was used. The 1965 Immigration Act abolished the quota system and set up an annual numerical limitation of 170,000 immigrants from the Eastern Hemisphere, with a per-country ceiling of 20,000. It also imposed a numerical limitation of 120,000 per year on Western Hemisphere immigration, which went into effect on July 1, 1968.

[b]Unrestricted prior to July 1, 1968.

[c]For 1991 to 2000: because the 1990 Immigration Act became effective in fiscal year 1992, the number for 1991 includes immigrants with third-preference, sixth-preference, and special immigrant visas and their spouses and children.

[d]Includes diversity (1995 to 2000), diversity transition (1992 to 1997), and legalized dependents (1992 to 2000).

Employment-Based Preferences[c]	Other Preferences[d]	IRCA Legalizations	Refugees and Asylum Seekers	Others Not Under the Numerical Cap[e]	Total Immigrants
—	—	—	—	—	1,762,610 (100%)
—	—	—	—	—	528,431 (100%)
—	—	—	—	—	1,035,039 (100%)
—	—	—	—	—	2,515,479 (100%)
—	—	—	—	—	2,589,772 (100%)
65,779 (9.0%)	327,609 (44.8%)	—	39,079 (5.3%)	–24,690 (–3.4%)	731,905 (100%)
321,382 (7.2%)	1,295,033 (28.8%)	—	539,447 (12.0%)	–168,322 (–3.7%)	4,493,314 (100%)
518,966 (7.1%)	118,589 (1.6%)	1,359,186 (18.5%)	1,013,620 (13.8%)	202,088 (2.8%)	7,338,062 (100%)
980,826 (10.8%)	550,150 (6.0%)	1,329,638 (14.6%)	1,021,266 (11.2%)	247,289 (2.7%)	9,095,417 (100%)
1,611,123 (15.3%)	453,463 (4.3%)	—	1,325,365 (12.6%)	350,481 (3.3%)	10,501,053 (100%)

[e]For 1991 to 2000: includes Amerasian, cancellation of removal, children born abroad to alien residents, Cuban/Haitian entrants, NACARA, nationals of adversely affected countries, nationals of underrepresented countries, parolees, registered nurses and their families, registry, entry prior to July 1, 1972, and other; for 2001 to 2010: includes parolees, children born abroad to alien residents, NACARA, cancellation of removal, Haitian Refugee Immigration Fairness Act (HRIFA) of 1998, and other.

[f]Includes transitional quarter (1976 to 1977).

[g]Compiled from U.S. Department of Homeland Security *Yearbook of Immigration Statistics 2000*, "Table 4. Immigrants Admitted by Type and Selected Class of Admission: Fiscal Years 1986 to 2000." (In the *Yearbook of Immigration Statistics 2000*, an immigrant was defined as a person lawfully admitted for permanent residence.)

[h]Compiled from U.S. Department of Homeland Security, *Yearbook of Immigration Statistics 2010*, "Table 6. Persons Obtaining Legal Permanent Resident Status by Type and Major Class of Admission: Fiscal Years 2001 to 2010."

sanctions intended to penalize employers who knowingly hired undocumented workers, IRCA provided an important pathway to legal status for hundreds of thousands of immigrants who had been in the country without authorized status. By 1990 the law had provided amnesty to 1.6 million unauthorized immigrants who had been in the United States since January 1, 1982, and it had allowed 1.1 million special agricultural workers (SAWs) who had been employed during the twelve-month period ending May 1, 1986, to legalize their status.[42] In time, these newly authorized immigrants sponsored family members to join them.

The growth in family-sponsored immigration that followed the 1986 law and the backlog it created for some categories pushed immigration restrictionists and some legislators to look to eliminating the fifth preference in the 1986 law—provisions that covered the brothers and sisters of U.S. citizens and these siblings' spouses and children. Despite concerted attacks by some lawmakers arguing that brothers and sisters did not constitute the intended meaning of family—specifically limited, they argued, to a nuclear one with two parents and children—the provision survived in the 1990 Immigration Act. Family preference provisions remained substantively the same while employment-based preferences were expanded. The first and second preferences were left largely unchanged. Married sons and daughters of U.S. citizens got the third preference, and brothers and sisters of adult U.S. citizens now had the fourth preference. The law created a separate preference system for employment-based immigration. Additionally, the 1990 act substantially increased legal immigration, raising the total limit to 675,000 in 1995 and thereafter—up from 290,000 in the 1965 act.

THE IMPACT OF FAMILY UNITY PROVISIONS

Family unity provisions have greatly altered the size and origin of immigration to the United States. Table 2.4 shows the general provisions under which immigrants have entered the United States since 1925. Family unity provisions have been the main source of immigration, comprising about 60 percent of authorized entries for the last two decades. In some ways this official number undercounts the extent to which family reunification dominates immigration. Consider the number of immigrants who entered in 2011 under the employer-based preference section: of the 139,339 immigrants who entered this way, an estimated 74,071 (53 percent) were spouses and children.[43] This reinforces the point that family reunification is the most significant mode of entry for authorized immigrants.

There have been critical changes in the continental sources of immigrants to the United States over the last two centuries. Table 2.5 shows

Table 2.5 Legal Permanent Immigration to the United States, by Region, 1820 to 2010

Period	Europe	Asia	The Americas	Africa	Oceania[a]	Total
1820 to 1850	2,199,610	230	107,844	126	156,388	2,464,200
	(89.3%)	(0.01%)	(4.4%)	(0.005%)	(6.3%)	(100%)
1851 to 1890	11,525,127	300,399	1,072,338	1,737	72,241	12,971,842
	(88.8)	(2.3)	(8.3)	(0.01)	(0.6)	(100)
1891 to 1920	15,933,279	645,641	1,544,531	16,161	79,149	18,218,761
	(87.5)	(3.5)	(8.5)	(0.1)	(0.4)	(100)
1921 to 1960	4,757,634	318,931	3,028,501	29,495	51,597	8,186,158
	(58.1)	(3.9)	(37.0)	(0.4)	(0.6)	(100)
1961 to 2000	4,045,147	7,549,649	11,801,140	641,565	210,969	24,248,470
	(16.7)	(31.1)	(48.7)	(2.6)	(0.9)	(100)
2001 to 2010[b]	1,263,937	3,784,554	4,511,094	860,447	81,021	10,501,053
	(12.0)	(36.0)	(43.0)	(8.2)	(0.8)	(100)

Source: Author's calculations based on U.S. Department of Homeland Security, *Yearbook of Immigration Statistics 2010.*

[a]Includes others unidentified by nationality.

that immigrants have increasingly arrived from regions other than Europe over the last half-century. Whereas Europe was the dominant source of immigrants through the exclusion and post–World War II eras, immigrants today come mostly from the Americas and Asia—specifically, Mexico, the Philippines, and China.[44] They have arrived through family connections in ways unexpected and perhaps unintended by the supporters of the family reunification provisions outlined in the 1965 act.[45] As family reunification has been formally codified and expanded, it is not surprising that immigrants who enter through such measures dominate current immigration. Family unity provisions provide a path or chain for migration. That is, a permanent legal resident or naturalized citizen who sponsors a spouse, child, or parent can become the initial source for a much larger web of immigrants—as, for example, a sponsored spouse eventually calls for his or her sister or brother.[46]

FAMILY UNITY PROVISIONS AROUND THE WORLD

Although in terms of degree and length of history the U.S. experience with family reunification may be unique, family reunification provisions are important features of many other immigrant-receiving nations as well, as table 2.6 shows. European countries have offered various provisions for

Table 2.6 International Family Unification Provisions

	Permanent Immigrants Using Family as a Category of Entry in 2010 (in Thousands)[a]	Citizens and Permanent Residents[c]: Sponsor's Conditions for Family Reunification
China	n.d.	No conditions specified
Japan	21.9 (39.3%)	Must reside in Japan for more than ten years (five years of which with working or residency visa)
South Korea	31.2 (19.9)	No conditions specified
Taiwan	n.d.	Must hold either a valid permanent resident certificate or an alien resident certificate or hold residence in Taiwan; Hong Kong and Macau residents and Mainland Chinese nationals need proof of legal residence; public documents to prove kinship ties

Citizens and Permanent Residents	Foreign Workers[d]	
Included Family Members	Temporary Workers/ Migrants	Included Family Members
Foreign parents, spouses, children under eighteen years of age, foreign relatives over sixty (resident permit)		
Spouses who lived in Japan for more than three years and continuously more than one year, children who lived continuously more than one year	Foreign workers on temporary visas Nikkeijin (Japanese descent)	Not allowed to enter Family members based on family registry in Japan
Spouse of permanent residency holder (residency visa); minor children under twenty of a permanent resident parent (permanent residency visa); Korean-born children of a registered foreigner (dependent family visa); Korean-born children of a foreigner with trainee or nonprofessional status (family visitation visa)	Foreign workers Overseas Koreans in China and former Soviet Union	Not allowed to enter, but family visitation available Family members allowed to enter, depending on sponsor's employment period
Spouses who are Taiwanese nationals without household registration in Taiwan, foreigners, Hong Kong and Macau residents, or Mainland Chinese nationals; children under twenty years of age (resident visa)	Foreign contract workers	Permanent settlement and family reunification prohibited

Table 2.6 Continued

	Permanent Immigrants Using Family as a Category of Entry in 2010 (in Thousands)[a]	Citizens and Permanent Residents[c]
		Sponsor's Conditions for Family Reunification
Singapore	n.d.	No conditions specified
Canada[b]	170.6 (60.8)	Must provide financial support (sign a sponsorship agreement); basic income requirement

Citizens and Permanent Residents	Foreign Workers[d]	
Included Family Members	Temporary Workers/ Migrants	Included Family Members
Spouse and unmarried children under twenty-one years of age	Employment pass holders (salary requirements)	Spouse and unmarried children under twenty-one (dependent's pass); common-law spouse, unmarried daughters above twenty-one years of age, handicapped children above twenty-one years of age, stepchildren, and parents/parents-in-law (long-term visit pass)
	Work permit holders	Not allowed
Spouses, common-law partners, conjugal partners; dependent children, including adopted children; other eligible relatives Effective November 5, 2011, no new application to sponsor parents or grandparents is accepted for processing for up to twenty-four months, but the parent and grandparent super visa (December 2011) is available for a visit to Canada for up to two years	Foreign workers	Allowed (especially for highly skilled workers) but may not work; spouses/ common-law partners/minor and dependent children

Table 2.6 Continued

	Permanent Immigrants Using Family as a Category of Entry in 2010 (in Thousands)[a]	Citizens and Permanent Residents[c]
		Sponsor's Conditions for Family Reunification
France	82.8 (42.9)	Must be legal for one year to apply for family reunification; proof of financial resources; language test; "reception and integration contract"
Germany	54.9 (24.7)	Must have public documents to prove family relationships; interviews for spouses; basic German knowledge for spouses under family migration
Italy[b]	94.8 (28.6)	Housing requirement
United Kingdom[b]	109.3 (26.4)	Maintenance and accommodation requirements; sponsor must sign an undertaking

Citizens and Permanent Residents	Foreign Workers[d]	
Included Family Members	Temporary Workers/ Migrants	Included Family Members
Spouses, partners in a long-term relationship, registered partners (PACS); minor children, older children with strong family ties in France; parents and other relatives in case of strong family ties (discretionary)	Foreign workers	Allowed for highly skilled workers
Spouses, registered same-sex partners; children under sixteen; children between sixteen and eighteen in exceptional circumstances; parents over sixty-five	Foreign workers	Allowed for temporary workers with a residence permit
Spouses (older than eighteen); minor children, dependent adult children, children of spouses from previous relationship if other parents give consent; dependent parents	Foreign workers	Not allowed
Spouses, partners in a long-term relationship; minor children, older children for humanitarian reasons, minor children of single parent only if parent has sole custody; parents over sixty-five and under sixty-five for humanitarian reasons only; aunts, uncles, siblings of sponsor for humanitarian reasons	Foreign workers	Allowed for skilled workers (contingent upon worker's resources and accommodations); spouses/partners and minor children under 18 years of age

Table 2.6 Continued

	Permanent Immigrants Using Family as a Category of Entry in 2010 (in Thousands)[a]	Citizens and Permanent Residents[c]
		Sponsor's Conditions for Family Reunification
The Netherlands	20.8 (21.7)	Age (twenty-one years or older) and maintenance requirement; basic knowledge of Dutch language and society
Spain	56.1 (18.7)	Minimum of two years of living together; independent working and resident permits required; income and housing requirements
Denmark[b]	7.5 (18.2)	Includes residence permit holder; both spouses/partners over twenty-four years of age; condition of ties; pass a Danish language and society test; housing, maintenance, collateral requirements
Sweden	25.5 (39.6)	DNA analysis may be performed; maintenance requirement

family reunification, admitting not only immediate family members but also parents and siblings of permanent residents and naturalized citizens. In particular, the European Union Council Directive of 2003 specified the right to family reunification, which many EU member countries incorporated into their national legislation. As a condition of family reunification, most countries have established income, housing, and maintenance re-

Citizens and Permanent Residents	Foreign Workers[d]	
Included Family Members	Temporary Workers/ Migrants	Included Family Members
Spouses, registered partners; minor children, adult children if non-admission would cause hardship; solitary parents over sixty-five years of age	Foreign workers	Spouses and minor children allowed for workers with permit to remain in the country for a least one year
Spouses; children (under eighteen years of age), children from previous marriage, children of single parent if sponsor has sole custody; dependent parents; dependent grandparents	No specific reference to temporary workers	
Spouses, cohabitants, registered same-sex partners; children under fifteen years of age	No specific reference to temporary workers	
Spouses, cohabiting partners; children up to twenty-one years of age; people intending to marry or become cohabiting partners; other close family members (members of the same households as sponsor or special relationship of dependence)	Foreign workers usually on 2-year permits	Not specified

quirements for applicants; several EU members, including Denmark, France, Germany, and the Netherlands, also require that family immigrants have knowledge of the host country's language(s) and familiarity with its culture. Canada imposes financial support and basic income requirements on sponsoring family members. Mindful of growing immigrant and labor migrant populations, Asian countries have begun to de-

Table 2.6 Continued

	Permanent Immigrants Using Family as a Category of Entry in 2010 (in Thousands)[a]	Citizens and Permanent Residents[c] Sponsor's Conditions for Family Reunification
Norway	10.1 (18.0)	Also includes Nordic citizen and foreign national with a residence permit (would-be permanent resident); income requirement; employment or education (four years for a foreign national who has set up a family since coming to Norway) requirement

Source: Compiled from Kraler 2010, "Table 1: Definition of the Family (Reunification with Third Country Nationals)," Organization for Economic Cooperation and Development 2012; Jin Zhu and Zhu Zhe, "Residence Permits to Aid Visits by Family," *China Daily*, May 21, 2010; Tsuda 2008; HiKorea, E-Government for Foreigner, "Grant Sojourn Status," February 1, 2008; Bureau of Consular Affairs, Ministry of Foreign Affairs, Republic of China (Taiwan), "Resident Visas"; Lin 2012; Government of Canada, "Citizenship and Immigration Canada"; Norwegian Directorate of Immigration, "Which Family Members Can Be Granted a Family Immigration Permit?"; Government Offices of Sweden, "Labour Immigration"; Organization for Economic Cooperation and Development 2001; Ministero Dell'Interno, "Entry of Foreign Nationals into Italy."

[a]Compiled from "Fig. I.4. Permanent inflows into selected OECD and non-OECD countries, total and by category of entry, 2010," OECD 2012. In 2010, 66 percent of the immigrants to the United States used family as a category of entry. Family migration accounted for 36 percent of the flows in OECD countries, while work-related migration constituted 21 per-

velop family reunification provisions for permanent residents, but they strictly regulate the admission of family members of temporary workers or migrants. In Japan, for example, foreign workers on temporary visas are not allowed to bring their family members. Singapore allows employment pass holders—foreign professionals—to bring over their family members but has no such provision for work permit holders, who are mostly low-skilled or unskilled laborers. Unlike many European countries and Canada, Asian countries lack social integration policies for immigrants.

The variations in policy outlined in table 2.6 suggest an important and distinctive difference between Europe and Canada versus Asia. Officially,

Citizens and Permanent Residents	Foreign Workers[d]	
Included Family Members	Temporary Workers/ Migrants	Included Family Members
Spouses, partners, or cohabitants; fiancés (fiancé permit); children; single mother or father over the age of sixty living in Norway; full sibling under the age of eighteen without a living parent or caregiver in home country; citizen or permanent resident children, regardless of age, residing in Norway can bring over parents for parent visit up to nine months	Highly-skilled workers and specialists Low-skilled workers	Allowed (same as permanent residents/ citizens) Spouses or partners that have or are expecting child or have lived together for at least two years; biological/adopted children under 18 years of age

cent, free movements 20 percent, accompanying family of workers 8 percent, humanitarian migration (asylum seekers) 7 percent, and "other" 7 percent of the total migration flows.
[b]This number (percentage) includes the category "accompanying family of workers." The percentage for "family" alone is 21 percent for Canada, 27 percent for Italy, 12 percent for the United Kingdom, and 12 percent for Denmark.
[c]In all countries, citizens and permanent residents (in some countries, residence permit holders too) are allowed to sponsor family members. While Asian countries lack provisions on sponsorship conditions, European countries have specific requirements that sponsors need to fulfill to bring over their family members.
[d]Temporary workers in Europe, unless they are highly skilled, generally cannot bring over their family members. Many European countries have a generous policy for family reunification and this might explain the lack of discussion on temporary workers and their rights to family reunion.

the former countries have more family-friendly policies than the latter. Immigration experts cite a number of factors for why immigration policy is generally more liberal in Europe than in Asia, including the active role of the judiciary and the importance of the ideals of social justice and human rights, particularly after the horrors of World War II.[47] What may be obscured, however, is the fact that controlling family migration and settlement is crucial to immigration control more generally in most of these countries. Thus, for example, the rhetoric of "the death of the nation," which is tied to declining birth rates by native-born citizens, is commonly heard in both regions.[48] Although the declining population numbers in many western European countries are easily reversed when increases in population attributed to immigration are considered, those additions have never been regarded as appropriate methods by which the nation can be maintained. This is even truer in Asia. Japan, for example, faces a serious problem with its aging population, but it has refused to consider mass immigration as a possible solution.[49] Hence, the effort to regulate family reunification is tied not simply to questions of who will be allowed to immigrate but also to decisions about which immigrants will be permitted to reunite with their families, allowed to settle permanently, and counted as members of the nation.

Despite the continental variation and difference in official policy, the provisions outlined in table 2.6 and the related debates surrounding family and migration suggest that family reunification is becoming much more of a globally important issue. Furthermore, as international migration grows and as family reunification increases as a percentage of that total, how family unity is handled in one country or region may have impacts on migration flows elsewhere in the world. As chapter 4 demonstrates, international relations and pressures can affect domestic policies.

CONCLUSION

The historian John Demos writes, "To study the American family is to conduct a rescue mission into the dreamland of our national self-concept. No subject is more closely bound up with our sense of a difficult present—and our nostalgia for a happier past."[50] The very malleability that makes family such a powerfully suggestive metaphor for a host of issues also suggests that the meaning, function, and role of family are ever changing. The diversity in form, function, and experience of families documented by social scientists belies a fixed definition. For many immigration stakeholders, these shifts in meaning underlie their unease about immigration. New immigration may highlight the difficult present and arouse desires for a past concept of the nation that may have never existed. As I show in chapters to come, the immigration stakeholders engaged in family ideation have claimed a definition of family and attached racialized and gendered meanings to immigrants and the process of immigration in an effort to forge and preserve a national identity.

Chapter 3

"I Have Kept My Blood Pure": Gender Propriety, Class Privilege, and Racial Purity in Family Reunification During the Exclusion Era

On September 1, 1916, Quok Shee, age twenty, arrived on Angel Island from Hong Kong. She accompanied Chew Hoy Quong, a fifty-five-year-old Chinese immigrant living in San Francisco who had originally landed in the United States in 1881. Chew Hoy Quong was a partner in a business that sold herbs and medicines and as such was a merchant who had the right to leave and reenter the United States and the privilege of bringing over a wife and children. Having found and married his young bride while on a visit to Hong Kong, Chew Hoy Quong was eager to have the comforts of a wife after decades of life as a bachelor in the United States. Unfortunately, he and Quok Shee met formidable challenges and endured nearly two years apart. Immigration officials at Angel Island Immigration Station interrogated the husband and wife at length. Suspicious immigration officers questioned the validity of their marriage and eventually denied Quok Shee entry. During the lengthy appeals process, Quok Shee endured isolation, depression, and smallpox before finally being allowed to enter in August 1918.[1]

Just a few years earlier, another couple faced a very different experience. On December 23, 1913, Kiyo Urakawa arrived in San Francisco from Japan with her eight-year-old son. They joined Kiya Urakawa's husband, a Japanese laborer, who was already living in the United States. Her immigration case file mentions no interrogations with immigration officials or long detentions.[2] In comparison to Quok Shee's case file, Kiyo Urakawa's case file is exceptional for how unproblematic the Urakawa family's efforts to reunite seemed to be.

There are two striking points about these women's immigration experiences and their husbands' efforts to reunite their families. First, Kiyo Urakawa's husband had an unremarkable, rather easy, time bringing over his wife and son, in contrast to Chew Hoy Quong's experience. Second, although the effort to reunify was heartbreakingly long for Quok Shee, both she and Kiyo Urakawa were able to join their husbands during an era of growing exclusion against immigrants, especially those from Asia.

The United States implemented the first federal immigrant exclusion policy, the Page Act, in 1875; that law excluded all immigrant prostitutes and prohibited the entry of Chinese women in particular for "lewd and immoral purposes."[3] In 1882, Congress enacted the Chinese Exclusion Act; banning all Chinese laborers, it was the first, last, and only ethnic-specific exclusionary law.[4] In 1907, following the Gentlemen's Agreement between the United States and Japan, Japanese laborers were also denied entry. Over the decades between and following these policies, anti-immigrant sentiments grew, and the United States issued increasingly more exclusionary policies, culminating with passage of the Immigration Act in 1924. Despite such sentiments and measures, immigrants—including those who were deemed undesirable, inassimilable, and even ineligible for citizenship—used family provisions that were available to bring over their spouses and children in an effort to settle more permanently.

How do we explain these family provisions? Why was the family protected in some sense and immigrants given the right to reunify their families during an era of increasing immigrant exclusion? Even the most draconian, anti-immigrant laws included provisions for family unity, or at least seeming reverence for the preservation of family. Most immigration scholars and politicians think about family reunification as a uniquely modern feature of American immigration policy. However, as the examples at the beginning of this chapter illustrate, there were family reunification provisions in earlier policies.

Although there are many excellent studies of the immigrant exclusion of this era, no studies have been conducted on family reunification policy during this period—let alone research to find explanations for why such provisions were included as part of the larger exclusionary immigration policies. This chapter shows that the expression of gendered ideals of marriage, home, and family created a liminal space and opened up opportunities for family reunification. I argue that these gendered expressions were part of family ideation (the conceptualization of family and its idealized features) that provided lawmakers, intellectuals, and moral reformers with a narrative framework for making sense of the changes they confronted—increasing numbers of strange new immigrants and changing roles for women, both in the family and in the larger society.

As more and more immigrants landed, would-be exclusionists evaluated whether the new immigrants were assimilable and "like one of the family"—that is, whether they could be incorporated into the national body. Family ideation and talk of idealized features of the family included not only racial but also gender claims. Politicians and intellectuals articulated these ideals in debates surrounding immigration law—expressing, for example, patriarchal claims about a man's right to his family if he had proper class standing. These ideals were formally codified or simply practiced informally by immigration officials. Family ideation provided a liminal space in which some racially undesirable immigrants who nonetheless possessed appropriate class and gender characteristics could exercise family unity claims.

Although family ideation opened up opportunities for family reunification for some eligible individual immigrants, it also provided a way to define deviance and degeneracy in the familial arrangements of many other immigrant groups, helping to racialize them as undesirable and inassimilable into the nation and making their exclusion more possible. When did family ideation create a liminal space for some individuals to make claims to family unity even though they seemed racially undesirable, and when did family ideation create opportunities for exclusionary policymaking? We must consider the larger framework of political opportunities, changing social and cultural milieus, and demographic shifts to answer these questions. Family ideation does not necessarily cause a particular policy outcome for immigrants. Rather, it is through family ideation that certain meanings about immigrants, race, gender, and class emerge and become attached to immigration policymaking. Thus, the goal of this chapter, as well as the book, is to understand the process of meaning construction around concepts of family, race, and nation in immigration policy. This explanation adds a deeper layer of meaning to how immigration control has operated than a focus simply on why a particular policy arises. I show this by first comparing the initially varying treatment experienced by Chinese and Japanese immigrants.

While the Chinese Exclusion Act of 1882 banned Chinese laborers and effectively denied family reunification efforts for most immigrants already in the United States, following the 1907 Gentlemen's Agreement, Japanese immigrants in the United States could call for their family members to join them. Most Asian American and immigration scholars argue that this varying treatment can be attributed to the difference in geopolitical power wielded by the two countries: while China was a declining power, Japan was an increasingly more formidable geopolitical player. These scholars thus conclude that anti-Asian racist sentiments explain the eventual exclusion faced by both countries in 1924, when Congress used Asians' racial ineligibility for citizenship as a way to ban their entry.[5] Unfortunately, this explanation ignores the complex ways in which changing racial and gender logics operated to make different methods of regulating Chinese and Japanese immigration both possible and desirable.[6] In addition, a geopolitical and racism argument cannot capture the nuanced ways in which seemingly contradictory meanings of race and gender operated to create opportunities for family unity *and* immigrant exclusion.

An ideational approach that looks at how notions of family, race, and immigrants were constructed can help to capture these subtle complexities in immigration policymaking. In comparing the experiences of the two immigrant groups, I show how exclusionary efforts against the Chinese operated through family ideation, which attached meanings of inassimilability, sexual degeneracy, and filth to Chinese immigrants. They would sully the American family and the nation—they were a threat to the purity of both. In contrast, Japanese immigrants enjoyed ethnic differentiation rooted in part in Japan's geopolitical might. Eventually, Japan's growing strength, including the permanent settlement of immigrants in the United States, incited alarm that the Japanese would "colonize" the nation, introducing undesirable elements that would threaten its sanctity. Japanese exclusionists referred to the deviant and offensive characteristics of the Japanese—particularly their sexual impropriety and Japanese women's high fecundity—as a way to attach negative meanings to their immigration while idealizing racial, gender, and class features of the family. Nevertheless, despite the convergence toward racial exclusion, some members of both immigrant groups experienced crucial gender and class privilege. In both cases, some Chinese and Japanese immigrants, specifically men (and usually men with class privilege), succeeded in exploiting the liminal space opened up by family ideation.

In the second half of the chapter, I show how other immigrants found this liminal space, which offered them opportunities for family reunification as well. The landmark legislation that created a national origins policy in the 1920s effectively curtailed southern and eastern European immigration. Despite focused and concerted efforts to limit their entry, however, legislation permitted family reunification among these immigrants. Legislators claimed that a man had a right to hearth and home, and they expressed patriarchal ideas of coverture—the Anglo-American legal tradition that placed a woman's legal status under that of her husband. I trace the history and role of coverture in determining women's status and permitting family unity provisions for supposedly racially undesirable immigrants.

Governmental oversight, the policing of these gendered assumptions about family, and the expression of family ideals in a given immigration policy (such as derivative status) sometimes intensified the very same gender relations among immigrants that politicians and moral reformers denounced earlier as deviant and cited to justify exclusion. I demonstrate this by concluding with a look at Chinese immigrants' claims in the early decades of the twentieth century to derivative citizenship as the sons of native-born citizens—claims that promoted an administrative structure of exclusion that further facilitated a gender-imbalanced migration—and at the government program created to purge fraudulent familial ties.

In examining these histories, this chapter illustrates the importance of investigating the expression of gendered ideals about family. Examining family in immigration policy does not mean simply looking for the development and use of family provisions. Rather, I explore conceptualizations and discussions of family alongside immigration and immigrants as a way to understand how racial, class, and gender meanings were deployed to attach to immigrants notions of assimilability and desirability or of inassimilability and threat. In so doing, this chapter demonstrates how family ideation enabled immigration policymaking not only to include racially exclusionary goals but also to preserve gender and sexual norms and class ideals.

CHINESE IMMIGRATION

A poor and weakened China helped to push many emigrants to the United States, which lured them with tales of gold and other riches.[7] There were over 63,000 Chinese immigrants in the United States by 1870, and over 105,000 by 1880. Most of the early Chinese immigrants were male sojourning laborers who came alone, leaving behind wives and children—a familial arrangement that, in challenging strict claims about an ideal family's heteronormative and nuclear organization, drew suspicion and criticism for being illegitimate.[8] Not surprisingly, Chinese men accounted for over 90 percent of the Chinese immigrant population. The ratio of male to female was nearly thirteen-to-one in 1870, twenty-one-to-one in 1880, and never lower than twelve-to-one until 1920.[9] The first measures adopted by the United States to regulate immigration targeted the Chinese and exacerbated this early gender imbalance. After passage of the Page Act, Congress enacted the Chinese Exclusion Act in 1882 and denied entry to all Chinese laborers. Since the Chinese Exclusion Act made no explicit mention of Chinese women, the Page Act continued to regulate their coming.[10] The laws banned practically all Chinese women from entering, for immigration officials assumed that most were prostitutes.[11] While the merchant class was exempt—in theory, if not always in practice, as discussed later in the chapter—these laws prohibited Chinese male laborers (who made up the majority of Chinese immigrants) from bringing over their wives and family, thus limiting permanent settlement in the United States and creating a bachelor society.[12] Given antimiscegenation laws that prevented whites from marrying most nonwhites at the time, these single men—like many other nonwhite men in frontier locations who, in the absence of representative numbers of coethnic women, nevertheless did not marry other nonwhite women, such as American Indians or Mexicans on the West Coast—faced the likelihood of a bachelor life.[13]

Earlier studies of Chinese exclusion have provided robust accounts that identify the roles of racism, labor competition between European American workers and immigrants, and opportunistic congressional leaders and moral reformers in the development of the exclusionary measures.[14] Unfortunately, these accounts have largely failed to explain why the policies themselves and the surrounding discourse focused so significantly on women, gender propriety, and idealization of the family. For example, as discussed later, many of the early anti-Chinese attacks focused on the effect that their cheapened labor would have on depressing the wages of native white workers and these workers' ability to provide for their families.[15] The imagined family figured centrally in how political leaders and intellectuals conceptualized the assimilability of Chinese immigrants and the supposed threat they posed to the American family and nation. Furthermore, these accounts are unable to explain why family reunification was extended to some Chinese immigrants. Thus, we can still gain a deeper understanding of Chinese exclusion in particular and of immigration exclusion in general by exploring how racialized and gendered meanings attached to immigrants—articulated through discussions of family—constituted efforts to regulate their entry.

The fact that Chinese merchants had the privilege of bringing over their wives, as illustrated by the story of Chew Hoy Quong, complicates the story of Chinese exclusion, particularly in regard to Chinese immigrant women. There are two ways to look at the official family provision for merchants. On the one hand, in one of the first examples of family as a factor in immigration law, Chinese merchants had family reunification rights that were not available to most Chinese immigrants. One immigration historian suggests that Chinese merchant men's limited success following the Chinese Exclusion Act in bringing over their wives in the 1890s and early 1900s reflects to some degree the way a Chinese woman's marital status "trumped" her racial classification, at least initially.[16] What was more crucial was their husbands' class standing. Merchants' class status aligned with the class bias of the idealized family. On the other hand, as the Chew Hoy Quong example demonstrates, Chinese merchants had tremendous difficulty exercising this privilege. Regarding questions of marriage validity, the slightest hint or suggestion that a Chinese woman was a prostitute or even just "connected" to a brothel was offered as proof that she was not a proper wife and the man was not a proper husband.[17] Immigration officials relied on such claims to render the women excludable. They rarely took Chinese merchant men's familial claims at face value. Furthermore, immigration officials questioned the validity of the Chinese men's merchant status. Indeed, many Chinese men gained entry and sought reunification through the use of fraudulent certificates identifying them as merchants, as discussed later in the chapter.[18] The veracity of these claims is less important to the current discussion than the fact that these provisions existed at all and permitted a mode of legal entry.[19] Although these features of Chinese immigrant regulation seem at odds with one another—that is, an official respect for coverture that emphasized gender privilege versus an administrative practice that exercised ethnic exclusion—they were both part of the family ideation that helped to spell out notions of gender and sexual propriety, class ideals, and racial fitness and desirability. This family ideation was crucial for the characterization of the Chinese as inassimilable and a threat to the nation, even as gendered ideals of family opened up opportunities for Chinese immigrants.

Chinese immigrants did not constitute the desired family type in the settlement and making of the nation. Exclusionists declared that Chinese immigrants were "a distinct race of people . . . wholly incapable of assimilation."[20] Their inassimilability—constituted by illicit drug use, debauched sexuality, disease, ability to live under depressed wage conditions, and illegitimate family formation—all purportedly undermined permanent white family settlement and threatened national identity. The Chinese were a threat to the purity of both family and nation. These claims were made meaningful by the symbolic linking of race and gender with specific references to immigrant women's sexuality. Thus, family ideation, with an emphasis on gender and sexual propriety, helped to racialize the Chinese, who were seen as a threat to the purity and sanctity of white families. Invoking such meaning constructions of the Chinese as an undesirable race that imperiled the nation, anti-Chinese politicians in Congress—supported by moral reformers, intellectuals, and labor leaders—pushed for exclusion.

Exclusionists' rhetoric focused on the racial inferiority of the Chinese and referred to their supposedly deviant and degenerative practices in both China and the United States, such as opium use. For example, the chief of police for San Francisco, James Rogers, submitted a report to the California Senate in 1878 outlining the activities and effects of the Chinese in the city. He complained that white men and women visited opium dens during all hours of the day and night. He also wrote that the police department had even found "white women and Chinamen side by side under the effects of this drug—a humiliating sight to any one who has anything left of manhood."[21] Politicians and other government officials found both the activities and the increasing proximity of the Chinese to whites, especially white women, abhorrent. These officials, in making it clear that such intimate contact was unacceptable, attempted to sexually and racially discipline both Chinese immigrants and white women.

Thus, anti-Chinese rhetoric intertwined racial claims with notions of sexual propriety. This was most evident in the arguments of lawmakers, moral reformers, and leading intellectuals. They claimed Chinese women were active carriers of pathogens whose presence would sully the purity and strength of the nation. Identifying sources of contagious disease in the activities and bodies of Chinese immigrants, particularly the prostitute women, provided justification for efforts to limit their coming and to quarantine their places of work and residence. Unfortunately for many Chinese women, being identified as a prostitute was difficult to avoid.[22] In his introduction of the bill that became the Page Act, Rep. Horace Page (R-CA) declared 90 percent of Chinese women in the United States to be prostitutes.[23] Such rhetoric was repeated again in 1882 in debates over Chinese exclusion when Chinese women were pronounced to be "all prostitutes or concubines."[24] Many moral reformers and health officials denounced Chinese women as the biggest source of disease and the greatest threat to the health of families and the nation.

The growing popularity and acceptance of the science of race combined with a newly developing germ theory that explained disease and health to lend credibility and serious weight to generalizations about the Chinese as an undesirable and inassimilable race.[25] Scientists and other leading intellectuals, moral reformers, and politicians could more easily connect race, gender, and nation to one another—both figuratively and literally—with the prudence and strength of science backing up meaningful claims about Chinese degeneracy. For example, in his official address as president of the American Medical Association, the world-famous gynecologist J. Marion Sims claimed at the centennial jubilee of the AMA in 1876 that syphilis had reached epidemic proportions, and he sounded the alarm about the particularities of the "Chinese syphilis tocsin." He stated that Chinese prostitutes on the West Coast had already spread syphilis not only to men but to boys as young as eight and ten.[26] Young boys were supposedly going to Chinatown, where the price for sexual favors was "so cheap," but the Chinese prostitutes were "inoculat[ing] the youth with diseases."[27] Frequenting Chinese brothels not only would bring shame upon the men and their families, but could kill them. Chinese prostitutes' virulence presented both moral and physical threats to families.

Besides criticizing the Chinese for their sexual depravity, politicians and labor leaders also claimed that Chinese immigration and settlement depressed wages and furthered unemployment.[28] Chinese frugality drove down living conditions, prohibiting settlement by the *right* kind of families. Speaking on the U.S. Senate floor in 1876, California Republican senator Aaron Sargent stated that the Chinese living conditions were so despicable that they were driving out white residents in places like San Francisco.[29] Local and state political leaders also directly lobbied Congress for action. In a letter sent to the U.S. Senate in December 1881, the Board of

Trade of San Francisco wrote: "It is evident that a continuance of an unrestricted Chinese immigration is prejudicial to the interests of the Pacific Coast, tending to prevent a desirable immigration from Europe and our Eastern States and causing a prejudice which operates against the settlement of our unoccupied lands by permanent settlers."[30]

Exclusionists stressed Chinese immigrants' seemingly inassimilable character as a threat to American institutions and to American families as well. Charles Wolcott Brooks was an American who worked for the Japanese government and was the former Japanese consul in San Francisco. He had spent some time in China and testified before the Special Committee on Chinese Immigration convened by the California State Senate in 1878. When asked whether the Chinese cared for American institutions, he stated: "The very fact of their retaining their own dress and customs, and keeping themselves so entirely separate, as a people, shows that they have not [love for our institutions]." Brooks continued: "The Chinese are bad for us, because they do not assimilate and cannot assimilate with our people. They are a race that cannot mix with other races, and we don't wish them to." He concluded: "The Chinese are bad for us, because they come here without their families. Families are the centers of all that is elevating in mankind, yet here we have a very large Chinese male population. The Chinese females that are here make this element more dangerous still."[31] Thus, Brooks and other political and intellectual leaders equated the problems of racial degeneracy, illicit sexuality, and improper family formation with Chinese immigrants. Though these leaders did not want family formation and a permanent Chinese settlement, they nevertheless pointed to the lack thereof as proof that Chinese immigrants were debased and unfit for inclusion in the nation.

Convinced by such arguments and motivated to appeal to the labor vote and to Western congressional delegates, national lawmakers sounded the alarm. Sen. James Blaine (R-ME) spoke on the Senate floor in 1879 in debates over whether the United States ought to abrogate the Burlingame Treaty, which had enabled Chinese immigration thus far, in a step toward making Chinese exclusion possible. He echoed Brooks's argument and declared, "The Asiatic cannot go on with our population and make a homogenous element." He further claimed that the Chinese had "no regard to family," did not "recognize the relation of husband and wife," and did "not have in the slightest degree the ennobling and civilizing influences of the hearthstone and the fireside."[32] In the explicit message that Chinese immigrants did not care about family was an implicit message that *their* kinds of families were unwanted and could also threaten *our* kinds of families.

In many ways, exploiting Chinese immigrants' labor and preventing them from permanently settling were key elements of the grand plans of many political and intellectual leaders for national expansion. In a letter to historian, writer, and publisher Henry Bancroft, Judge Lorenzo Sawyer, a federal district judge in California, outlined a pattern of immigration that would be most beneficial to business, capitalist development in the West, and the nation. Writing about Chinese men, Sawyer stated:

> If they would never bring their women here and never multiply and we would never have more than we could make useful, their presence would always be an advantage to the State. . . . So long as the Chinese don't come here to stay . . . their labor is highly beneficial to the whole community. . . . The difficulty is that they are beginning to get over the idea that they must go back. Then they will begin to multiply here and that is where the danger lies in my opinion. When the Chinaman comes here and don't bring his wife here, sooner or later he dies like a worn out steam engine; he is simply a machine, and don't leave two or three or half dozen children to fill his place.[33]

Although it was written in 1886, after passage of the exclusion laws, Sawyer's sentiments illustrate how many economic, political, and intellectual leaders envisioned Chinese immigrants' role in developing the nation with their labor but not in constituting the national fabric, reflecting a continuing theme regarding the value and desire placed on the productive labor provided by immigrants but not on their reproductive labor.[34] Chinese immigrants would be quite successful in making Judge Sawyer's vision come true.

JAPANESE IMMIGRATION

Whereas Congress made the Chinese Exclusion Act permanent in 1902 (it would not be reversed until 1943, when the United States and China became wartime allies), the United States implemented a more favorable policy toward Japan. Japan and the United States negotiated the terms of an immigration policy outlined in the so-called Gentlemen's Agreement, a series of six memos exchanged between late 1907 and early 1908. The Japanese government pledged not to provide passports to laborers, skilled or unskilled, to go to the continental United States in exchange for concessions regarding laborers already residing in the United States and their right to bring over families.[35] Japan was permitted to continue issuing passports to parents, wives, and children of laborers already in the United States. The family reunification provisions were short-lived; based on their racial ineligibility for naturalization, Japanese immigrants were banned in the Immigration Act of 1924. Nevertheless, the varying treatment was hugely consequential in that it created a viable, American-born

Table 3.1 Chinese and Japanese Wives Coming to the United States Between 1908 and 1924

	Chinese Wives Admitted		
Fiscal Year Ended June 30	Wives of U.S. Citizens	Merchants' Wives	Japanese Wives of Residents
1908 to 1917	985	1,095	18,404[a]
1918 to 1924	1,833	1,509	17,660
Total	2,818	2,604	36,064

Source: Compiled from U.S. Department of Labor, Bureau of Immigration *Annual Reports of the Commissioner General of Immigration to the Secretary of Commerce and Labor, 1908–1924* (to the *Secretary of Labor*, 1914 and thereafter), "Table E. Japanese Arrivals in Continental United States, Showing Various Details Bearing on the Japanese Agreement (Wives to Residents)," and "Table 2. Chinese Seeking Admission to the United States, by Classes and Ports (Wives of U.S. Citizens and Merchants' Wives, Admitted by Final Disposition)."
Note: The number of Japanese wives arriving in Hawaii was not included in the table. No data for Japanese wives of U.S. citizens were available in the reports, perhaps because the number of U.S. citizens of Japanese descent was too small to be significant. Pre-1908 annual reports had data only for merchants' wives, not for wives of U.S. citizens.
[a]Included the number of Japanese wives arriving in the United Stated during June 1908. No such data were available before the month of June 1908.

second generation (Nisei) for the Japanese but not for the Chinese. By 1920 there were over 111,000 Japanese and Japanese Americans in the continental United States, and over one-quarter of them were native-born citizens.[36] Facilitating this settlement and formation of the Nisei was the number of Japanese women who entered as wives. Although some Chinese wives were able to enter, their numbers paled in comparison to the number of Japanese wives who arrived in the United States in the early 1900s (see table 3.1). Between 1908 and 1924, just over 5,400 Chinese wives were admitted, whereas over 36,000 Japanese wives were permitted to enter. In addition to wives initially left behind, Japanese men also called for women they married by proxy with photographs in Japan. These brides were euphemistically called "picture brides" or "photograph brides" by American immigration officials and politicians, though that description elicited a negative response from the Japanese government.[37]

A number of factors explain why policies toward Japanese immigration began with partial restriction and family reunification yet resulted in exclusion.[38] During the height of Chinese immigration, Japan and its subjects were characterized as superior to China and its people. Ethnic differentiation from the Chinese was part of the early history of Japanese immigration. Although politicians, labor union leaders, medical experts, and newspaper editors regularly derided China and Chinese immigrants, many of them initially spoke and wrote glowingly of the Japanese. For example, in 1869, when there were only a few Japanese immigrants in the city, the *San Francisco Chronicle* noted the difference between the two groups: "The objections raised against the Chinese . . . cannot be alleged against the Japanese. . . . They have brought their wives, children and . . . new industries among us."[39] Crucial differences between the two groups highlighted by many commentators centered on gender relations and notions of proper family arrangements.

Most significantly, the United States conceded a more favorable immigration policy to Japan (agreeing to the terms of the Gentlemen's Agreement) because Japan was a major geopolitical power. Unlike China, which faced declining influence as it was besieged by domestic and international crises, Japan emerged as an important international player after its defeat of Russia in the Russo-Japanese War of 1905. Thus, geopolitics, as other scholars have documented, mattered greatly.[40] Other important factors included the timing of Japanese immigrants' arrival. They followed Chinese immigrants just as the United States began to recover from a national economic recession, beginning in the 1890s and increasing more significantly after 1900. Owing in part to Chinese exclusion, cheap labor had become less available. In addition, Japanese immigrants engaged in agricultural work, and demand for agricultural laborers ran high along the West Coast. While Chinese agriculturists had been rather plentiful through the end of the nineteenth century, they became scarcer with the boom in a more intensive form of agricultural production that required a greater number of farm laboring hands.[41] As Japanese seeking agricultural work settled in more rural areas, they drew less attention from white labor organizations, which had a largely urban focus and concentrated on making Chinese exclusion permanent.

Thus, men like the farmer Rihei Onishi, who was able to visit Japan and return with the wives of the other settled agriculturalists who worked with him—as discussed at the beginning of the book—benefited from geopolitics and more advantageous comparisons to China and its immigrants. For those who might not have cared to protect these immigrants' right to family formation, the coming and settlement of some Japanese families nevertheless had beneficial qualities. The Japanese family served the economic development needs of the growing nation. Therefore, Japanese women as wives provided helpful labor on the farms on which their husbands worked, something understood by the men working on Onishi's rice farm.[42] These small yet significant opportunities for reunification made possible primarily by Japan's geopolitical position hinged on the gender propriety, class privilege, and proper family arrangements that the Japanese supposedly had. As Japanese immigrants successfully used available family provisions to gain entry, form families, and settle more permanently, however, their growing presence solicited hostilities and a negative characterization. The negative rhetoric focused on the threat to the very qualities that politicians and other commentators had originally declared that the Japanese possessed: gender and sexual propriety and racial fitness. Specifically, they claimed that Japanese immigrants—especially men—threatened racial purity and the sanctity of white womanhood. In addition, they argued, Japanese women threatened the nation with their high fecundity, which allowed them to gain land ownership. Thus, the meaning construction of Japanese immigrants as desirable and assimilable or as a threat to the nation operated through family ideation, which enabled political leaders, intellectuals, and others to conceptualize racialized and gendered ideals about Japanese immigrants in their efforts to control their entry and construct a national identity.

As in the Chinese case, gender and sexual propriety and efforts to discipline both native-born Americans and immigrants featured prominently in exclusionists' discourse. For many moral reformers, politicians, and other exclusionists, protecting native-born white women meant protecting the nation.[43] The discourse and set of practices that disciplined and engendered the settlement patterns of immigrants (family-centered or bachelor; more male or more female) were firmly entrenched in the larger dialogue over the gender and sexual propriety of white women. Women's purity and sexual propriety ensured the supposed sanctity of a pure, untainted nation. Thus, white women's sexuality had to be "protected" above all else in defense of the nation.[44] Such discourse and practices help to demarcate the symbolic boundaries of the nation.

The anxieties over protecting white women's virtue served many useful purposes—or rather, the discourse of protection did. Chivalrous claims helped to legitimize exclusionary practices based on apprehensions concerning the inferiority of immigrants and the allegedly detrimental effects of racial miscegenation. Antimiscegenation laws and the "one-drop rule" codified strictures aimed at prohibiting racial mixing, which could challenge the existing racial hierarchy.[45] Immigrants, particularly nonwhite men, and white women risked fines and even imprisonment for marrying across accepted racial lines. Thus, attempts to control white women's sexuality had the added benefit of controlling immigrants' sexuality.

As both men and women became solicitous over sexual norms and gender roles at the end of the Victorian era—the period of Chinese and Japanese exclusion and regulation—they attempted to identify proper womanhood (and manhood).[46] Concerns over these changing gender roles, industrialization, and immigration were encapsulated in the fight against white prostitution, which was euphemistically called the "White Slave Traffic."[47] Although the pairings of Japanese men and white women were rare, politicians and immigration officials identified them as one of the worst features of Japanese immigration and tried to link such mixing to prostitution. Immigration officials' handling of a case involving a Japanese man and a white woman exemplified the stereotypical assumptions about Japanese men and their sexuality. A European American woman named Louise McElwain and her Japanese husband, named Manzo Goto, were arrested and investigated by the Bureau of Immigration in 1914 when it was suspected that Goto had led McElwain into prostitution.[48] In interviews, she confessed that she earned money for sex with Japanese men, though she contradicted this statement on several occasions. During one of these interviews, the investigators asked if Goto ever slapped her, suggesting violence was used to keep McElwain in prostitution. When Goto was ordered deported for having committed the crime of prostitution, the Bureau of Immigration sought to send McElwain to her parents with the hope that she could be "reformed."[49]

Moral reformers in particular feared that foreign men were leading native white women into lives of prostitution.[50] Louise McElwain's entrance into some prostitution work was not unusual. Many women, with limited opportunities for financial independence, moved in and out of prostitution during their life course.[51] Japanese men or other foreign men were not necessarily to blame for these women's entrée into prostitution. To the immigration officials, however, McElwain represented the fallen woman who fell victim to the predatory Japanese man. She, like other white women, had to be protected from the likes of Manzo Goto. Like the Chinese men, the Japanese men were often brandished as hypersexual and menacing. The immigration officials who interrogated Goto and McElwain sought to identify him as lecherous and their relationship as deviant. In so doing, they were able to make chivalrous claims to protecting white womanhood while racializing Japanese men as deviant. The imputed purity of white womanhood metaphorically represented the purity of the nation, whose sanctity had to be protected against contaminating immigrants.

These fears over racial mixing intensified as the increasingly more permanent features of Japanese immigration produced two growing problems: American-born Japanese children, and Japanese immigrants' purchase of precious land. Although several states, such as California, Oregon, and Washington, had legislated alien land laws, prohibiting noncitizens from buying land in the state,[52] first-generation Japanese immigrants, the Issei, found ways to buy land through their native-born citizen children, the Nisei. Politicians and other leaders saw the purchase and control of land as a symbolic and physical challenge to supposed racial purity of the nation and the white race. Articulating such sentiments before the California Assembly during debates surrounding a proposed alien land law that sought to limit Japanese land ownership was a former congregational minister named Ralph Newman, who clamored: "Near my home is an eighty-acre tract of as fine land as there is in California. On that tract lives a Japanese. With the Japanese lives a white woman. In that woman's arms is a baby. What is that baby? It isn't Japanese. It isn't white. It is a germ of the mightiest problem that ever faced this state, a problem that will make the black problem of the South look white."[53] The Japanese man transgressed twice, according to Newman: by taking land and by cohabiting with a white woman, thereby sullying the purity of the nation. The woman herself was a traitor to her race and the nation. While man, woman, and child might constitute a family, for Newman this construction was unfathomable and instead represented the precipice of racial and national ruin. His argument relied on the imagery of women and their bodies as both physical and symbolic boundaries of the nation. Women, land, and nation were interchangeable in nationalist and nation-building discourse, and such discursive work was central to the kind of family ideation that shaped exclusionary policy.

Similarly, in a letter to Secretary of State Robert Lansing, Democratic senator James Phelan of California echoed Minister Newman's comments regarding the problem of Japanese land ownership. Referring to Japanese immigrant women, he wrote: "She also bears children, and, born on the soil, are American citizens, and take real estate as citizens; in other words, the Japanese are circumventing the [alien land] law." These Nisei children were a dangerous threat to the American nation, as were their parents. Though American-born, they could not be assimilated. Whereas the possibility of Japanese men socially and biologically mixing with white women had been considered earlier the gravest danger facing the nation's population, Japanese fecundity was now equally menacing. Phelan had specific remedies in mind:

> The Chinese Exclusion Law has operated to reduce the number of Chinese from year to year, but so long as women are admitted from Japan, so prolific are they, that even with an exclusion law, we shall have the economic evil of their presence for a great many generations. The Japanese are, as you are aware, non-assimilable, and we are inviting, unless checked, a race problem more serious than that in the south. Every day is a day lost, and therefore action is earnestly demanded.[54]

Phelan very clearly conveyed the magnitude of the problem with his reference to the South and in likening Japanese immigrants to blacks.

In addition to lawmakers, other influential speakers decried the alarming growth associated with Japanese women's fecundity. Speaking before the Senate during hearings on Japanese immigration, the anti-Japanese forces, including V. S. McClatchy (former publisher of the influential *Sacramento Bee* and director of the Associated Press), testified against continued

Japanese immigration, condemning their inassimilability and the danger their large families posed to the United States.[55] McClatchy argued:

> They do not come here with any desire or any intent to lose their racial or national identity. They come here specifically and professedly for the purpose of colonizing and establishing here permanently the proud Yamato race. They never cease being Japanese. . . . In pursuit of their intent to colonize this country with that race they seek to secure land and to found large families.[56]

Like Phelan, McClatchy identified Japanese women's reproductive abilities, which enabled Japanese immigrants to make their settlement increasingly more permanent through family formation and land ownership, as the root of their growing threat to the nation. Referring to the idea of "colonization," McClatchy invoked the horror and threat of the theme of the "yellow peril," which was first used to conjure fears about a Japanese (and eventually an Asian) invasion.[57] Congressional leaders heeded their cautions. In the Immigration Act of 1924, as Congress instituted a quota system that essentially favored the "older stock" of English and German immigrants,[58] it could have extended the quota system to Japanese immigrants or let the Gentlemen's Agreement continue to regulate Japanese immigration, albeit in modified form. Congress did neither, but instead voted to exclude all who were "ineligible to citizenship." The Supreme Court in Ozawa v. United States (1922) determined that the Japanese might be "white" in color but are not "Caucasian," rendering them ineligible for citizenship.[59] Following the 1924 law, Japanese were barred entry.

The act devastated the Japanese American community. First-generation Japanese in the United States were unable to call for their families, and many left, leading to the attrition of the Issei. Though the exclusionists feared and dreaded the possibility of a permanent Japanese American community and had agitated to prevent such a development, they succeeded only partially. With over 111,000 Japanese and Japanese Americans in the continental United States by 1920 and over 30,000 second-generation Nisei, the more permanent features of Japanese settlement survived. And because Congress never made the "aliens ineligible to citizenship" status hereditary, the development and growth of a native-born population was critical in ensuring the economic, political, and social development of a permanent Japanese American community. Nevertheless, the legacy of their ineligibility to naturalize was profoundly and painfully significant. By further cementing the notion that the Japanese were inassimilable and a foreign element within the nation, it helped to justify their internment during World War II.[60]

The history of Chinese and Japanese immigration and eventual exclusion clearly highlights the importance of family unity provisions, even limited ones, for immigrant settlement. More importantly, their history shows that family ideation was central to immigration policymaking. Examining how immigration stakeholders talked about the meaning of family and its ideal features and the coming of these new immigrants illustrates how family provided a narrative structure or touchstone for characterizing immigrants' efforts to join the nation. Perhaps unexpectedly, family ideation provided an important liminal space for otherwise racially undesirable immigrants *and* a powerful discursive tool for identifying them as deviant and inassimilable. Nonetheless, the gendered ideals of family expressed by lawmakers and other immigration stakeholders occasionally provided unexpected policy framings and outcomes. The history of coverture and the battle over women's citizenship status further demonstrate how family ideation shaped immigration policymaking.

COVERTURE: MEN'S PRIVILEGE AND WOMEN'S DIVESTMENT

The seeming reverence for family continued even as the United States passed increasingly more exclusionary measures. The Immigration Act of 1917 barred idiots, imbeciles, epileptics, persons suffering from tuberculosis or other contagious diseases, the mentally ill, anarchists, beggars, prostitutes, and the poor. The act also became known as the Asiatic Barred Zone Act for creating, through a language of latitudes and longitudes, an excludable geographic area that was equivalent to Asia (although immigrants from China and Japan continued to be regulated by the Chinese Exclusion Act and the Gentlemen's Agreement until passage of the Immigration Act of 1924, respectively). And after more than twenty years of lobbying by exclusionists, Congress passed a literacy test as part of its effort to stem immigration, overriding a veto by President Woodrow Wilson. Although the 1917 act required aliens to pass a literacy test for admission, it exempted close family members of immigrants already in the United States. In addition, the Immigration Act or National origins Act of 1924, which set annual quotas for each nationality and dramatically curbed southern and eastern European immigration to the United States, provided nonquota visas for the wives and children of U.S. citizens (initially for men only, as explained later in the chapter), including naturalized immigrants (see table 3.2).[61]

This followed the uproar after the Emergency Immigration Act of 1921 included a preference for wives, children, parents, and siblings of citizens and permanent residents who had applied for citizenship but counted their visas toward the annual quotas for each country.[62] For example, on February 26, 1921, Rep. William E. Mason (R-IL) objected to the quota sys-

Table 3.2 The Immigration Act of 1924

	Major Provisions and Family Preferences
Limit	150,000[a] (2 percent of the total population of foreign-born persons of each nationality recorded in the 1890 census, minimum of 100)
Per-country limit	After July 1, 1927: overall cap of 150,000 determined by national origins of the total U.S. population recorded in 1920, minimum of 100 (became effective July 1, 1929)
Nonquota	Wives and unmarried children[b] of U.S. citizens, Western Hemisphere immigrants, religious or academic professionals,[c] and students at least fifteen years of age
Preferences within quotas[d]	1. Unmarried children,[e] parents or spouses of U.S. citizens twenty-one years of age or over 2. Skilled agricultural laborers and their spouses and children under the age of sixteen[f]: no more than 50 percent of the nationality quota

Source: The Immigration Act of 1924 (43 Stat. 153).
[a]Initially 165,000. After July 1, 1927, the total quota was set at 150,000.
[b]Nonquota status was granted to the unmarried child under eighteen years of age. The Act of May 29, 1928 (45 Stat. 1009) changed the limiting age of an unmarried child from eighteen to twenty-one. Husbands were added under the 1928 act provided that they were married before June 1, 1928. The Act of July 11, 1932 (47 Stat. 656) changed the date to July 1, 1932. Those who were married after that date were put under a preference category.
[c]Included accompanying wives and children under eighteen years of age
[d]Under section 6(a)(2) of the 1924 Immigration Act, this preference for skilled agricultural laborers "shall not apply to immigrants of any nationality the annual quota for which is less than 300." The preferences within quotas (1) and (2) were not ranked; that is, family preference did not take precedence over skilled laborer preference.
[e]Under twenty-one years of age. By the 1928 act, they were moved up to the nonquota category.
[f]By the 1928 act, the age of children had increased from sixteen to eighteen. This act also gave preference to unmarried children under twenty-one years of age and wives of alien residents lawfully admitted for permanent residence.

tem, stating that in Illinois "there are hundreds and hundreds of people who have made a success here in the United States who want to bring their aged and dependent people here. They are not a burden to the American people. They are consumers, and they become patrons of the farmer and the manufacturer, and the son or brother who has been able to lay by his money to take care of those old people ought to be allowed to bring them in."[63] Referring to these family members as "consumers" helped to convey the meaning that family reunification would not encumber the state and would instead help to generate demand for American products. In addition, immigrant aid associations expressed concern that families would be separated. The Hebrew Aid Society argued that Congress should allow "the reunion of families" and "a more just attitude toward minority peoples."[64]

Nonquota exemptions in the National Origins Act of 1924 retained racial restrictions consistent with earlier citizenship and immigration laws. Men and women were unable to secure nonquota exemptions for their foreign spouses who were ineligible for citizenship, which included anyone of Asian descent. Thus, family provisions in immigration policy helped to construct not only racially permissible individuals but also racially eligible families. Nevertheless, the earlier class privilege enjoyed by merchants continued. On May 25, 1925, the Supreme Court declared alien wives, being ineligible for citizenship, ineligible for entry—even if they were the wives of American citizens (Chang Chan et al. v. Nagle). On the same date, the Court also ruled that alien Chinese wives and minor children of alien Chinese merchants in the United States could enter for permanent residence as nonquota immigrants (Cheung Sum Shee et al. v. Nagle).[65] Despite these limits, family provisions accounted for over 32,000, or 13 percent, of the nearly 242,000 immigrants who entered between 1925 and 1930.[66]

There were fine, yet important, distinctions in these family provisions for men and women over the years. In general, men—including naturalized citizens—faced better prospects of reuniting their families during the decades of exclusion, in large measure because marital decisions and familial choices for men were significantly less consequential, especially politically. Even as Congress passed exclusionary laws aimed at reducing immigration, it protected citizen men's right to family unity. While the National Origins Act of 1924 offered citizen men the right to bring in their wives and minor children, women did not have rights to such family reunification provisions until 1928, when foreign husbands of American citizen wives were exempted from quota restrictions. However, this provision was offered only to those who were married before June 1, 1928.[67] Some congressmen feared that American women were being fooled into marriage by foreign men seeking entry into the United States.[68] Women citizens did not achieve parity in family reunification until the 1952 McCarran-Walter Act, which replaced the word "wives" with "spouses" of U.S. citizens who were eligible to enter on a nonquota basis.

These legislative actions and the surrounding discourse illustrated the anxiety about women's "foolish" marital decisions and the state's efforts to regulate their most intimate relations—not unlike the chivalrous claims of protecting white womanhood that justified antimiscegenation and anti-prostitution laws. Such legislative action and discourse also demonstrate that gendered notions of coverture and family ideation were critical to the regulation of immigration during this era. In articulating the characteristics of assimilable individuals and desirable families, political leaders, intellectuals, and moral reformers mapped meanings of racial worth and gender propriety onto the bodies of immigrants and controlled their entry. Concomitantly, such family ideation regulated the lives of native-born citizens, especially women.

In 1855 Congress enacted a law that declared that a woman who married an American male citizen gained American citizenship, thus giving her derivative citizenship.[69] Questions arose, however, concerning the status of American women who married foreigners. Congress clarified the issue by passing the Expatriation Act of 1907, which stripped citizenship status from American women who married an alien man. An American woman who lost her citizenship could regain it only upon her husband's death, the dissolution of the marriage, or her husband's naturalization. In contrast, foreign women who gained American citizenship by marrying an American man continued to possess it after their husband died or their marriage was terminated. Virginia Sapiro argues: "While the 1855 Act could be interpreted as the generosity of a nation of immigrants concerned with family unity and therefore extending to foreign wives (but not husbands) immediate recognition as part of the 'family,' the 1907 law also constituted a rejection, an alienation, of those women who dared to marry a foreigner."[70]

While American women who married foreign men were all negatively affected, rendering many women stateless, the 1907 act was particularly harsh in its effect on American women who married men who were racially ineligible for citizenship. This meant that American-born women who lost their nationality after 1907 could not expect to gain derivative status through their Asian immigrant husbands. This negative consequence was even more deleterious for American women who were themselves racially ineligible for citizenship. Thus, an American-born woman of Chinese or Japanese descent who married a coethnic foreigner lost her citizenship status forever, even after the death of her husband or the dissolution of her marriage.

Neither the 1855 act nor the 1907 act drew much public outcry. Growing anti-immigrant sentiments and the ratification of the Nineteenth Amendment giving women the right to vote changed this. Immigrant foes worried that foreign women who gained citizenship through marriage could vote. Thus, exclusionists lent support to women's rights groups that pursued independent citizenship for women as full political expression, as well as to congressional leaders who increasingly grew concerned about a women's "bloc vote."[71] Of course, their seeming support for greater gender equality in citizenship status did not challenge patriarchal notions of women's sexuality and their particular roles in preserving the boundaries of racial purity. Opponents of a bill amending the Expatriation Act that would have returned independent citizenship status to American women who had lost it through marriage believed that such an amendment would only encourage "mixed" marriages and that the risk of losing their American nationality was "a good lesson to our American girls to marry American boys."[72]

Women reformers saw independent citizenship status as vital to their full independence as women, especially financially. Nevertheless, many women recoiled at the possibility of the polluting and inassimilable qualities that women could introduce through international marriage. Thus, when Kate Waller Barrett, a physician, social reformer, and president of a women's charitable mission, spoke before the House Committee on Immigration and Naturalization in 1917 on amending the Expatriation Act, she spoke against the injustice lobbied against American women who married foreigners, especially their loss of property. She explained that she was supportive of these "international marriages." However, she drew the line at racial mixing. When asked about marriages to persons of Chinese or Japanese descent, she replied: "I do not believe in indiscriminate international marriages. For myself, I am Anglo-Saxon, and I would not marry anybody who was not an Anglo-Saxon. . . . At the present time the Anglo-Saxon is the highest type, and I have kept my blood pure and have kept my children's blood pure and my grandchildren's blood pure."[73] Even as they supported the principle of independent citizenship, advocates continued to question a woman's allegiance to her race and nation based on her marital decision. Her intimate decisions had consequences for the preservation of racial and national purity.

In 1922 Congress passed the Cable Act, which gave women independent citizenship. It was part of a larger omnibus immigration bill that Congress considered and eventually passed as the Immigration Act of 1924 (which included the National Origins Act). Congress's overriding concerns over immigration control, including efforts to reduce the immigrant vote and maintain racial purity, were expressed in its effort to divest women's citizenship status from their marital status. Following the Cable Act, immigrant women did not automatically gain American citizenship upon marriage to a citizen husband. Instead, they had to go through naturalization, although their residency requirement was just one year as opposed to the usual five. American-born women who married racially eligible men did not lose their citizenship. Such women who lost their citizenship prior to the Cable Act could regain their citizenship status, although they would be considered "naturalized" citizens, not "native-born." In defending the treatment of native-born wives of eligible aliens as naturalized rather than native-born citizens, the chair of the Immigration Subcommittee stated: "If she goes abroad and permanently resides for two years she ought to by that act, voluntarily on her part, lose the right granted to her by this law, because she has, in the first place, married an alien. She has determined by her own motion and her act and her conduct that she is not thinking of the United States and therefore ought not to be an American citizen."[74] A woman had by agreeing to marriage consented to its consequences, and her most intimate relation remained a fair site for state regulation.

Racial restrictions on independent citizenship continued with passage of the Cable Act, and the consequences of marriage remained particularly precarious for many women. American women who married men ineligible for citizenship continued to lose their citizenship status, and thus, native-born women who were expatriated prior to the Cable Act for marrying ineligible men had no avenue for regaining their citizenship status while they remained in their marriage. American-born women who were themselves racially ineligible to naturalize could not regain their citizenship, even after their husband's death or their divorce.

Other gender and racial inequalities remained following passage of the Cable Act, including differences in men's and women's ability to confer citizenship status on minor children and streamlined naturalization processes for alien wives versus alien husbands. Congress addressed these inconsistencies and contradictions in a series of amendments passed in 1930, 1931, and 1934. Following the last amendment, American women no longer lost their citizenship for marrying a man ineligible for citizenship, and Congress finally fully separated a woman's citizenship from her marriage.[75]

Does this decoupling suggest that gendered and racialized notions of familial propriety and national identity faded or that women no longer stood for the boundaries of racial and national purity? Quite to the contrary—women continued to represent symbolically crucial features of racial and national boundaries. For example, the United States and other developing nations used such characterizations to advance state- and nation-building activities in international efforts to halt the trafficking of women into prostitution.[76] Nancy Cott argues that U.S. policymakers aimed for world leadership and saw the claim to the principle of "equal nationality" as critical to their efforts not to be upstaged by the Soviet Union on sex discrimination in a time of growing fascism. This suggests that the amendments to the Cable Act were part of the early reform efforts guided by international policy pressure and framed by family ideation.[77]

GENDERED DEVIANCE: PAPER SONS AND THE CHINESE CONFESSION PROGRAM

Although the Cable Act of 1922 ended derivative citizenship status for women, the status was still valid and available to children born of American citizens, regardless of their place of birth. This derivative status was particularly meaningful for racially ineligible immigrants like the Chinese. An ethnic Chinese born in the United States possessed birthright American citizenship, which could be passed on to his or her children. Along with merchant status, derivative citizenship status permitted ethnic Chinese applicants to enter legally during the Chinese exclusion era. Many Chinese relied on fraudulent claims to do so. As entry claiming merchant status became more difficult, Chinese turned to derivative status.[78] The great San Francisco earthquake of 1906 facilitated their efforts at subterfuge, for no official records survived to counter Chinese claims of birthright citizenship. Chinese men asserted derivative citizenship status as the sons of men whose birth records were supposedly destroyed. Derivative citizenship claims enabled 71,040 Chinese to enter between 1920 and 1940.[79]

Although immigration officials questioned the veracity of these familial claims and claims to birthright status, the legal architecture of exclusion helped to create the very foundation of evidence upon which other Chinese applicants could lay a claim to rightful entry. As Lucy Salyer explains, the courts upheld the right to hear habeas corpus arguments in cases brought by Chinese who were denied entry by immigration officials for lack of proper documentation.[80] Although many of these judges held strong anti-Chinese views (including Judge Sawyer, whose anti-Chinese position was shared in a letter discussed earlier), they ruled in favor of Chinese claimants in over 60 percent of cases brought to the U.S. District and Circuit Courts in San Francisco. In so doing, Mae Ngai writes, the court records in these cases "*created* documentation of native-birth citizenship where none had previously existed."[81] Chinese applicants memorized the details of these documents, including information on entire villages and up to three generations of eligible applicants, in their efforts to make a claim for entry.[82]

The gender arrangement of these claims—"paper sons" of citizen fathers—continued the gender imbalance that characterized early Chinese immigration. As discussed, the Page Act and the Chinese Exclusion Act had exacerbated the gender imbalance of early Chinese immigration. The exclusionary efforts that continued into the twentieth century added to this imbalance. As much as the earlier administrative structure of exclusion had encouraged Chinese men to leave their wives behind in China,[83] the later system did as well as Chinese men learned to pose as "paper sons." The number of "paper sons" led immigration officials to cry foul and to conclude that each Chinese woman in the United States prior to the 1906 earthquake would have had to produce hundreds of sons to account for the number of Chinese men claiming native-born and derivative citizenship status.[84] These men were imposters, taking advantage of a system and a body of evidence constructed in large part by the very government that sought to exclude their entry.

This evidence and the continued arrival of "paper sons" represented a serious loophole and security breach in the American immigration system. Growing fears over communism and the supposed threat of an infiltration by the Chinese reds moved government officials to act. Fraudulent families posed a security risk; using familial claims, Communist elements could enter, threatening national security. However, the only way to ferret out the truth and plug the loopholes for entry in the system was to encourage Chinese immigrants to confess. Government officials instituted the Chinese Confession Program in an effort to document and shore up the false claims of familial ties for future entry. Eventually, the program was able to document at least 11,336 Chinese Americans, who implicated 19,124 people, as having entered under false papers and ties.[85] In addition to illustrating the importance of a gendered analysis in immigrant exclusionary history, the consternation over "paper sons" also highlights the theme of governmental concerns about notions of legitimacy—that is, about what familial ties are real and appropriate as bases for entry. The issues raised by "paper son" claims also illustrate the growing relevance of international relations and national security as critical engines for shaping immigration control, which I turn to in the next chapter.

CONCLUSION

Beginning with the Page Act in 1875, the U.S. government reversed its long-standing tradition of an open immigration policy and instituted over the next half-century a series of exclusionary policies that limited people by ethnicity, national origin, class, occupational status, likelihood to "become a public charge," literacy, political affiliation, moral turpitude, and health status, culminating with the National Origins Act in 1924, which effectively ended large-scale immigration. Most scholars are familiar with this history of exclusion. What has been neglected or perhaps simply misunderstood is the history of family reunification during this period. In no way do I want to suggest that the level of family reunification during this era paralleled what we are witnessing today. However, there were important and consequential opportunities for some immigrant families to reunite and to settle in the United States. To have even limited rights to family unity provisions spelled the difference between the formation of a bachelor society (Chinese immigrants) and the development of a viable second-generation community (Japanese immigrants).

Although we have rich accounts of why the United States enacted immigrant exclusion laws, no explanation has been offered as to why family reunification provisions existed at all during this period. That is, given the anti-immigrant tide that swelled over the decades from the mid-1800s through the 1920s, why did the government ever show reverence for the preservation of family and concede by passing family unity provisions?

This chapter has explained that family and family ideation played central roles in how immigrants and immigration were understood and regulated. The imagined family provided, in some sense, a blueprint for political leaders, intellectuals, moral reformers, and other stakeholders to construct the notions of gender and sexual propriety and racial fitness that would be most desirable in a national identity. Family, with its metaphorical and synecdochic properties capable of representing the nation, provided a narrative structure about what families and their members can and should do. In this era, immigration regulators asked that families serve to protect the putative claims of racial purity and ensure gender and sexual propriety. By engaging in family ideation—talking about what family is and should do—immigration stakeholders were able to articulate and attach racialized and gendered meanings to immigrant groups. Family ideation thus guided policy that denied entry to immigrants as members of ethnic or racial groups because of their inassimilable ("not like one of the family") characteristics but still permitted family unity provisions based on gender and class ideals. Declarations of gender ideals of family, in particular, protected immigrant men's right to hearth and home, even when their racial assimilability remained questionable. Luckily for exclusionists, the imagined family also provided a powerful arsenal for constructing discourse and exclusionary policy that defined racially undesirable immigrants as degenerate and inassimilable for the family writ large—the nation.

Chapter 4

"Reason of Elemental Humanity": The Urgency of Uniting Families in the Postwar Era on the Road to Immigration Reform

On October 11, 1945, nearly one thousand British women from all parts of Great Britain lined up outside Caxton Hall in London, many with babies in their arms, for a meeting organized by the Married Women's Association. The women had earlier planned to march with some ten thousand participants before the police canceled the scheduled event; their pent-up frustrations only grew over the following days. Finally, on that crisp fall day, the aggrieved women protested the continued delay in their efforts to unite with their U.S. military servicemen husbands who had been returned home. The women eventually made their way to the U.S. embassy, shouting, "We want our husbands!" Standing before the frustrated women, Comm. Herbert Agar, special assistant to John Winant, the U.S. ambassador, tried to calm the women and responded, "A lot is being done." Commander Agar assured them that the U.S. government had not forgotten them—a message he extended to the British Parliament, which was also clamoring for action on the women's behalf.[1]

Indeed, something was being done. The stories of wives and babies left behind captured the public's imagination and the attention of President Harry Truman's administration and congressional leaders. As newspapers and popular magazines reported the growing anger and desperation among the wives (and to a lesser extent the husbands) left behind or published stories of stowaways sneaking aboard ships to join their betrothed stateside, members of Congress and President Truman received both personal pleas and official requests from Great Britain for action. There were an estimated 75,000 to 100,000 spouses of American armed forces personnel, with 54,000 from Great Britain alone.[2] Specifically, the protesting British wives wanted ship transport to the United States. More generally, foreign wives and husbands wanted assistance in immigrating to the United States. The government had to respond to their demands.

Although spouses of American military members lamented the long wait in joining their spouses, many of them nevertheless had avenues for family reunification. The 1924 National Origins Act had curtailed immigration from southern and eastern Europe by instituting a quota policy based on national origins and had made Asians an excludable class by declaring racial ineligibility for citizenship a cause for exclusion (although Congress made exceptions to this during and immediately after the war by passing legislation exempting Chinese, Filipino, and Indian immigrants).[3] However, as the previous chapter showed, even in this draconian, exclusionary policy, an important family unity provision was that the spouses of U.S. citizens did not count against the national origins quotas. Of course, permanent resident immigrants did not have this much latitude. Furthermore, citizens could not bring over spouses who were racially ineligible for citizenship, which included most Asians. Thus, for example, native-born Japanese American citizen husbands could not sponsor their Japanese wives for entry.[4] Despite the formal avenues available for reunification for eligible families, given the patchwork nature of the family unity provisions, the applicable quota limits, and the slow speed at which reunifications were granted, Americans who had served in the military during World War II and their spouses grew frustrated and made demands for change. Beginning with a response to their cries, family reunification—as a feature of the official U.S. policy, as a policy objective for immigration reformers, and as the method of entry for thousands of immigrants—became crucial to how U.S. immigration evolved over the period following World War II on the road to reform. Both supporters and opponents of the national origins system laid claims to the meaning of family and family reunification in defending American interests and the nation's very identity in the aftermath of World War II.

Because family as a category of immigration already existed, lawmakers could make piecemeal changes to immigration policy by altering the groups eligible. To this extent, policy legacy shaped some of the policy choices available.[5] Nevertheless, for initial reform efforts, policymakers had to identify both the family in a general sense and the affected groups more particularly as deserving of the policy change and attention. Whereas in the exclusion era family reunification was implemented without much expressed thought or consideration of it as a policy—highlighting more the unstated gender and class biases of the era and of the leading political and intellectual leaders—these actors now increasingly talked about family and the importance of their reunification was more explicit. They engaged in family ideation as a way to further the goals of immigration control in the postwar era with its particular configuration of domestic and international pressures and objectives arising from the status of the United States as a superpower. That is, they invoked family and made appeals for change on families' behalf as a way to attach meanings about merit, sacrifice, humanity, morality, and race to immigrants and immigration.

Family ideation—the conceptualization of what family means, constitutes, and features in terms of its idealized characteristics, such as gender or sexual norms, class ideals, and racial or ethnic attributes—provided a framework for talking about a specific human dimension of Immigration—separated families. Immigration reformers stressed the need for an urgent response to the problem of separated military families who had sacrificed for the nation, helping to shift the discussion of immigration away from something inextricably limited to the issue of race, especially the maintenance of racial purity or of the racial status quo. For immigration reformers, national origins policy was a clearly racially discriminatory law that had no place in a modern world with the United States as a democratic leader. Nevertheless, they faced significant challenge in recasting immigration and its beneficiaries as meritorious while redirecting focus away from race. It was a difficult, at times seemingly contradictory, task. On the one hand, reformers—particularly those in Congress—had to suggest that doing away with national origins policy would not alter the meaning of race in the United States. On the other hand, they had to show that the change in policy was not only humane but a clear moral response to the criticism of racial discrimination, a growing concern as demands for civil rights for African Americans in the United States and the battle against communism shaped the larger domestic and international political landscape. International pressure added a growing perception of urgency to the issue.

Talk about the family, however, is not inherently liberalizing for policy. Family rhetoric did not necessarily equal support for immigration reform generally or for ending racially discriminatory immigration policies specifically. Exclusionists and defenders of national origins policy also idealized the family in their efforts to uphold the discriminatory policy. Despite the more expansive meaning of national identity that reformers' talk of family afforded, the inherently conservative characterization of family (with assumed heteronormative features and functional roles in forming the next generation) helped to limit reform opportunities as well. As political pressure for overturning national origins policy grew, exclusionists sought to preserve it and to limit reform by arguing that national origins policy did not run counter to efforts to unite and protect American families. They did not challenge the characterization of the targeted group—military families—as meritorious. Exclusionists accepted limited family unity provisions for military families as they insisted their reunification would preserve the racial status quo. Even as debates and the focus of immigration policy moved away from regulating racially excludable groups, exclusionists assumed that family reunification would preserve the racial status quo that national origins policy had helped to protect. Thus, immigration stakeholders on both sides of the issue talked about the importance of serving the family, highlighting the crucial symbolic and metaphorical role of family in political debates.

The ability to speak and to be heard, however, is conditional on crucial institutional arrangements and balance of power. Thus, this chapter locates these discursive acts and efforts at meaning construction in policy in a broader context of shifting power relations, interests, and resources. As Francesca Polletta argues, "Configurations of power and resources determine what kind of a hearing particular stories secure." In the post–World War II era, these power configurations and institutional resources had a great influence on the ways in which framing immigration as an issue of family unity would affect policy outcome.[6]

IMMIGRATION IN A NEW WORLD ORDER

World War II altered power relations and resources in ways that had been unimaginable just a few decades prior. The new world order created by the war included the discrediting of scientific racism in general and of eugenics in particular, which had provided fundamental support for the creation of national origins policy but whose legitimacy was forever tarnished by the link to Nazi Germany.[7] The decoupling of the conceptualization of family from nationalist "race betterment" programs helped to open up new meaning construction opportunities for race and immigration.[8] Although this did not mean the end of racial prejudice in American immigration policy (or even the end of eugenics in the United States), the U.S. defeat of Germany in World War II ushered in a period when overtly racially discriminatory policies could be challenged from both within and outside the country.[9] At the domestic level, challengers of national origins policy and advocates for civil rights reform for African Americans pressured lawmakers to overturn racially discriminatory policies. Internationally, the United States risked losing an important propaganda war with the Soviet Union as critics questioned its commitment to democracy. Critics argued that Jim Crow segregation and national origins policy were anathema to the tenets of democracy. Domestic and international criticisms threatened to undermine U.S. legitimacy and the nation's domestic and international policy objectives.

As the U.S. government itself recognized, the official U.S. position on race (with respect to Jim Crow segregation and in national origins policy) left it vulnerable to attack. After World War II, President Truman's Committee on Civil Rights, charged with assessing the status of the nation's civil rights, issued *To Secure These Rights,* a report that recommended the formation of a permanent Commission on Civil Rights, congressional action against lynching and voter discrimination, and new laws to end employment racial discrimination. The report stressed that:

> our position in the postwar world is so vital to the future that our smallest actions have far-reaching effects. . . . We cannot escape the fact that our civil rights record has been an issue in world politics. . . . Those with competing philosophies . . . have tried to prove our democracy an empty fraud, and our nation a consistent oppressor of underprivileged people. . . . The United States is not so strong, the final triumph of the democratic ideal is not so inevitable that we can ignore what the world thinks of us or our record.[10]

Civil rights scholars have argued that this concern for the reputation of the United States on the world stage greatly shaped the development of civil rights legislation during the 1950s and 1960s.[11] They claim that the Cold War and national security concerns helped to push through legislation such as the Civil Rights Act of 1964 and the Hart-Celler Act of 1965. The rhetoric of national security introduced a sense of both urgency and legitimacy to these legislative efforts. A question remains, however: how did lawmakers talk about immigration to make policy change possible given the long-standing support for exclusion? Policymakers and other immigration stakeholders had to specify the changes that potential immigrants' entry would generate and their potential impact on the national identity. Both supporters and opponents of immigration reform turned to family to help make sense of these demands, to articulate or to frame new possibilities, to rationalize a political position, and to convince other lawmakers and a skeptical public. The struggle over immigration reform occurred around and through the meaning of families.

Another important postwar development was the formation of new coalitions around immigration reform. While restrictionists still dominated Congress, new and unexpected alliances made reform more feasible than in decades past. For example, although the American Federation of Labor (AFL) continued to take an anti-immigration position, it eventually changed its tune following its merger with the Congress of Industrial Organizations (CIO) in 1955. The racially progressive CIO was supportive of overturning national origins policy and attacked that policy in part for the way it separated families as early as 1940.[12] The merger of the two labor organizations spelled a critical change in organized labor's position on immigration and an end to its reliable support for exclusionary policies. In addition, groups like the Immigration Restriction League, which had been home to leading intellectuals with connections to major political leaders and had provided crucial support for national origins and other exclusionary policies, folded, with no successor group to follow. Instead, coinciding with the official fall of scientific racism, academics and social science organizations sided with more politically liberal causes, including black civil rights and immigration reform.[13]

Strong presidential support for immigration reform also helped to keep the issue alive in Congress. Every president after World War II, from Truman to Johnson, sought to overturn national origins policy, although a bill to abolish the system would not be sent to Congress until the Kennedy administration. As I show later, these presidents framed the issue of immigration reform as vitally important to the well-being of the nation—as a national interest. For the White House, national origins policy was an embarrassment with the potential to damage American legitimacy and national security.[14] In urging reform, each successive administration stressed the inhumanity of separated families and pushed for family reunification as they increasingly identified united families as a moral objective.

Despite these important developments, which led to more reform opportunities, significant barriers to immigration reform remained. Although racism against previously excluded immigrant groups like Asians declined in the postwar years, public opinion polls continued to show little support for overturning national origins policy or for increasing immigration.[15] In Congress, immigration restrictionists continued to hold major leading roles, particularly the chairmanship of the judiciary committees and the immigration subcommittees. During and immediately after World War II, restrictionists focused on increasing immigration control. Southern Democrats such as Sen. James Eastland (D-MS) allied with Western Democrats like Sen. Pat McCarran (D-NV) to block legislative reform efforts. (Both Eastland and McCarran served as chairman of the Senate Judiciary Committee.) In addition, concerns over national security and Communist propaganda did not guarantee an attack on national origins policy. To the contrary, citing such concerns, Congress passed strict border control measures like the Internal Security Act of 1950, which, among other things, toughened exclusion and deportation laws for subversives, particularly Communists. Furthermore, immigration competed with other weighty domestic and international issues for attention, including civil rights and postwar realignments in Europe, which pitted the United States against the Soviet Union in Cold War détente. These political exigencies, however, created some opportunities for legislative action as well.

Given the demands of the new world order and shifting configurations of power and resources, how did reformers and restrictionists attack or defend national origins policy? As in the earlier era, family provided a narrative structure for discussing American national interests and for changing meanings of immigration, race, and nation. In the sections remaining, I show how reformers and restrictionists battled over immigration policy and trace the construction and discursive use of family by policymakers and other immigration supporters and foes.

IMMIGRATION REFORM AS A WAR MEASURE

World War II and the resulting new world order were important catalysts for immigration reform, with international relations providing crucial pressures and opportunities for domestic policymaking. Even before the war ended, changing international alliances demanded a change in American immigration policy. As the United States entered World War II with China as an important ally against Japan, the decades-old policy of prohibiting Chinese immigration stood as an embarrassingly hypocritical policy for a country at war to end fascism. Opponents of Chinese exclusion, such as Richard Walsh, the husband of the Pulitzer Prize–winning author of *The Good Earth,* Pearl Buck, helped to form the Citizens' Committee to Repeal Chinese Exclusion in 1943. This small yet active lobbying group contributed to efforts to galvanize greater support for repeal.[16] That year Congress began considering a number of bills to abolish the Chinese Exclusion Act and replace it with provisions that would extend an official quota of 105 visas for Chinese.

As a war measure, ending Chinese exclusion was crucial to preventing the loss of American legitimacy, the collapse of morale in China, and a diminished position in the war. Japan argued that Asia had to unite in a race war against the United States, citing the discriminatory laws against the Chinese as proof that the United States did not live up to its supposed ideals of democracy. Fearful of the possibilities of an Asian racial conflict, congressional leaders warned that if China were to side with Japan, the rest of Asia would do so as well, resulting in a "campaign of Asia for Asiatics."[17] Congress declared that the exclusion laws had to be repealed, not only as war and peace measures and to uphold American legitimacy, but also because the "salvation of the white race" depended on continued friendly relations with China.[18] The military consequences would be significant as well. One retired Navy officer told Congress that the Chinese exclusion laws were equal to "twenty divisions" of the Japanese Army. President Franklin Roosevelt announced his support for the repeal in a letter to Congress on October 11, 1943.[19]

Opposition to the end of Chinese exclusion, even in symbolic terms, still remained. Given the long history of racially exclusionary discourse that had supported all earlier immigration restrictions, it is not surprising that a bill seeking to reverse Chinese exclusion and provide a quota of just 105 continued to generate the debate that it did. Southern congressional leaders balked at repeal efforts, raising concerns that abolishing Chinese exclusion would lead to an end of other Asian exclusions. Organizations such as the American Federation of Labor and the American Legion lobbied against any repeal bills. Opponents of the law's cancellation raised arguments about the racial superiority of Europeans over Asians and the assimilability of the Chinese. However, supporters found ways to sidestep the issue of racial assimilability. For example, Pearl Buck refused to address the question of whether she believed in "full social equality of the races," which was posed by Rep. A. Leonard Allen, a Democrat from Louisiana, during House hearings on the repeal. Instead, she argued that the repeal was a war issue.[20] The bill backers successfully framed the repeal in terms of national security to quiet opposition and to draw support. Even some Southerners, such as Rep. Ed Lee Gossett, a Democrat from Texas, voted for the bill, declaring that it "is not an immigration bill. This bill is a war measure and a peace measure."[21]

Thus, as a war and peace measure and not as an immigration bill, the bill passed. The new law ended Chinese exclusion, finally provided Chinese immigrants with the opportunity to naturalize, and permitted the admission of up to 105 Chinese immigrants to the United States per year. This quota was based on ethnicity, not on national origin, which meant that Chinese coming from countries other than China, such as Brazil, would count as part of the total quota. During the first ten years the law was in effect, an annual average of just 59 Chinese immigrated under the quota visas. Chinese immigrants who chose to become naturalized numbered only 1,428 between 1944 and 1952.[22]

Immigration reform as a form of national security and as part of the wartime effort continued to effectively resonate with political leaders. Before the war ended, Congress introduced bills to repeal exclusion for those coming from India, Korea, the Philippines, and Siam (Thailand), in 1944 and 1945.[23] As resistance to reform waned, members of Congress and the White House used immigration reform as a tool against "Jap propaganda."[24] And as long as quotas for these groups remained at the symbolic 100 or 105, the gains made in strengthening the U.S. position in fighting the war or communism greatly outweighed any foreseeable problems at the time.

INTERNATIONAL LEGITIMACY AND LEGITIMATE IMMIGRANTS

The link between immigration reform and international diplomacy in general and national security more specifically created opportunities for characterizing immigration in new ways. The isolationist position taken by the United States in the 1910s and 1920s (despite its role in World

War I) helped to underscore its exclusionary and anti-immigration position as necessary for national security—since tighter immigration control would prevent the entry of potentially seditious and anarchist elements as well as the racially inassimilable. The nation's position as the leading Western power after World War II, however, eviscerated any hopes entertained by restrictionists that it could lock the gates and turn out the lights.[25] As much as Chinese exclusion created problems of legitimacy for the United States during the war, afterward its racially discriminatory national origins policy continued to pose challenges to U.S. claim as a world leader.

As one of the first orders of business, the plight of war brides like the ones who rallied in London demanded attention and quick legislative action. As the opening vignette illustrates, brides and babies left behind by American military servicemen created powerful images, drawing attention to the many constraints in the national immigration policy. As the women in London protested, a bill addressing their demand to be reunited with their stateside husbands made its way through Congress. The bill proposed to expedite the admission of alien wives, husbands, and minor children for a period of three years by processing their mental and health examinations more quickly.

Two features of the bill and its introduction highlight the ways in which lawmakers coupled family and immigration and shaped reform following the war. First, policymakers supported the importance of uniting families without advocating any significant reform. The bill altered little in the existing immigration policy and did not challenge any quota laws. For example, it did not cover racially ineligible spouses or children. Instead, the bill merely quickened the process of admission. Previously, eligible spouses gained admission eventually, but the process was unnecessarily long and required administrative action or private bills introduced through Congress (which burdened its workings). The nearly identical House and Senate reports that accompanied the bill argued that the new legislation would simply facilitate this process and reduce the potential run-up in costs associated with implementing these alternative measures or with sending public health officials overseas to conduct the medical examinations required for immigration.

Second, lawmakers linked family reunification with U.S. legitimacy by pointing to the sacrifices of military personnel. The reports accompanying the House and Senate bills identified the beneficiaries of the proposed law—those who had served in the military during the war—as deserving and legitimate, making their efforts to reunite with their families seem meritorious. The reports stated that "strong equities run in favor of these service men and women in the right of having their families with them."[26]

Furthermore, the reports reminded Congress that these spouses, mostly women, faced challenges to entering because they no longer gained American citizenship upon marriage the way spouses of American servicemen in World War I did; women no longer had derivative status after the Cable Act of 1922 (as discussed in the previous chapter). The bill generated little debate on the floor of either house, and supporters argued that the new law would simply "cut red tape."[27] With no objection, the bill passed and was signed into law on December 28, 1945. Known more commonly as the War Brides Act, the law expired three years later.[28]

During these three years, over 95,000 immigrants—or nearly one-quarter of all legal immigrants to the United States—entered under this law, as table 4.1 shows.[29] Most immigrants came from Europe, with Great Britain sending 30,316 wives, 43 husbands, and 419 children.[30] Given the fact that the national origins quota allotted entry to just 154,000 per year, these military service personnel's family immigration represented a sizable number of legal immigrants during this period.

Family-sponsored migration also came from China during the immediate years after World War II. From China, 3,759 wives, 4 husbands, and 363 children landed in the United States, representing a far more significant number of legal immigrants from China than the 105 immigrants per year the national origins quota permitted.[31] Congressional action in 1946 facilitated the immigration of these Chinese wives (mostly) and children under a newly legislated family reunification provision. On August 6, 1946, Congress permitted Chinese wives of U.S. citizens to enter on a nonquota status (under the Chinese War Brides Act, P.L. 79-713, 60 Stat. 975), putting them in the same position as other wives of U.S. citizens who gained nonquota status under the 1924 Immigration Act. In its report to the full House of Representatives, the Committee on Immigration and Naturalization reminded Congress that the repeal of Chinese exclusion and extension of the small annual quota of 105 was not intended to sug-

Table 4.1 Spouses and Children Admitted Under the War Brides Act, 1946–1948

Year Ended June 30	Children	Husbands	Wives	Total
1946	721	61	44,775	45,557
1947	1,375	101	25,736	27,212
1948	968	94	21,954	23,016
Total	3,064	256	92,465	95,785

Source: House Committee on Judiciary, *Admission into U.S. of Certain Alien Fiancés and Fiancées of Members or Former Members of Armed Forces* (1949), 3.

gest their racial parity with others eligible for naturalization. However, the small quota had created extremely long waits for Chinese wives of American citizens who wished to reunite with their husbands.

As with the War Brides Act of 1945, supporters of the bill for Chinese war brides in both the House and Senate advocated its passage by emphasizing two points. First, they suggested that the proposed legislation would not change practices very much. Therefore, they anticipated no problem with implementing its provisions. For example, the Senate Committee on Immigration and Naturalization report highlighted what was likely to be a numerically inconsequential effect of the law given the small number of American citizens of Chinese descent in the United States. The report reminded lawmakers that from 1931 to 1942—the years when Chinese wives who had married American citizens prior to the enactment of the 1924 Immigration Act were admitted, following an act passed in 1930—only 767 had entered the country.[32] In addition, lawmakers assumed that American citizens bringing over Chinese wives would themselves be of Chinese descent. They did not entertain the possibility of any racial mixing. For example, in House hearings, Rep. Joseph Farrington (R-HI) declared, "A very large number of those soldiers . . . are Hawaiians, Chinese, and many other races, and the normal thing for them is to marry into these other races."[33] Second, as with the War Brides Act, they framed the beneficiaries of the bill as deserving because of their sacrifices and service in the military. On the Senate floor, for instance, Sen. William Knowland (R-CA), the chair of the Committee on Immigration and author of the Senate report, reminded his colleagues that the Chinese in the United States had been both "good citizens" and "good soldiers in the Army during the war."[34]

The War Brides Act and the Chinese War Brides Act demonstrated that lawmakers could achieve limited reform around the issue of family reunification by shifting the focus on immigration from race to family and meritorious or deserving military personnel. However, such talk of family necessitated neither an expansion in policy nor, more importantly, the end of national origins. Besides reformers, immigration restrictionists also talked increasingly about families and even supported family reunification in their own efforts to *limit* challenges to national origins policy. Thus, talking about the family could lead to some changes in the existing immigration policy, but not inevitably to relaxation of the racist views that upheld national origins policy. For example, some policymakers emphasized the importance of extending family reunification provisions to previously ineligible groups as a way to maintain racial segregation and thwart the possibility of mixing. In so doing, they identified the family as a racially pure one, continuing the earlier era's tradition of situating the work of maintaining racial purity in the family. Such family ideation was at work when Congress passed a law making previously racially ineligible spouses (according to the 1924 quota system) eligible for entry under the War Brides Act provisions.[35] Congress extended the benefit to both citizen and noncitizen military service men and women. Lawmakers stressed two crucial points: first, the law was not intended to encourage racially mixed unions, and second, the measure was to be temporary. In the accompanying House report, the Committee on the Judiciary stated that many U.S. citizen soldiers of Japanese or Korean descent had married "girls of their own race." Unfortunately, under existing laws, these brides were ineligible for admission. Referring to a judicial decision by the Ninth Circuit Court of Appeals to deny entry to a GI bride who was half Japanese, both the Senate and House reports declared that "this discrimination should be eliminated." Nevertheless, Congress clearly intended for this relaxation of racial admissibility to be a temporary measure, stating that the law was to expire on December 28, 1948. Furthermore, Congress did not want to encourage future marriage between U.S. citizen soldiers and racially inadmissible brides; after first considering whether to make the provision available only to those who had been married prior to 1947, it relented and extended it to those married within just thirty days of the act's passage.[36] The act ensured the entry of 5,398 husbands, wives, and children from Asia.[37]

After the War Brides Act sunset at the end of 1948, the American military presence in Japan and the growing conflict on the Korean Peninsula, which would lead to the Korean War, revived new demands for family reunification for members of the armed forces. On August 19, 1950, Congress voted to bring back the War Brides Act, allowing for the entry of Japanese and Korean spouses.[38] The 1950 law, originally good for six months, was renewed for another six months. As in earlier legislation that extended family reunification provisions to previously racially ineligible citizens, lawmakers expressed concern over racial mixing. In the accompanying report by the Senate Judiciary Committee, Senator McCarran explained that many of the citizen servicemen who would benefit from the expansion of the War Brides Act to Japanese wives and children were themselves Japanese. In making this assumption, the committee report stated that it expected just 760 spouses would enter under the law. Of course, Congress predicted this number incorrectly in part because non-Japanese American men brought their Japanese wives stateside.[39] In 1950 the number of wives of U.S. citizens from Japan was nine. In 1951 the number increased to 125, and in 1952 it reached 4,220; most of these wives were "admitted under special legislation which was passed to permit the admission of war brides racially ineligible for admission."[40]

THE MCCARRAN-WALTER ACT AND PRESERVING NATIONAL ORIGINS

For reform advocates, these military personnel–related measures helped to connect the meaning of deserving categories to immigrants by offering immigration reform efforts as a fair response to the sacrifices that brave military men and women had made. This made the expansion of family reunification or simply the quicker facilitation of these provisions easier to legislate since the affected groups appeared legitimate and meritorious. It also helped to strengthen the state-subject relationship around immigration. Lawmakers declared immigration benefits like family reunification to be a reward for those individuals who act responsibly in service of their nation. Given the limited nature of reform, even supporters of national origins policy and the racial status quo could stand behind these new laws. As policy scholars have often noted, incremental policy expansions face lesser opposition when the core of the policy issue remains unchanged.[41] Thus, the central focus or core of American immigration policy—limiting immigration through national origins policy—persisted despite the various measures proposed during and after World War II. Although emphasizing the merit and legitimacy of military families' efforts to reunite helped to shift attention away from racial exclusion to some extent, race still featured centrally in the conversation on how families could be reunited while legislators left core existing immigration objectives untouched. Thus, as the extension of the War Brides Act to previously racially ineligible spouses illustrates, lawmakers could engage in talk about the significance of family and family unity to stress the importance of preserving the racial status quo.

Despite the apparent limits, liberal Northern Democrats in Congress felt emboldened by these piecemeal reform developments and by their success in the passage of laws such as the Displaced Persons Acts of 1948 and 1950, which helped over 400,000 refugees who had fled Nazi rule or were escaping Communist persecution. With support from the Truman administration and immigrant advocacy groups, these lawmakers targeted national origins policy. They articulated themes they would use later in their more successful legislative efforts in 1965—justice (linking immigration reform to civil rights), humanity for separated families, national interest (the need for new and more immigrants who would provide new skills to fuel industry), and international relations (the U.S. role as a democratic leader). In 1952 Sen. Hubert Humphrey (D-MN), Sen. Herbert Lehman (D-NY), and Rep. Franklin D. Roosevelt Jr. (D-NY) sponsored a bill that would overthrow national origins policy and replace it with an immigration policy consistent with these declared goals. In the joint statement, Humphrey, Lehman, and eleven other sponsors of the bill affirmed:

> This bill would enable us to meet the emergency world situation by providing a haven for religious and political persecutees from eastern, southern, central, and northern European countries behind the iron curtain. . . . This bill would reunite divided families, some members of which are already in the United States as citizens of permanently resident aliens. . . . At the same time this bill would eliminate from present law the damning and damaging stigma of racial discrimination, and discriminations based on sex. . . . Another purpose of this bill is to couple justice with humanitarianism as the twin symbols of America in immigration as well as in other fields.[42]

Increasingly, the reform effort emphasized the morality of reuniting families and leading a just society, a focus that stood up to the charges of racial discrimination both domestically and internationally.

Senator McCarran and Rep. Francis Walter (D-PA), both restrictionists, issued their own alternative bill—one that would preserve national origins policy but allocate existing quota visas for each country through a new preference system that would favor job skills and family reunification. In offering this alternative formulation, McCarran and Walter responded directly to the claim that national origins policy was unjust and inhumane or did not address the national interests represented by new immigrants.[43] They identified separated families and an economy in need of new skilled workers as beneficiaries of the proposed legislation. Speaking on the Senate floor on May 13, 1952, McCarran explained that his bill would remove from immigration law "the present racial discriminations in a realistic manner" and "discrimination based on sex,"[44] referring to language in the family unity provisions for husbands to bring over wives rather than the gender-neutral term "spouses." He emphasized that "one of the most significant changes made by the bill is the introduction of the principle of selectivity into our quota system. Under the provisions of the bill, 50 percent of each quota is allocated to aliens whose services are needed in this country because of their special knowledge or skills."[45] Like reformers who advocated ending national origins policy, McCarran, Walter, and their supporters talked about ending racial discrimination while still preserving the core of national origins policy.

McCarran and Walter's bill benefited from the power that their sponsors wielded in Congress, particularly as chairs of the Senate Judiciary Committee and the House Subcommittee on Immigration, respectively. They led a joint House and Senate subcommittee hearing on the immigration bill in 1951 and controlled the list of speakers who came before the group, which McCarran chaired. Most of the speakers before the subcommittee supported the bill sponsored by McCarran and Walter. Even the Japanese American Citizens League (JACL) supported the bill, for it ended Asian exclusion and the bar to naturalization while offering small, token quotas for previously inadmissible groups, including the Japanese. The JACL wanted Japanese Americans to be treated equally and their families to enjoy the right of reunification. Thus, for determining the allocation of immigration quotas, Mike M. Masaoka of the JACL declared: "The wives, husbands, and unmarried minor children under the age of 21 of all American citizens, regardless of race, ancestry, and national origin, should, of course, be nonquota immigrants as proposed in all the pending bills before this Joint Committee."[46]

Because the bill ended Asian exclusion, the State Department supported it as well, and Secretary of State Dean Acheson wrote to President Truman to argue in favor of the proposed legislation. In particular, he noted the recent signing of the Treaty of Peace with Japan, which formally ended Japan's colonial rule in Asia and established U.S.-Japanese relations. Secretary Acheson worried that Japan would be offended by existing racial bars to entry for Japanese immigrants. He further warned: "Our failure to remove racial barriers provides the Kremlin with unlimited political and propaganda capital for use against us in Japan and the entire Far East."[47] Secretary Acheson referred to the national security concern of maintaining a positive international image in pressing for immigration reform that included the symbolic change of ending Asian exclusion even as it maintained national origins policy.

On April 25, 1952, after debating for three days, the House passed the Walter bill with amendments, and the Senate passed the McCarran bill by a voice vote on May 22, 1952, after seven days of debate.[48] President Truman, who had voiced strong opposition to the bill for its failure to end national origins policy, vetoed it. However, he was outvoted in Congress, which passed the Immigration and Nationality Act of 1952 (McCarran-Walter Act) on June 27, 1952. It was the first major overhaul of the nation's immigration and naturalization laws and still stands, albeit in modified form, as its main basis.[49] The act changed the formulation for allocating an annual quota to one-sixth of 1 percent of the number of persons of that national origin who were in the United States in 1920 (see table 4.2).[50]

The minimum quota remained at one hundred. The act removed racial barriers to naturalization and thus ended racial ineligibility for immigration. However, it still made Asian ancestry a target. The law allotted just two thousand visas to applicants whose ancestry could be traced back, at least by 50 percent or more, to the "Asia-Pacific triangle," thus treating Asian descent racially.[51] The new law extended nonquota status to spouses of U.S. citizens without regard to date of marriage—previously, only husbands married prior to January 1, 1948, qualified—although professors were excluded from the nonquota status. Presented with some fanfare by the legislation's supporters, the act revised the quota preference structure. The first preference, amounting to 50 percent of visas, went to immigrants

Table 4.2 The McCarran-Walter Act of 1952

	Major Provisions and Family Preferences
Limit	154,657
Per-country limit	Modified the 1924 national origins system and set the annual quota for an area at one-sixth of 1 percent of the number of inhabitants in the United States in 1920 whose ancestry or national origin was attributable to that area, minimum of 100, ceiling of 2,000 for Asia–Pacific triangle countries
Nonquota	Spouses and children of U.S. citizens
First preference	Highly skilled immigrants whose services were urgently needed in the United States and the spouse and children of such immigrants (50 percent)[a]
Second preference	Parents of U.S. citizens[b] (30 percent)[c]
Third preference	Spouses and children of aliens lawfully admitted for permanent residence (20 percent)[d]
Fourth preference	Brothers, sisters, sons, and daughters[e] of U.S. citizens[b] (25 percent maximum of any unused visas for first three preferences)[f]
Nonpreference	Applicant not entitled to one of the above preferences

Source: The Immigration and Nationality Act of 1952 (66 Stat. 163).
Note: A "child" is defined as an unmarried person under twenty-one years of age, unless otherwise noted.
[a]Plus any not required for second and third preferences.
[b]To sponsor parents or siblings, the petitioning U.S. citizen had to be age twenty-one or older.
[c]Plus any not required for first and third preferences. Unmarried sons and daughters (over twenty-one years of age) of U.S. citizens were moved up from the fourth preference by the Act of September 22, 1959.
[d]Plus any not required for first and second preferences. Under the 1959 act, unmarried sons and daughters (over twenty-one years of age) of permanent residents were added.
[e]Accompanying spouses and children were included in the preference by the 1959 act. Now "sons and daughters" referred to married sons and daughters, regardless of age.
[f]Increased to 50 percent under the 1959 act.

with high qualifications. Thirty percent plus unused visas went to parents of adult citizens (the second preference), and 20 percent were reserved for the third preference plus unused visas for spouses and children of permanent residents. Any unused visas, with a maximum of 25 percent, were to go to other relatives of U.S. citizens (brothers, sisters, sons, and daughters).[52] Immigrants from the Western Hemisphere still enjoyed nonquota status, although newly independent former colonial states of the Caribbean were allotted a quota, which drew criticism that the provision was racist, for it restricted entry of blacks from the region.[53] The earlier piecemeal reform successes did not translate into full-scale reform and the overturn of national origins policy.

URGENCY FOR HUMANITY AND THE END OF NATIONAL ORIGINS

Before national origins policy could be ended, political alliances and leadership had to change. With the continued dominance of restrictionists in leadership roles in the House and Senate, especially McCarran as chairman of the Senate Judiciary Committee, and with critical alliances in Congress between Southern and Western Democrats and Republicans who supported national origins policy, reformers lacked the institutional setting for their telling of immigration reform needs. Opportunities for successful legislative action directly challenging national origins did not emerge until the retirement of key political figures, such as McCarran, who retired from the Senate in 1954. Representative Walter, McCarran's cosponsor in the 1952 law, served in the House until his death in 1963. In addition, other central supporters of national origins policy, including Rep. Michael A. Feighan (D-OH) and Sen. James Eastland (D-MS), had to be outmaneuvered through the orchestration of an increasingly more engaged White House.[54]

As political space opened up, reform advocates continued to mount pressure for change. They stepped up the claim that family reunification was important by emphasizing that the effects of denying family unity by enforcing national origins policy undermined American interests internationally. They reiterated claims made during the war and its immediate aftermath: immigration reform was vital for serving the national interest—for presenting the United States as the leader and defender of democracy. As had happened during World War II, an international crisis—now the exigencies of a détente with the Soviet Union—gave reformers an opportunity to frame the issue of immigration as one requiring ever more urgent action. Thus, for example, in a series of notes, Democratic representative Emanuel Celler from New York, the eventual sponsor of the 1965 Immigration Act in the House, identified a number of problems—both family-related and not—that he saw in the workings of national origins policy. In preparation for a speech on immigration he was to deliver, he noted, "The history of our immigration legislation since World War II is a clear example of the ineffectiveness of our present national origins law to meet our national and international needs," referring to displaced persons and GIs desiring to bring in alien wives. He continued: "The most recent example of how the national origins law prevents us from doing what is right and proper is the Hungarian situation, where an explosion of freedom fighters against communism enabled us to show our traditional humanitarian belief in the right of asylum only through disregard of the provisions of the law."[55] Lamenting that the United States could respond to the "Hungarian situation" only by acting contrary to the official immigration policy, Celler added: "Something must clearly be wrong with a law that stands in the way of so many important and critical national objectives."[56] He concluded that "the national origins theory does not work, is not being applied and is broken down by all kinds of special legislation including refugee provisions."[57] He believed that "national origins [was] more honored in the breach than in the observance."[58]

Celler and other immigration experts knew that the United States regularly ignored official policy and that there was a disconnect between the law in action and the law on the books. It was a policy gap—one in which the existing national origins policy was unable to address extant circumstances. For example, family reunification was the dominant mode of entry between 1953 and 1965, the years when the Immigration and Nationality Act (INA) of 1952 was in effect. During those thirteen years, some 3.5 million documented immigrants entered the United States, and only a little over one-third were quota immigrants. The rest were nonquota immigrants and represented the majority of all immigrants in all thirteen of those years. Over 237,000 Asian immigrants, whose entry was officially limited to just 2,000 per year by the "Asia–Pacific triangle" clause of the INA, arrived—mostly as nonquota family members of Asian Americans who as citizens had invoked newly gained family unity provisions.[59]

In addition to framing immigration reform as a national interest that benefited U.S. international policy objectives, reform advocates made family reunification increasingly the focus and explicit goal of a new law that would overturn national origins. That is, reformers made family reunification itself a primary reform goal instead of simply pushing for the end of national origins policy. Quite significantly, such a discursive reference and shift in policy goal came from the president: the White House played an ever more important role in setting the agenda for immigration reform. Since the Truman administration, immigration reform had been an important issue for the White House, and over successive administrations the president and his advisers more explicitly focused on family reunification as a major priority of the reform effort. For example, in his address to Congress on February 8, 1956, President Dwight Eisenhower stated that family reunion was an important element—albeit of many—of a reformed immigration policy, including the need for skilled workers or for improving U.S. relations with sending countries. According to him, these elements included "the needs of this country for persons having specialized skills or cultural accomplishments; close family relationships; the populations and immigration policies of countries sending immigrants to this country; their past immigration and trade relationships with this country; and their assistance to the joint defense of the friendly free nations of the world."[60]

Within a few years, political leaders identified family reunification as *the* fundamental goal of immigration reform. In 1960 the presidential nominees, Democratic senator John F. Kennedy from Massachusetts and Vice President Richard Nixon, offered their thoughts on immigration reform when Rep. Alfred Santangelo (D-NY) asked both candidates to weigh in on his proposal to liberalize the existing immigration policy. Vice President Nixon replied that "the United States has been built by immigrants from other countries" and "humanitarianism itself calls for action to bring about a reunion of immediate family members under preferential quotas."[61] Expressing similar sentiments, Senator Kennedy wrote that he was "concerned with reforming our immigration laws so they will better meet our national needs and international responsibilities." After noting that he had upheld Truman's veto of the McCarran-Walter Act, Kennedy continued:

> I believe that the most important immediate objective of immigration reform is the reuniting of families. There are many new citizens in America whose immediate families are in other lands, waiting patiently to join them. In countries which oversubscribe their quotas, they have been waiting for many years. We have a social obligation to bring these families together. For this purpose, I have suggested that nonquota status be granted to parents, minor children and spouses of citizens and resident aliens, provided they are otherwise eligible under the law. . . . Ours is a nation of immigrants. . . . And if our country is to be the leader of democracy in the world, our immigration policies should conform more fully to the principles of equal justice on which our country was founded.[62]

Unlike earlier discussions of family reunification, which referred to family reunification as a rightful action toward meritorious and deserving military service personnel and their families or as a way to preserve the racial status quo, Kennedy identified family unity as a just goal in and of itself. In their references to U.S. immigrant history and to the "principles of equal justice" and "humanitarianism," Kennedy and Nixon, respectively, conceptualized a national identity and the family in new moral—and not racial—terms.

Despite Kennedy's affirmation of family reunification and immigration reform, as president, he did not offer an immigration bill until after Representative Walter's death in 1963. That year Representative Celler and

Sen. Philip Hart (D-MI) introduced the Kennedy administration bill that proposed a preference system with 50 percent of visas reserved for family reunification and the other 50 percent for persons with needed skills and education. The legislation stalled in Congress, however, as restrictionists Senator Eastland and Representative Feighan blocked it, preventing even hearings for the bill.[63] Again, the configuration of power provided an important and crucial context for how immigration reform would be debated and how the calls for reform would be heard, if at all.

After President Johnson's election and the Democratic Party's landslide victory in 1964, immigration reformers finally had a more favorable Congress. President Johnson transmitted a bill to Congress on January 13, 1965, for reforming the Immigration and Naturalization Act. The bill, introduced in the House and Senate by Celler and Hart, respectively, proposed to end national origins policy, abolish the Asia-Pacific triangle, and establish a preferential system for those with skills and for close relatives of citizens and permanent residents.[64] In hearings for the proposed legislation, the administration's attorney general, Nicholas Katzenbach, spoke on behalf of the bill, arguing the need for urgent action:

> I say urgency for three reasons, any of which alone justifies prompt remedy. The first is the reason of elemental humanity. Under present law, we are requiring the separation of families—indeed, in some cases, calling on mothers to choose between their children and America. The second reason is one of domestic self-interest. Under present law, brilliant and skilled residents of other countries are prevented or delayed from coming to this country. We are depriving our selves needlessly of their talents. As President Johnson observed in his immigration message, "This is neither good government nor good sense."
>
> The third reason for urgency is our self-interest abroad. Under present law, we choose among potential immigrants not on the basis of what they can contribute to our society or to our economic strength. We choose, instead on the basis of where they—or in some cases even their ancestors—happened to be born. There is little logic or consistency in such a choice, when we proclaim that our system of freedom is superior to the rival system of fear; when we proclaim to all the peoples of the world that every man is born equal and that in America every man is free, to demonstrate his individual talents.
>
> H.R. 2580 would eliminate such illogic and such injustice to immigrants.

Katzenbach concluded by saying, "We must be concerned, above all, with justice."[65]

In debates on the House and Senate floors, supporters stressed these moral and humane dimensions. Rep. Jacob Gilbert (D-NY) claimed: "Under the new immigration system, immigrants will be selected not on the basis of their race but primarily on their family relationship to American citizens and on the talents and skills that they possess." He added: "The bill [H.R. 2580], then, goes far toward eliminating the cruelties of family separation which the United States has inadvertently been responsible for committing under the old law."[66] On the Senate floor, the bill's cosponsor, Sen. Philip Hart, stressed: "Moral and national interest reasons justify a new immigration policy. Aside from its racial and ethnic discrimination, the Immigration and Nationality Act of 1952 fails to give sufficient recognition to the principle of family unity." He argued that "a compelling priority in any reform bill is the urgent need to facilitate the reunion of families," and he discussed "the historic value of immigration to our economy."[67]

The White House and the bill's supporters added pressure on the remaining restrictionists and maneuvered to quiet their opposition. In particular, they had to contend with interference from Representative Feighan, who tried to introduce his own bill. In private conversation with Sen. Edward Kennedy (D-MA), President Johnson acknowledged that they had to "work on him a little bit," to which Senator Kennedy replied, "He's a tough cookie."[68] Supporters were successful in placating the restrictionists, and Congress passed the Hart-Cellar Act on October 3, 1965.

The Hart-Celler Act phased out the national origins system over a three-year period before eliminating it permanently. An overall quota of 120,000 visas was set aside for Western Hemisphere immigrants and 170,000 for Eastern Hemisphere immigrants, with a cap of 20,000 per nation (see table 4.3). Family reunification became the centerpiece of the new American immigration policy as 74 percent of all visas were reserved for family members of American citizens and permanent residents. The remaining 26 percent were divided between professionals and those with special talent and education, skilled or unskilled laborers who fulfilled particular labor needs in the United States, and refugees fleeing communism or the Middle East. U.S. citizens continued to have the right to bring over their immediate family members on an unlimited, nonquota basis.

For the first time "immediate family" included the parents of these U.S. citizens. In debates, congressional members stated the importance of including the parents of U.S. citizens. For example, Rep. John V. Lindsay (R-NY) argued: "The family relationship is the most important standard of all in this problem of priorities in immigration, and parents of U.S. citizens should be included in the high priority list."[69] By adding parents to the category of immediate family, Lindsay and other leaders helped to legitimize those ties as appropriate for family reunification. These political leaders might have assumed that this was a largely symbolic, yet inconsequential, endorsement for enlarging the meaning of "immediate family." In the early 1960s, only about 30,000 spouses and children en-

Table 4.3 The Hart-Celler Act of 1965

	Major Provisions and Family Preferences
Limit	290,000[a]
Per-country limit	20,000
Family preferences limit	74 percent
Not limited	Immediate family members (spouses, children, and parents) of U.S. citizens[b]
First preference	Unmarried sons and daughters[c] of U.S. citizens (20 percent) (58,000)
Second preference	Spouses and unmarried sons and daughters[d] of permanent resident aliens (20 percent) (58,000)
Third preference	Members of the professions of exceptional ability in sciences and arts and their spouses and children (10 percent) (29,000)
Fourth preference	Married sons and daughters[e] of U.S. citizens and their spouses and children (10 percent) (29,000)
Fifth preference	Brothers and sisters of U.S. citizens[b] and their spouses and children (24 percent) (69,600)
Sixth preference	Skilled or unskilled workers in occupations in which labor is in short supply and their spouses and children (10 percent) (29,000)
Seventh preference	Refugees[f] (6 percent) (10,200)

Source: The Immigration and Nationality Act of 1965 (79 Stat. 911).
Note: A "child" is defined as an unmarried person under twenty-one years of age, unless otherwise noted.
[a]The 1965 Hart-Celler Act (Immigration and Nationality Act) set a ceiling of 170,000 on Eastern Hemisphere immigration. It also limited Western Hemisphere immigration, effective July 1, 1968, to 120,000 annually without per-country limits. The 1976 Immigration and Nationality Act amendments applied the 20,000 per-country limit to the Western Hemisphere. The Immigration and Nationality Act amendments of 1978 set a single worldwide ceiling of 290,000, and the Refugee Act of 1980 set the worldwide ceiling at 270,000.
[b]To sponsor parents or siblings, the petitioning U.S. citizen had to be age twenty-one or older.
[c]Age twenty-one or older.
[d]The second preference "unmarried sons and daughters" included both minor and adult children.
[e]Married sons or daughters were persons who had a recognized parent-child relationship and were married, regardless of age.
[f]The seventh preference category of the 1965 act reserved 6 percent of Eastern Hemisphere immigrant visas to refugees. As the ceiling for the Eastern Hemisphere visas was initially set at 170,000, the number for the category was 10,200. It increased to 17,400 when the 1978 law set a single worldwide ceiling of 290,000. By the 1980 Refugee Act, refugees were admitted separately and were not under the preference system. The 6 percent preference for refugees from 1965 was added to the second preference, increasing it from 20 percent to 26 percent.

tered. Lawmakers may have guessed that the addition of parents would add few immigrants to that total. Since 2006, however, over 100,000 parents of U.S. citizens have entered annually.[70] This, like many other demographic changes generated by the post-1965 immigration, has been perhaps an unintended consequence. Critics might argue that such developments have been the cost associated with the expansion of family reunification provisions as the policy definition of "immediate family" has been enlarged.

Representative Feighan's actions led to the greater emphasis on family unity provisions. Feighan changed Senator Kennedy's proposal, which allocated half of visas to skills-related immigration and half to family reunification. Feighan made family reunification the centerpiece of the new law, and in some sense this focus lessened the reform impact of the original Kennedy-Johnson proposal. He ensured that there were four preference categories for family reunification and just two for immigrants with needed skills and educational backgrounds; the White House proposal originally wanted to set aside more visas for the latter. Because the largest preference category was for brothers and sisters, with 24 percent of visas, the act acquired the label of "the Brothers and Sisters Act."[71] Feighan spoke passionately in support of uniting families and objected to "the large number of families in our Nation, split and separated by war, tyranny and human upsets, with some members living abroad waiting for a quota number to join their loved ones in the United States. The waiting period in many instances is long and trying, difficult if not impossible to justify in light of the primary moral value our society attaches to the integrity of the family."[72]

Feighan also offered a narrative about the value of family for the nation—one that was central to its history and vital for the future. In a speech delivered in February 1965, he declared: "The highest values of our free society are the integrity of the family and the sanctity of the home. The strength and stability of our nation flows from a firm adherence to these values. Families, split and divided by peculiarities of law rather than free choice, are at variance with our long standing tradition. Our first obligation should be to correct this inequity of law and to prevent its recurrence."[73] In talking about the importance of a united family, Feighan defined the new core goal of family reunification as central to American immigration policy—not the earlier effort to limit entry of the racially undesirable through a system of national origins quotas.

However, the two goals of family reunification and maintenance of the racial status quo were amenable and perhaps even equivalent. Few lawmakers could have anticipated that those taking advantage of family reunification provisions would be anyone other than immigrants who had assimilated into the United States by then—the southern and eastern European immigrants who had been previously considered inassimilable but were now simply "white"—and whose close family members, as prospective immigrants, needed someone to sponsor them.[74] Given the oversubscription of the fourth preference for brothers and sisters in the 1952 act and the resulting backlog of brothers and sisters waiting to enter, lawmakers were perhaps right to presume that most of the immigrants entering under the revised policy would be the siblings of earlier European immigrants.[75] Even supporters like Sen. Hiram Fong (R-HI) could not fathom the racial and ethnic shift in immigration flows. He dispelled as groundless the fear that "an increase in the number of Asian immigrants would upset the historical and cultural pattern of American life." Basing his argument on the 1960 census, he emphasized the small number of Americans of Asian descent currently in the United States and claimed that the expected allocation for Asians in the proposed immigration bill was too small to cause fear among Americans. He also pointed out the economical and cultural contributions of "Americans of oriental ancestry."[76] Lawmakers did not anticipate the eventual dominance of Asian and Latin American immigration (an unintended consequence), as immigration scholars have argued.[77] Thus, for most lawmakers—reformers and restrictionists alike—the new law may have been a way to end national origins policy, but without making significant changes to immigration flows and, more importantly, the nature of American racial and national identity. Nonetheless, by altering the law to end national origins policy, they explicitly made family reunification and the importance of family core features of American immigration policy. Talk of family provided a framework for making this policy change happen in small incremental moves over a period of decades following World War II.

CONCLUSION

The end of World War II created a new world order with a changed set of opportunities and constraints for immigration supporters and foes. Families separated by the cruelties of war and the ideological war between the United States and the Soviet Union demanded action. As in previous years, the meaning of family and the role that family reunification should play in regulating immigration shaped immigration policymaking. Specifically, both supporters and opponents of the national origins system could lay claims to a national identity and national interests around the issue of family and family reunification.

Through family ideation, immigration supporters constructed a meaning of immigration and nation that shifted the focus away from race to meritorious and deserving military families. This opened up new policymaking opportunities. However, defenders of national origins policy also found ways to talk about legitimate families while still arguing for the maintenance of the racial status quo preserved through the national origins system. Both immigration reformers' and restrictionists' advocates and foes engaged in family ideation to help make sense of shifting political realities and new domestic and international challenges. Referring to family in general and to separated families in particular, immigration stakeholders found ways to talk about the meaning of race and nation and to frame the increasingly urgent issues that the United States faced in the post–World War II era. As configurations of power and institutional arrangements of resources shifted to strengthen immigration reformers' position, immigration reform supporters invoked the meaning of the morality of uniting families, stressing their humanity, while calling for urgent action. In so doing, they not only ended national origins policy but conceptualized family and family reunification as central to the nation's history and vital to American interests, helping to make them core features of a new immigration policy.

Chapter 5

"Our Nation's Efforts to Protect Families Has Fallen Far Short": Pluralist Ideals and Vulnerable Families

In a letter dated June 11, 1984, and addressed to Rep. Peter Rodino (D-NJ), chair of the House Subcommittee on Immigration and Nationality, regarding a bill proposing to alter family reunification provisions, Hyman Bookbinder of the American Jewish Committee reminded the congressman: "America's commitment to fair and humane entry preferences for relatives [has] historically expressed our highest values and [has] brought to the U.S. newcomers who have enriched our social, economic, and cultural life."[1] It was an unnecessary reminder. One lawmaker after another during the debates related to addressing unauthorized immigration—which eventually led to passage of the Immigration Reform and Control Act (IRCA) of 1986—spoke in favor of preserving family reunification, regardless of their position on the proposed legislation to extend amnesty to the estimated two million undocumented immigrants in the country.[2] For example, Sen. Kent Conrad (D-ND) argued, "Family immigration must continue to be the mainstay of this country's immigrant flow—our culture, our economy, and our national character have been shaped by the diverse and vital communities who make up the fabric of this country."[3] In addition, Sen. Edward Kennedy's claim that the "country's historic commitment to family reunion" was "the principal goal of our immigration policy" was not surprising given his long-standing support for family unity provisions.[4]

Even congressional leaders who supported tighter controls on immigration, particularly undocumented flows, and opposed an amnesty program prefaced their position with a statement of support for family reunification. On the House floor, Rep. James Scheuer (D-NY) questioned the impact of an amnesty program, especially "the phenomenon of chain migration" and its strain on the social and economic system, while still articulating support for family reunification.[5] He argued:

> Once we make millions of illegal aliens legal residents, they will be eligible to bring in spouses and unmarried sons and daughters under the preference

> system. Family reunification is a longstanding goal in this country and one I continue to support. But if we are suddenly going to have several million people given legal resident status, we must take some time to look at what the impact of that amnesty will be. How will it affect our ability to provide social services, health care, housing, and above all, jobs to both our citizens and the newly legalized aliens? Can we absorb virtually unlimited legal immigration on top of unhampered illegal immigration? No.[6]

In addition to illustrating the official commitment to family reunification that most immigration scholars and the lay public associate with contemporary immigration, Representative Scheuer's statement demonstrates three additional points that have come to dominate discourse surrounding immigration in the era after the 1965 reform. First, lawmakers like Representative Scheuer have been alarmed by the increase in immigration generated through family sponsorship and reunification. Second, concern over unauthorized immigration, which has increasingly been conflated with legal immigration, has grown. Until 1965, the central immigration debate was about whether national origins policy should be continued, but after the Hart-Celler Act the attention of both lawmakers and the public shifted toward undocumented immigration. Third, Scheuer's comments reflect unease regarding immigrants' use of social welfare provisions. Anger over supposed misuse of welfare support helped Congress and the White House to undertake the massive legislative effort of reforming welfare. In 1996, Congress enacted the landmark Personal Responsibility and Work Opportunity Reconciliation Act (PRWORA) and the Illegal Immigration Reform and Immigrant Responsibility Act (IIRIRA). The meaning of family, legal status, and welfare support all came to a head in the decades after the 1965 Hart-Celler Act ended national origins policy and firmly cemented family reunification in American immigration policy.

Politicians and scholars who have heralded the 1965 reform as a liberal political achievement—part of the civil rights reforms of the 1960s—and a continuing symbol of a pluralist national ideal can surely find abundant evidence to support this claim in the patterns of entry and settlement of the diverse immigrant families who dominate American immigration.[7] The end to national origins policy facilitated the immigration of previously excluded groups. In addition, family unity provisions now account for nearly two-thirds of all authorized immigration.[8] Officially, these developments are celebrated, and immigration stakeholders—from conservative politicians to liberal immigrant activist groups—nearly unanimously support the continued centrality of family unity in American immigration policy. This has made for what many immigration scholars call "strange bedfellows."[9] For example, traditionally conservative religious organizations, liberal immigrant advocacy groups, and business interest groups have regularly worked together to fight for continued family reunification provisions. However, this endorsement across the political divide and hortatory language in public pronouncements in support of family reunification do not necessarily signal a commitment to a liberal, culturally pluralist vision of the nation or even a commitment to protecting immigrant families. What, then, does family mean after the end of national origins policy and the codification of family reunification? Is family indeed protected in American immigration policy? What is the role of family after family reunification in American immigration policymaking?

As in previous chapters, I turn to family ideation in immigration policymaking to answer these questions. The simple answer is, yes, family is protected in American immigration policy. As I discuss here, family appears to be a firmly entrenched, privileged category in American immigration policy. Despite repeated political efforts to limit the definition of family to a nuclear one and to alter family provisions accordingly, these measures have failed. However, this has not meant that families—in all their diverse forms and experiences—have been protected and supported in their efforts to reunite and settle in the United States. As I argue, the postreform era has been marked by a strong contrast between official, public pronouncements of support for family unity and legislative and administrative policies that leave families vulnerable. This divergence appeared most strikingly after welfare reform in the 1990s, which required immigrants to pass more eligibility requirements for gaining access to benefits and for entry itself. Family sponsors of relatives seeking to immigrate have had to demonstrate financial independence and to vouch for their relatives' ability not to become a public charge. In addition, mixed-status immigrant families—families with some members who are authorized and some who are not—are particularly vulnerable, as unauthorized immigrants face greater prospects of deportation after September 11, 2001, leaving their families separated. Furthermore, would-be immigrants and their sponsoring family members have had to prove the veracity of their familial claims by arguably ever more technologically exact measures. These developments are all part of the government's demands that familial claims—as a basis for entry and access to welfare provisions—are legitimate.

The question of legitimacy, in part, goes back to the definitional issue of what constitutes a family. Sibling sponsorship opponents like Representative Scheuer argued that sibling relations as a basis for family unity provisions were illegitimate—that they were somehow not as real or as deserving as nuclear family relations. Talking about these kinship ties as less important or less legitimate helped to attach the meaning of less deserving to them. Meritorious entry is crucial to public perceptions of fairness.[10] As I showed in chapter 4, attaching meanings of merit and legitimacy to familial claims and efforts to reunify through immigration following World War II helped to decouple racial exclusion from immigration. The Hart-Celler Act made family reunification a rightful claim to be exercised by permanent residents and U.S. citizens. Opponents of immigration, including those interested in curbing total numbers or the eligible categories of immigrants, had to attack the basis of family reunification itself—familial claims—in order to link illegitimacy to the policy provisions. They did this even as they lauded the role of family reunification and the diversity of families. The ways in which politicians and other immigration stakeholders have talked about family in the postreform era illustrate less a commitment to cultural pluralism in American immigration and more a discursive move to appropriate the diverse family frame for purposes of disciplining American families in general and crafting a particular meaning of race in a post–civil rights society. Despite the continued references and rhetorical commitment to the narrative of the United States as a nation of immigrants and the importance of diversity, for many of the actors involved the family dinner table has run out of seats.[11] Their family ideation suggests that the discourse surrounding family and immigration in the post-1965 era is a way to officially declare support for civil rights era reforms while still limiting the extension of these reforms. Immigration, as it has for its entire history, is crucial for shaping the meaning of both race and nation.

PRESERVING A DIVERSE FAMILY DEFINITION

As in the previous periods, the larger context, including international relations and institutional arrangements of power, has mattered for shaping immigration policy in the contemporary era. After passage of the Hart-Celler Act, immigration reached levels unseen since the decade prior to the implementation of national origins policy. The American public's attitude toward growing immigration evolved to reflect increasing unease about unauthorized versus legal immigration. As legal immigration gained the support of the American public, opinion pollsters found firm and consistently negative attitudes toward illegal immigration. The public offered a bifurcated public response, equating fair with legal immigration, in contrast to criminal with unauthorized immigration.[12] After 1965, with the job of ending national origins policy over, both lawmakers and the public directed their attention to the problem of unauthorized immigration.

Despite earlier attempts to bring legislation onto the House and Senate floors, Congress was unable to get serious traction on the issue of unauthorized immigration until 1982, when Sen. Alan Simpson (R-WY) and Rep. Ron Mazzoli (D-KY) coauthored an omnibus bill on legal and illegal immigration. It included many of the recommendations made by the Select Commission on Immigration Refugee Policy (SCIRP)—a panel composed of academics, congressional members, White House cabinet secretaries, and several members of the public that had been charged with reviewing immigration laws and practices. In addition to proposing employer sanctions for those who hired undocumented workers and an amnesty program for unauthorized immigrants already in the United States, the bill called for an annual cap of 425,000 for family-sponsored immigration and essentially eliminated the fifth preference visas for U.S. citizens' brothers and sisters. (Table 5.1 shows the family reunification provisions in place in the early 1980s.)

The bill faced stiff opposition, and groups ranging from business organizations such as the U.S. Chamber of Commerce to liberal immigrant advocacy groups like the American Civil Liberties Union formed a broad coalition against the measure. After the bill died, the coauthors introduced another bill. In the new reform bill, Simpson pushed for the elimination of the fifth preference, which was later dropped, and added a provision putting a three-year restriction on the use of welfare benefits by those granted amnesty. However, the bill remained largely the same as the previous one.[13]

As lawmakers debated the specifics of these bills in the early 1980s, the proposal to end the fifth visa preference for siblings of citizens in particular drew criticism. Immigration stakeholders clarified their position on the goal of immigration and laid a claim, whether or not they supported the specifics of the bill, to a narrative about the nation as one built on the work and diversity of families. The Bookbinder and Kennedy quotes that opened this chapter illustrate these points. Their family ideation articulated the meaning and role of family in the national narrative. Bill supporters like cosponsor Senator Simpson argued in vain that the new proposed family preference system clarified the meaning of family as a "nuclear" one that still upheld the central value of family reunification in American immigration policy:

> Immigrants can still greatly benefit America, but only if they are limited to an appropriate number and selected within that number on the basis of immediate family reunification and skills which would truly serve the interest of a highly developed nation. . . . The family preference categories will not include what is now referred to as the fifth preference, that is the brothers and sisters of adult U.S. citizens. This is done in order to reserve for the closer relatives the limited visas available for family reunification and to allow an increase in immigration opportunities for those who have no close relatives in the United States but who do have skills which will benefit the American people as a whole. Those who had already received fifth preference status and were on the waiting list as of March 1, 1982 will be pro-

Table 5.1 Existing Family Preference Provisions in 1980

	Major Provisions and Preference Categories
Annual immigration limit	270,000[a]
Per-country limit	20,000
Family preferences limit	80 percent of the annual immigration limit (216,000)[b]
Not limited	Immediate family members (spouses, children, and parents) of U.S. citizens[c]
First preference	Unmarried sons and daughters[d] of U.S. citizens (20 pecent) (54,000)
Second preference	Spouses and unmarried sons and daughters[e] of permanent resident aliens (26 percent) (70,200)
Third preference	Members of the professions of exceptional ability in sciences and arts and their spouses and children (10 percent) (27,000)
Fourth preference	Married sons and daughters[f] of U.S. citizens and their spouses and children (10 percent) (27,000)
Fifth preference	Brothers and sisters of U.S. citizens[c] and their spouses and children (24 percent) (64,800)
Sixth preference	Skilled or unskilled workers in occupations in which labor is in short supply and their spouses and children (10 percent) (27,000)

Source: The Immigration and Nationality Act of 1965 (79 Stat. 911); the Immigration and Nationality Act Amendments of 1978 (92 Stat. 907); the Refugee Act of 1980 (94 Stat. 102).
Note: A "child" is defined as an unmarried person under twenty-one years of age.
[a]The Refugee Act of 1980 set the ceiling at 270,000, lowered from a single worldwide ceiling of 290,000 under the 1978 law. By the 1980 act, refugees were admitted separately and were not under the preference system. The 6 percent preference for refugees from 1965 was added to the second preference, increasing it from 20 percent to 26 percent.
[b]Included first, second, fourth, and fifth preferences.
[c]To sponsor parents or siblings, the petitioning U.S. citizen had to be age twenty-one or older.
[d]Age twenty-one or older.
[e]The second preference "unmarried sons and daughters" included both minor and adult children.
[f]Married sons and daughters were persons who had a recognized parent-child relationship and were married, regardless of age.

> tected. For the same reasons, the definition of second preference [for spouses and children of permanent residents] will be narrowed somewhat to cover spouses and minor children of permanent residents—their "nuclear family." The percentage of family reunification visas allocated to this category is increased greatly.[14]

Simpson sought to define family and those deserving preference for immigration as limited to what he considered the "nuclear family," which would not include brothers and sisters of adult U.S. citizens. In addition, by contrasting these siblings whom he believed should not qualify for existing family provisions to other potential immigrants "who have skills which will benefit the American people," Simpson portrayed both the expanded definition of family and sibling sponsorship as illegitimate and undeserving.

One way by which lawmakers suggested the illegitimacy of the extended family categories was by referencing the problem they supposedly created: an ever-growing waiting list for the immediate family members of permanent residents, that is, those trying to enter through the use of visas afforded by the second preference of the family provisions.[15] Because of the preference-category system and country ceilings, many spouses and minor children of permanent residents in the United States were having to wait for years to join their sponsoring family member. Thus, Rev. Theodore M. Hesburgh, chair of SCIRP, declared: "There is something wrong with a law that keeps out for as long as eight years the small child of a mother or father who has settled in the United States while a nonrelative or less close relative from another country can come in immediately. Certainly a strong incentive to enter illegally exists for persons who are separated from close family members for a long period of time."[16] Some lawmakers argued that the family preference provision for siblings contributed to the unfortunate wait. In 1982, Rep. James Sensenbrenner (R-WI) argued that the logjam created by the exercising of the fifth preference visas was keeping closer family members apart:

> If the fifth preference is not modified, then closer family members, i.e., spouses, sons, and daughters will continue to have problems being united. If family reunification is to be a preferred public policy, it should be for the closest relatives—not a loophole to bring "every" relative into the country. Because of the way in which the preference system is allocated, family reunification is becoming the principal way for immigrants, other than refugees, to enter this country. This will be felt even more a few years down the road when all the legal immigrants, which include refugees, become citizens; and, if amnesty is granted, the millions of now illegal aliens will be eligible for citizenship, and naturally will want to bring their relatives into the country.[17]

In addition to the problem of a backlog, Sensenbrenner saw the potential for abuse of the family reunification policy, calling the use of the fifth preference a "loophole." Furthermore, he saw a looming problem of extended family migration for immigrants who would benefit from the proposed amnesty program—continued, and perhaps growing, immigration through the chain migration effect that the family preference provisions would help generate. Despite Representative Sensenbrenner's worries about the misuse of the fifth family preference, he nevertheless argued that he supported family unification as a goal.

For immigration supporters who opposed any curbs on the fifth preference category, endorsing family reunification meant supporting all family members. Furthermore, an attempt to limit family reunification and alter the system was a fundamental challenge to immigration's goal of uniting families. Thus, at Senate hearings, Rev. Hesburgh reminded everyone that family reunification "is something I think everyone can agree with. Our country is built on families."[18] Other bill opponents saw efforts to curb family reunification as contrary to the goal of addressing unauthorized immigration. In early 1983, Joaquin Avila, president and general counsel for the Mexican American Legal Defense and Education Fund (MALDEF), questioned the rationale for pursuing both objectives, reasoning:

> While we see the logic behind the creation of two separate categories for family reunification and independent immigration, we believe that the inclusion of immediate relatives within the cap and the elimination of certain family members from immigrating will actually lead to *more illegal* immigration. The simple truth is that the desire to maintain the family as a unit is much stronger than the fear of violating our immigration laws.[19]

Although Avila sought to defend the existing family definition and provisions, he also helped to elide further the idea of illegality and family migration.

Despite the attacks on sibling sponsorship and the raised specter of illegitimacy, supporters of the existing family preference system prevailed. Family reunification provisions remained largely unchanged, and the fifth preference stood. Brothers and sisters of U.S. citizens still counted as family. The new law, the Immigration Reform and Control Act (IRCA), signed on November 6, 1986, by President Ronald Reagan, made important changes in other areas. The new legislation had three central features: sanctions against employers who knowingly hired undocumented workers; increased appropriations for the Immigration and Naturalization Services Border Patrol; and an amnesty program for the estimated two million unauthorized immigrants that would provide them with a pathway to citizenship. Lawmakers and other immigration stakeholders hoped that IRCA would solve the problem of unauthorized immigration. They believed the law could deter unauthorized immigration by removing economic incentives in the form of jobs. Yet for this to work, employers had to be prevented from hiring undocumented workers. However, with almost no fiscal or administrative support for employer sanctions, the first provision was doomed to fail from the beginning.[20] Financial resources went instead toward border control and enforcement.[21]

Efforts to alter the family preference system did not end with passage of IRCA. Through the 1980s, Senator Simpson sought to convince his colleagues that only "close" family members should have the privilege of being united. As before, however, lawmakers stood by the preference system awarding unity provisions to citizens' siblings when Congress reauthorized IRCA in 1990. The 1990 Immigration Act increased immigration limits from 290,000 to 675,000 per year and devised a new preference scheme of three categories—family-based, employment-based, and diversity (see table 5.2).

Family-based preference categories offered about 75 percent of the total

Table 5.2 The Immigration Act of 1990

	Major Provisions and Preference Categories	
Period	1992 to 1994[a]	1995 and after
Limit	700,000	675,000
Per-country limit	7 percent of the total preference	
Family preferences limit	465,000[b]	480,000
Not limited	Immediate family members[c] of U.S. citizens[d]	
First preference	Unmarried sons and daughters[e] of U.S. citizens	
	23,400	23,400
Second preference	Spouses and children of lawful permanent residents (2A)[f] and unmarried sons and daughters[e] of lawful permanent residents (2B)[g]	
	114,200	114,200
Third preference	Married sons and daughters[h] of U.S. citizens and their spouses and children	
	23,400	23,400
Fourth preference	Brothers and sisters of U.S. citizens[d] and their spouses and children	
	65,000	65,000

(continued)

Table 5.2 Continued

	Major Provisions and Preference Categories	
Employment-based preference[i]	20 percent of the total limit	20.74 percent of the total limit
First preference	Workers with special talents or skills (40,000)	
Second preference	Workers with advanced degrees or technical expertise (40,000)	
Third preference	Workers with needed job skills, professionals, and others (40,000)	
Fourth preference	Special immigrants and religious workers (10,000)	
Fifth preference	Investor immigrants (10,000)	
Diversity immigration[j]	40,000	55,000

Source: The Immigration Act of 1990 (104 Stat. 4978).
Note: A "child" is defined as an unmarried person under twenty-one years of age, unless otherwise noted.
[a]A transitional limit of 700,000 was allocated between 1992 and 1994 until the 1990 Immigration Act came into effect in 1995.
[b]This number does not include 55,000 legalizations under the Immigration Reform and Control Act of 1986 (8 percent). Between 1991 and 1994, 55,000 visas per year were allocated for the spouses and children of migrants who became legal residents under IRCA, with the 1990 Immigration Act extending the cutoff date to May 1988.
[c]The number of immediate family members (spouses, children, and parents) of U.S. citizens was not limited, but it was assumed to be 239,000 between 1992 and 1994, and 254,000 in 1995 and after. This number was used to determine the family preference limit for the next fiscal year. The annual floor of 226,000 for the family preference system was set. The U.S. Department of Homeland Security, *Yearbooks of Immigration Statistics* explain (for each data on the preference system): "Immediate relatives [of U.S. citizens] may enter without any limitation; however, the limit for family-sponsored preference immigrants [for citizens and permanent residents] in a fiscal year is equal to 480,000 minus the number of immediate relatives [of U.S. citizens] admitted in the preceding year. The limit of family-sponsored preference visas cannot fall below a minimum of 226,000—the worldwide limit of 480,000 minus 254,000 [the number of immediate relatives assumed to enter]."
[d]To sponsor parents or siblings, the petitioning U.S. citizen must be age twenty-one or older.
[e]Age twenty-one or older.
[f]2A: 77 percent of the total limit, of which 75 percent were issued without regard to the per-country limit.
[g]The second preference expanded by at least 62 percent after 1990.
[h]Married sons and daughters are persons who have a recognized parent-child relationship and are married, regardless of age.
[i]Total limit of 140,000: 120,000 plus 10,000 for religious workers and 10,000 for investors. Employment-based preferences include visas for spouses and children.
[j]Diversity immigration was determined by lottery. In 1995 the permanent diversity program came into effect, with 55,000 visas available annually. The Nicaraguan Adjustment and Central American Relief Act in 1997 reduced diversity to 50,000.

visas, which were set aside for unmarried adult children of U.S. citizens (first preference), immediate family members of permanent residents (second preference), married children of U.S. citizens (third preference), and siblings of adult U.S. citizens (fourth preference). Spouses and minor children of U.S. citizens continued to face no limits. Employment-based preference visas, 20 percent of the total (20.74 percent since 1995), were available to immigrants with special talents (first preference), workers with advanced degrees or technical experts (second preference), skilled workers and professionals (third preference), and special immigrants and religious workers (fourth preference). Because the new law raised the cap on total immigrants, the 20 percent allocation for employment visas nonetheless increased the total number of visas for workers. The new law also included a diversity program that made 55,000 visas available annually by lottery to diversify the ethnic composition of immigrants to the United States. By the 1990s, immigrants eligible for the program hailed from Europe, which had been the dominant source of immigrants for much of U.S. history but not after the 1965 reform.[22] Would-be immigrants without familial ties (and hence lower opportunities for admission) could apply for a diversity visa.

Senator Simpson and his supporters failed to alter the family preference system partly because of a focused effort by a diverse coalition made up of "strange bedfellows." The lobbying efforts by these coalition members also successfully pressured President Clinton to abandon his support for amending the preference system and reducing fourth preference visas for siblings of adult U.S. citizens, as recommended by the Jordan Commission. The Commission on Legal Immigration Reform, created by the Immigration Act of 1990 and chaired by Rep. Barbara Jordan (D-TX), had recommended the reduction of annual legal admissions by one-third by facilitating the admission of spouses and minor children of legal immigrants at the expense of parents and adult children of both citizens and permanent residents and siblings of U.S. citizens. The commission also proposed reducing the number of employment-based preference visas from 140,000 to 100,000.

In addition to liberal advocacy and business interest groups, immigrant ethnic organizations and religious groups argued against the recommendations. In particular, immigrant ethnic organizations, made up of newly naturalized immigrants, flexed greater political weight by the 1980s and 1990s.[23] In this sense, political interest groups were important for immigration policymaking. However, Simpson's defeats also highlight the extent to which the meaning of family had become central to immigration policy. Changing the definition of family was not a small incremental change in policy. As the previous chapter showed, family and family reunification had become core features of American immigration policy. Efforts to change the family preference provisions to exclude siblings met stiff resistance as defenders of the provision cast such a change as counter to a fundamental narrative of immigration policy—families should be united. Furthermore, as policy scholars argue, benefits once extended are hard to take back, because "the core of policy is resistant to change."[24]

Despite these failed efforts to alter the family preference system, debates over what constitutes a legitimate family claim and a meritorious entry have continued. Although President George W. Bush was unable to oversee passage of any new immigration laws, Congress considered several bills that dealt with challenges associated with unauthorized immigration, the need for skilled and unskilled laborers, and the growing backlog of would-be immigrants waiting to reunite with their family sponsors. One such proposal was a bill introduced in 2007 in the Senate that proposed a comprehensive reform of the existing policy. Among other features, the bill proposed to limit family reunification to spouses and children of U.S. citizens and permanent residents, shifting the annual visas to skills-based employment immigration. The bill went even further than the proposals of the 1980s and 1990s, which tried to end family reunification for siblings. Although the bill failed to become law, debates surrounding the proposed changes illustrate the ongoing efforts to question the legitimacy of familial claims and to suggest that family reunification is a drain on the United States. For example, on the Senate floor, Sen. Jeff Sessions (R-AL) engaged in the kind of hortatory language heard in earlier years, praising the importance of family in American immigration history as he also attacked immigrants who used family reunification to reunite an extended family. He argued:

> I reject the idea that a movement to a system such as Canada's or Australia's that is based on merit and skills for immigration is somehow, as I think Senator Reid said, an attack on the family. I am offended by that statement. A person who wants to come to this country, has to ask to be admitted into the United States of America, and say that: I have not been a criminal, I meet the standards for admission, and I want to be a productive citizen. Then after we give that person a green card, that person can become a citizen and have the right to demand that his or her parents be allowed to come here, the aging parents who will be fundamentally supported by the American taxpayers, demand that his or her brothers and sisters and their spouses and children be allowed to come. So how is this an attack on your family if we say: You can come, you can be a citizen, but right up front, you cannot bring your parents, adult children, and siblings, you don't have any special rights to do so, but they can apply if they qualify, just like everybody else, based on their own merit. But why should the fact that we give one person a glorious thing—citizenship in the United States—entitle them to bring maybe tens of other people? It just does not make sense. I reject the argument that moving to a merit based system is an attack on family.[25]

Sessions declared that an immigration system that emphasized, for example, worker skills over family reunification, such as the points system in places like Canada, was not anti-family. He claimed that such policies were based simply on merit. However, he argued that the use by siblings and parents of family reunification provisions was not meritorious, especially when their coming and their settlement could be a drain on American taxpayers. Thus, he criticized the use by immigrant families of a family-preference policy that had been in existence for over forty years as somehow illegitimate.

These legislative proposals to alter U.S. immigration policy from family-based to skills-based in general highlight the continuing tensions over what role immigration should play in the United States—promoting family unity or economic development. More specifically, despite Senator Sessions's protestations, his comments reflect the point that the allocation of visa preferences is a zero-sum game: allocating more visas for workers means fewer visas for family members. For some politicians and their constituents, this will always represent an attack on families. Sessions's defensive tone further illustrates the dominance of family—what it means, what it should mean, and the roles it ought to play—in how the United States as a nation should move forward. Even if Senator Sessions could convince his colleagues of the merit of his position, he had to counter the criticism that the new formulation was contrary to not only immigrant families and the goal of family reunification but also to the American narrative that families *matter*—that they are foundational to the meaning and identity of the American nation. If the national narrative is a story about the building and strengthening of the nation through the hard work and sacrifices made by families, a worker-based system could jeopardize national strength and vitality by severing family ties.

VULNERABLE FAMILIES AFTER FAMILY REUNIFICATION

Although family unity may be a professed goal and central value in American immigration policy, these pronouncements have not meant that immigrant families themselves are valued. Hortatory language about the U.S. commitment to family and the policy of family reunification itself are forms of family ideation. Politicians, intellectuals, immigrant advocates, and other stakeholders articulate particular gender, sexual, and racial ideals and attach these meanings to immigrants, the concept of family, and the nation. In so doing, they identify which immigrants are legitimate families and "like" members of the larger family that is the nation. Despite the expression of support for family unity and the commitment to family reunification policy, many immigrant families have experienced deep vulnerability in the postreform era. This is particularly true for the estimated 11.5 million unauthorized immigrants and the estimated 8.8 million families with a head of household or spouse who is unauthorized.[26] These mixed-status families include 16.6 million persons. More than 80 percent of the children in such families are U.S.-born citizens—an estimated 4.5 million children in 2011.[27]

The number of mixed-status families highlights the fact that issues and policies that supposedly affect "just" illegal aliens have far-reaching consequences. Legal permanent residents and citizens, including young children, can be ensnared in these policies and surrounding rhetoric when their family members are unauthorized immigrants. This was particularly true with respect to welfare reform in 1996. Both PRWORA and IIRIRA made crucial changes in whether, when, and how immigrants would be eligible for welfare benefits. PRWORA restricted legal immigrants' eligibility for welfare programs and barred unauthorized immigrants from most welfare benefits, including food stamps and cash assistance, for which unauthorized immigrants did not qualify even prior to the change in law. IIRIRA reduced noncitizens' access to benefits and specified unauthorized immigrants' ineligibility for public benefits, although it allowed them aid from nonprofit charities by exempting charity organizations from the immigration status verification requirement. Families with citizen or legal permanent resident children were and continued to remain eligible for welfare provisions. As discussed in greater detail in chapter 2, however, a number of researchers have shown that usage declined significantly as eligible families chose not to apply for benefits out of fear that doing so would trigger deportation against unauthorized members of the family or jeopardize the legal status of authorized family members.[28] Unfortunately, underutilization of such benefits may harm eligible families, especially those with children, who are most at risk for suffering from the negative effects of poverty.

The confusion for many immigrant families can be traced back to the arguments that lawmakers made about welfare, family, and immigration. Many of them elided the various concepts of legal and illegal status as they questioned the role of the state in the lives of families and vice versa. This family ideation attacked immigrant families, regardless of legal status, for seeking any state support and provided a framework for critiquing dependency on the state in general. The statement of Rep. Frank Riggs (R-CA) on the House floor in debates over welfare reform illustrates these points:

> I just wanted to respond since the question of immigrants came up and make clear again, reality check, we are not bashing immigrants, we are giving strength to the longstanding Federal policy that welfare should not be a

> magnet for immigrants, legal or illegal. To accomplish this, we do 4 things: We prohibit legal aliens from the big 5 magnet programs, cash welfare, food stamps, Medicaid, title 20, and SSI which has been an especially egregious source of abuse by legal aliens. We make the alien sponsor's affidavit legally binding and enforceable. We apply the existing deeming rule to all Federal means-tested programs so that in these programs the income of an alien sponsor is deemed to be the alien's. Lastly, we authorize Federal and State authorities for the first time to go after deadbeat sponsors. We are strengthening current immigration policy, not bashing anyone.[29]

Representative Riggs concluded by saying that the government ought to "go after" the family members who sponsor their relatives for family migration but fail to support them financially, leading their family members to seek welfare support. Riggs found a way to criticize not only the existing welfare program but also the family reunification program for not preventing such financial malfeasance. In these debates, Riggs also warned that reform was necessary in order to prevent, "through some sort of perverse incentive in the welfare system the hordes of illegal immigration."[30]

Some members of Congress charged that these welfare reform efforts, particularly those limiting benefits to legal immigrants, were simply "mean-spirited and punitive."[31] Still, Congress did indeed find a way to prevent the "perverse incentive" about which Riggs worried and to go after those "deadbeat sponsors." IIRIRA imposed on sponsors a minimum income requirement, defined as 125 percent of the poverty level. It also required all family unification immigrants to have U.S. citizen sponsors, who had to sign a binding affidavit of support.[32]

IMMIGRANT FAMILIES AS SECURITY RISKS

After the terrorist attacks on September 11, 2001, the meaning of security has taken on particularly important resonance. The government reorganized old agencies and created new ones to handle issues related to terrorist threats and attacks, enforcement of immigration laws, and border control.[33] In the post-IRCA amnesty and 9/11 era, immigration restrictionists warn that illegal immigration is a symbol of vulnerable borders and represents a nation at risk for another terrorist attack. Scholars who write about unauthorized immigration, particularly from Mexico, have written about the alarmist rhetoric that politicians use to connect terrorism and unregulated immigration.[34] They, along with other immigration researchers, argue that the long history of the U.S. system of deportation and securitization at the border predates the attacks on September 11, 2001.[35] For example, Dan Kanstroom explains that deportation has been an important element of immigration control in general for the United States.[36] Thus, security as a theme and one that immigration stakeholders invoke in family ideation is not new (also evidenced in the earlier discussion of the Chinese Confession Program in chapter 3). What is unique to the postreform era is the emphasis on security risk that diverse immigrant families represent *because* they are accessing the new rights and privileges generated by the reforms of the civil rights era, including immigration reform. Restrictionists warn that immigrants who gain unauthorized entry, access welfare benefits, or sponsor family reunification that is not based on *real* familial ties are committing fraud. The fact that the United States can be defrauded signifies a national security risk.

Immigrant families can become entangled in this security rhetoric and in policies aimed at protecting the nation's borders. Most gravely, the government's focus on immigration law violations as potential security risks has caused some immigrant families to face the risk of separation as unauthorized members of their families struggle with the possibility of deportation. In fiscal year 2012, the United States deported 409,849 immigrants. Although President Barack Obama's administration has stressed the importance of deporting immigrants with criminal records, more than 40 percent of those deported in 2012 had no such record.[37] Families, particularly mixed-status ones, face separation even as the Obama administration responded to criticism about its detention procedures by announcing a plan to overhaul its system of detaining unauthorized immigrants. In 2009 the administration agreed to change its network of jail and prison cells for detaining immigration law violators, to institute a "truly civil detention system," and to establish three family detention centers.[38] Immigration activists argue that the increase in detention and deportation separates families, many of which include minor children who are U.S.-born citizens. A report by one civil rights organization states that, as of 2011, there were at least 5,100 children in foster care as a result of their parents' detention or deportation, and it estimates that in the next five years at least 15,000 more children will be separated from their parents who are detained or deported.[39]

The assertion that these immigrants represent a security risk is another variation on the claim that some immigrant families are illegitimate—their ties are not close enough (brothers or sisters), and they represent "loopholes," in Representative Sensenbrenner's words. They are also illegitimate because they may not be real families at all. Politicians and immigration officials have long voiced concerns that fraudulent family claims undermine the immigration system—from the years when women gained derivative status to the years of "paper sons" to, more recently, passage of the Immigration Marriage Fraud Amendments in 1986. That legislation made legal permanent resident status conditional for the first two years of marriage. One INS survey estimated that as many as 30 percent of spousal petitions were fraudulent.[40] In related congressional hearings, INS commissioner Alan C. Nelson warned:

> Marriage has always played a crucial role in the laws and policies governing both the immigration and naturalization of aliens. The existence and preservation of close family ties form the basis for numerous benefits and waivers under the law. Unfortunately, these special privileges are being abused. . . . Marriage fraud and fiancée fraud now pose significant threats to the integrity of our lawful immigration procedures.[41]

Immigration officials have characterized fraudulent claims as potential security breaches. "Paper sons" could have introduced Chinese Communist elements into the United States, and likewise, false spouses could bring down an entire immigration system. In part, such fears motivate government efforts to truly and accurately test familial claims for family reunification purposes through the use of DNA testing, as the story of Isaac Owusu, which began the book, demonstrates. Although neither U.S. Citizenship and Immigration Services (USCIS) nor the U.S. embassy require genetic testing for confirming family ties for purposes of family reunification, they strongly encourage its use for applicants from certain countries. In particular, for would-be immigrants from countries and regions that the government suspects have unreliable documents verifying family relations, the use of genetic analysis can speed up their application process. Without such testing, applications can be delayed for years or even denied without proper proof of kin claims. The costs, which can be particularly high for applicants coming from developing countries, and the burden of proof lie with the applicants.[42]

Despite this concern over the possible burden on applicants, government agencies and critics of various family reunification programs have advocated the use of genetic testing to verify familial claims as evidence of supposed fraud appear. In 2008 the U.S. State Department suspended a humanitarian program designed to reunite African refugees with family members in the United States when DNA testing showed evidence of inconsistencies in familial claims among many applicants. Earlier that year, the government conducted a pilot program to test the DNA of applicants to confirm familial ties. The program administrators declared there were high levels of fraud in a number of east African countries, particularly in Kenya. Testing proved biological family ties in just 20 percent of the cases. In remaining cases, there was at least one genetically unverified relationship or no testing occurred. However, critics of the testing program argued that many of these applicants had familial ties that were perhaps not biological but adoptive.[43] With inadequate paper documentation, those familial relations are harder to prove. The veracity of these applicants' kinship claims rested on indisputable proof of blood ties—the *natural substance* of kinship.

The technological use of genetic analysis may be new, but the effort to verify familial ties is an old one. The question remains the same. Are immigrants' familial claims real and legitimate bases for entry? The efforts to answer this question with putatively more exact science demonstrate the growing fear among immigration officials that fraudulent and illegitimate families represent security risks for the nation.

RACE AND THE LIMITS OF CULTURAL PLURALISM

The tension between hortatory language and various policies that has left immigrant families vulnerable, as discussed in this chapter, reflects unease by many immigration stakeholders—including politicians, who might have supported an end to national origins policy—about immigrants' civil rights gains. Civil rights legislation like immigration reform—as part of the broader civil rights movement—has helped to alter the meaning of race in this country. Likewise, demographic changes that have resulted from immigration reform also have helped to change the meaning of race, particularly as it relates to a national identity. Consider one small example: the status and meaning of "Asian American" in the United States. Within a few decades since immigration reform, Asian immigrants are no longer considered inassimilable and excludable but rather "honorary whites." Some scholars lament the continuing "forever foreign" characterization of Asian Americans.[44] For example, following the arrest of Chinese American scientist Wen Ho Lee for alleged "mishandling" of sensitive information in 1999, 32 percent of Americans surveyed stated that Chinese Americans would be more loyal to China than to the United States.[45] However, other researchers also cite Asian American immigration, settlement, and mainstream white America's acceptance (as indicated by changes such as increasing rates of intermarriage with white Americans) as one reason for the shifting color line in the United States. That is, whereas the line of significance that ordered racialized hierarchy in the United States prior to the contemporary period was drawn between white and nonwhite, these scholars argue that it is now drawn between black and nonblack.[46] As Asian American acceptance has grown, the overall meaning of race has changed.

However, this important development does not mean that the United States as a whole has come to embrace the culturally pluralist ideas represented in immigration reform.[47] Even the shift in the perception of Asian Americans can be seen as a way to critique the civil rights ideals of racial equality. Politicians, activists, business leaders, journalists, and community leaders often use racial triangulation to position Asian Americans vis-à-vis blacks and whites.[48] Dominant whites may valorize Asian Americans for their relative success in relation to blacks (supposedly without the kind of civil rights legislations like affirmative action that African Americans enjoyed) yet still criticize them for being immutably foreign in an effort to deny their full civic participation in the body politic.[49]

Building on this idea of racial triangulation, I suggest that family ideation, which includes exalting the unique role of immigrant families in the making of the nation while questioning the veracity, legitimacy, and merit of their family practices, is a way to construct a racialized meaning of new immigrants who are mostly from Asia, Latin America, and increasingly Africa as illegitimate and not deserving—particularly those who are in the United States without proper authorization. Exclusionists may not distinguish the immigrant status of Asian Americans or Latinos who may be legal permanent residents or unauthorized immigrants. Thus, during the welfare reform debates, Rep. Norman Mineta (D-CA) lamented that lawful Asian American and Latino immigrants were being lumped together with unauthorized ones in an effort to deny them benefits. Referring to the anti-immigrant rhetoric that surrounded California's efforts to ban unauthorized immigrants from securing public state services, he argued:

> Asian Pacific Americans in California are second to none in our frustration with illegal immigration. Many in the community have waited patiently for years for spouses and children to join them through the legal process. But it quickly became clear to us that the rhetoric and the emotion went far beyond the issue of illegal immigration alone. Those who supported Proposition 187 told us repeatedly that legal immigrants had nothing to worry about. But sure enough, here we are today, debating on the floor of the House of Representatives whether taxpaying, lawfully admitted immigrants will be eligible for the services their taxes pay for.[50]

In addition, politicians who applaud immigrant families for their hard work and thrift use this valorization to critique both implicitly and explicitly the economic and social drain of poor native-born families, particularly blacks.[51] Politicians praise the accomplishments of "model minorities," who appear to have succeeded in the United States without the assistance of a state handout like affirmative action.[52] For example, in 1995 House Speaker Newt Gingrich (R-GA) argued that "Asian Americans are facing a very real danger of being discriminated against" at colleges that practiced affirmative action.[53] These claims continue today as conservative pundits decry the seemingly unfair treatment of Asian Americans applying to elite universities.[54] Thus, the hortatory language of Asian American success and immigrant families helps to subordinate native-born blacks and the poor to immigrants. Family ideation and political efforts to maintain or limit family reunification continue to be crucial for shaping American immigration policymaking and for constructing meanings of race and nation.

CONCLUSION

Like his predecessor, President Obama in his first term was unable to pass comprehensive immigration reform. Nevertheless, through executive orders, he instituted regulatory changes—both big and small—that have affected immigrant families. For example, in January 2012 the administration announced that USCIS would no longer require that unauthorized immigrants return to their home country to apply for legal residency, thus helping to preserve family unity in cases in which immigrants might have previously left behind spouses or children. By the summer of 2012, Obama had issued a more significant executive order that deferred deportation orders for qualified unauthorized immigrants who had been brought to the United States by their families when they were minors.[55]

Recognizing the importance of immigration as an issue for many voters—particularly Latinos—Obama's opponent for the White House in 2012, Republican presidential nominee Mitt Romney, reiterated many of the profamily sentiments that opened this chapter. Referring to immigration reform as a "moral imperative," Romney vowed to increase family reunification for immediate family members of permanent residents.[56] For many Latino and Asian American voters, such talk was too little too late: both groups voted overwhelmingly for Obama. The *New York Times* exit polls for the 2012 election showed that 71 percent of Hispanics and 73 percent of Asians voted for Obama.[57]

Bruised by the 2012 elections, the Republican Party expressed a willingness to consider a new comprehensive immigration reform bill. As the White House and both Democratic and Republican members of Congress debate the details of a number of thorny issues—including a pathway to citizenship for unauthorized immigrants; temporary worker visas; and more visas for science, technology, engineering, and math workers—all sides continue to talk about the importance of family and the need to preserve family unity in American immigration policy.[58] As various immigration stakeholders seek to make sense of a changing political landscape—one in which younger voters and more minority voters express greater support for immigration *and* flex political power—referring to the meaning of family and the importance of family unity may help to frame both the possibilities and the limits to policy change, as family ideation has done in previous debates.

As has been the case since the 1965 reform, official support for immigrant families and family reunification continues. However, as this chapter has shown, the hortatory language on family has not been matched by efforts to protect diverse immigrant families in practice. Immigrant families face great scrutiny in their efforts to reunite and to settle fully into the nation. The hurdles they face in securing social benefits are just one illustration of these difficulties. The seeming reverence for family and for preserving family reunification policy also does not equate with a commitment to cultural pluralism, as many politicians and scholars claimed after passage of the 1965 immigration reform. As part of the civil rights gains of the 1960s and 1970s, the Hart-Celler Act has been vital to changing the racial and ethnic character of the United States through new and previously unexpected immigration patterns, which family reunification facilitated. The changes the act has generated raise potential challenges to how new immigrants will be integrated and made "like one of the family." In the postreform era, immigration stakeholders continue to lay a claim to the meanings of family in an effort to define the nation.

Chapter 6

Conclusion: "What Basis Do We Use to Decide Who Gets to Come?"

In 2007, a year after hundreds of thousands of immigrants and their supporters demonstrated in Los Angeles and elsewhere to demand the liberalization of U.S. immigration laws, members of the Senate considered a proposal, the Comprehensive Immigration Reform Act (CIRA), to do just that. The bill had three critical features: a pathway to citizenship for the estimated 12 million unauthorized immigrants; a temporary worker visa program; and an overhaul of the preference program, which would have ended most of the existing family preference categories except for spouses and children of U.S. citizens. Instead of a family-based policy, the new legislation would have implemented a point-based or "merit" system in which applicants would have been evaluated for entry based on their education, job skills, and English proficiency in addition to family connections.[1] As in previous debates on proposals to significantly alter the family reunification provisions, senators objected. Sen. Russ Feingold (D-WI) argued that the proposed reform to legal immigration was a "radical shift away from reunification. That solution is not consistent with the core values of this Nation. In the past, our immigration laws have acknowledged that our country and our communities are stronger when families are united."[2]

If limiting the family preference system was not the right solution to the immigration problem, what kind of reform did it warrant? Lawmakers had to answer a fundamental question. Sen. Jeff Sessions (R-AL) asked: "If we can't accept everybody, what basis do we use to decide who gets to come?"[3] As the previous chapter and the debates over CIRA show, this question raises competing demands between family unity and economic interests. That is a rather simple characterization of the policy choices or goals. Nevertheless, in working toward immigration reform, lawmakers and other stakeholders must consider whether these goals are equivalent, operate in tandem symbiotically, or in opposition to one another. In Senate judiciary hearings on immigration reform, Sen. Patrick Leahy (D-VT) presented these concerns and offered a narrative that he hoped would reconcile the two policy objectives as compatible. Offering support for legislation that would reduce wait time for families wishing to reunite and would provide a pathway to legal status for unauthorized immigrants, he pushed for reform and stated, "Changes to our family-based immigration policies are not just the right thing to do for moral reasons; they would also be good for the economy."[4]

However, the more foundational issue—the one this book has sought to address—requires an answer to the question of what we imagine the nation to be. As immigrants alter, challenge, or affirm an existing identity, immigration policy is about regulating their settlement in order to preserve or fashion a new national identity. This book has shown that the meaning of family and the role of family reunification have been central to these efforts. Family reunification has been part of what I call family ideation—the conceptualization of what family means, constitutes, and features in terms of its idealized characteristics, such as gender or sexual norms, class ideals, and racial or ethnic characteristics. Family has provided immigration stakeholders with a narrative structure for talking about immigrants' assimilability and the meanings of race and nation, enabling them to claim which immigrants are "like one of the family" and can be incorporated into the "American family." Exploring family this way, I explained that family reunification provisions existed in American immigration policy long before politicians and immigration scholars celebrated family reunification as a modern political achievement.

Regardless of the diversity of arrangements and actual lived experiences of individual families, the narrative structure or framework of family has offered immigration stakeholders a way to make sense of the unfamiliar, to talk about related concepts of race and nation, and to shape policy development. The structure includes a story line about family members, their roles and functions, and family's purpose. Immigration stakeholders' discursive action around family helped to generate unexpected family support for otherwise excludable immigrant groups (chapter 3) as well as restrictions against immigrant families during a time of immigration expansion (chapter 5). Family narrative is malleable; the particular details of the narrative are diverse and open to varying interpretations. Different groups at different times, for example, can be thought of as meritorious or deserving of family unity (chapter 4).

In addition, this narrative structure offers a language for articulating the meaning of relatedness and the various affective roles attendant to those relations. More specifically, this framework provides the language for communicating family's two crucial elements: "relationship" (ties or connection) and "natural substance" (putative blood or genes), which become foundations or codes for conduct. These are the building blocks and elements of other forms of kinship like race or ethnicity and nation, and we often use the language and structure of family to talk about these other forms. The apparent interchangeability between family and other forms of kinship lend to the symbolic strength and significance of family. The idea of family constitutes the nature of relations between individuals, and it also delineates the boundaries of those relations. Clarifying the meaning or characteristics of these elements is therefore highly consequential. We talk about families in order to specify and to understand how we are related, what that relatedness means, and what privileges and responsibilities are conferred by our relations. Actors can refer to or borrow from this family narrative structure to understand and give meaning to new immigrants. Immigration stakeholders have assessed whether immigrants' familial ties are legitimate and whether the substance that connect family members are real. Their evaluations help determine if immigrants are "like one of the family," and hence, a member of the nation, or instead are too different or deviant and inassimilable.

Immigration policy that focuses on family and is born out of family ideation constrains the meanings that actors can attach to the goals, functions, or roles of immigration. Quite simply, the narrative structure of family is inherently conservative and thereby limits the political framing and storytelling of immigration—that is, the story of what purpose immigrants and immigration should serve and how. The conservatism of family ideation inheres not only in the possibility that individuals themselves have conservative beliefs about who and what constitutes a family but also in the point that family is a form of kinship. The two elements of "relationship" and "natural substance" are reproduced by gendered bodies, which are dictated by patriarchal and heteronormative rules. Thus, the "strange bedfellows" coalition of immigrant advocacy groups and conservative religious organizations is not so strange after all. Both groups gain by advancing a family-based immigration system. For immigrant advocacy groups, maintaining a system that brought its constituents into the United States ensures the continued immigration of future members. For conservative religious organizations, support for family reunification in immigration provides them with a large and public arena in which to advocate traditional family forms and gender relations.

The experiences, claims, and values of nontraditional families may speak in direct opposition to such patriarchal and heteronormative rules, but these families exist in a world in which such ideas dominate. Thus, for example, many queer activists have long criticized the mobilization for recognition of same-sex marriages for gays and lesbians in the belief that the political goal of state recognition of gay marriage will validate heteronormative ideals and a straight, mainstream definition of normalcy while further marginalizing queer lifestyles and relations.[5] Nonetheless, many gay and lesbian activists and organizations understand that state-recognized marriages confer real and important benefits and privileges.

Thus, for example, gay and lesbian activists and liberal organizations have legally challenged the Defense of Marriage Act (DOMA), passed by Congress in 1996, which declared marriage to be a union between one man and one woman.[6] In addition to issues such as inheritance and government spousal benefits, gay and lesbian activists have questioned the constitutionality of DOMA over their rights to sponsor spouses for family reunification.[7] Although the Obama administration announced on February 23, 2011, that it would not *defend* DOMA in federal court challenges, it stated that it would continue to *enforce* the law.[8] This means that same-sex married couples are unable to sponsor spouses for immigration through family unity provisions that are available to heterosexual married couples.[9] Whether or not they support the institution of marriage, the legal claimants challenging DOMA understand that the way family is defined and officially recognized by the state is central to their efforts—not only to collect spousal survivor benefits from the government or to sponsor their gay spouses to join them in the United States, but also to gain full incorporation into the nation as members whose rights are not limited by their sexuality.

Whether conservative or liberal, immigration policy—which, like so many other social policies, hinges on the meaning of family—has to confirm or validate the elements of relationship and natural substance. Defenders and critics of family unity provisions for siblings or same-sex married couples may believe that there is a vast gulf of difference in opinion about the meaning of family between them. However, fundamentally, both sides are seeking to extend the right to immigrate to people who can validate their ties and natural substance. Thus, reform efforts that seek to limit a family preference system to spouses and children as well as those that would also include siblings exist on the same policy plane that limits options about who is eligible to immigrate to individuals who can be identified to be "like one of the family." This policy orientation restricts the range of possibilities for granting immigration rights and privileges, identifying new or different goals of immigration, and constructing the family writ large—the nation.

Efforts to "improve" the current system are thus reduced to technocratic and technological innovations in better identifying familial elements of relationship and natural substance—hence, the government's growing emphasis on genetic analysis for facilitating family reunification claims.[10] As explained in chapter 5, U.S. citizens and permanent residents in the United States wishing to sponsor family members can turn to DNA testing to expedite their applications. Without necessarily requiring such testing, the government has nonetheless deemed genetic analysis not only a *more* accurate form of testing but also *the* accurate test for verifying familial claims.

The use of genetics for evaluating familial claims and extending family unity benefits further suggests a number of tensions inherent in kinship constructs that rely on ties and natural substance. I return to the case of Isaac Owusu, whose fourteen-year effort to reunite with his four sons left behind in Ghana illustrates these tensions and the conservatism of an immigration policy that focuses on family's elements of ties and blood. Despite the highly personal nature of his experience with genetic testing, Owusu's struggle to retain his role of father of all four of his sons, not just the one who proved to be genetically related to him, underscores three general points that arise from the increasingly geneticization of family.[11] First, as the case makes clear, genetic analysis does not always provide unwavering answers to how people are related, and certainly not to how they understand their attachments to one another. Owusu's test results did not nullify his feelings of affection and filial responsibility for the boys who were not his *biological* sons, although they altered the legal parameters of his relationship with them. A reliance on genetic analysis may obscure the complex and contested ways in which familial ties (also racial, ancestral, or national origins) are constructed, understood, and mobilized for particular goals or purpose. For example, genetics may flatten or ignore the sometimes thorny nature of family relations, including adoption cases that are not legally sanctioned. Didier Fassin writes about the case of an Algerian-born woman in France who adopted a son in Algeria and brought him to France.[12] Algeria does not recognize adoption but approves of kefala—a type of extended guardianship common in North Africa. France does not permit kefala to be transformed into adoption. Thus, the adoptive mother never registered the child as her legal son in France. When DNA tests (undertaken to prove the child's relation to the mother once he became known to the French authorities) determined the boy was not biologically hers, the state placed him in foster care. Genetics and the legal architecture of family and immigration laws could not authenticate the affective tie between the mother and her son. Both Owusu's case and that of this mother in France show that genetics is increasingly not only *an* answer to questions of kinship and belonging but instead a *way* of answering or even framing questions of how collective ties ought to be formulated, evaluated, and understood for purposes of connecting individuals across time and space. DNA testing embodies the growing emphasis on seeing family in ever more technologically "precise" terms.

The Owusu case illustrates a second point about the increasing geneticization of family: there is an evolving tension between the supposedly absolute nature of genetic tests and the seemingly contingent nature of personal accounts. Seen through the lens of genetic analysis, the stories we repeatedly tell about ourselves and our origins—passed down from one generation to the next—are deemed to be less real than the results of a buccal swab test. Of course, nationalism scholars have long shown that such ancestral storytelling is part of the mythologizing of nations, and this continues to be true in the era of genetic analysis.[13] The putative claims of nativists and nationalists and of business entrepreneurs marketing genetic ancestry testing are entrenched in various and overlapping measures of fact and fiction.[14] In replacing personal, familial, or national narratives with DNA analysis, some scientists, government officials, business entrepreneurs, and consumers of ancestral testing have failed to recognize that genes tell stories as well—stories rooted in equivocal and challengeable claims.[15]

Third, Owusu's experience highlights the role of gender in molding the boundaries and meanings of family, race or ethnicity, and nation. The issue has been paradoxically absent from discussions of genetics and kinship but is critical to how notions of family, race or ethnicity, nation, and state are constructed, in two important ways. First, gender frames the questions that individual family members, government officials, and nationalists may demand that genetics provide answers to, since gender helps to structure the relations we have with one another, a larger ethnic or racial group, the nation, or the state. Second, gendered rules govern intimate relations such as marriage and reproduction, as well as more formal ones related to migration and settlement. In Owusu's case and in countless other families, gender relations and expectations may determine who moves where and when. For example, men may move first (like Owusu), or women may make the initial journey, thereby challenging earlier gender dynamics in a given family or immigrant group.[16] In turn, these relations shape the development of physical materials, including populations, genome banks, and even DNA and cell lines. For example, church regulations and recordings of marriage in colonial Quebec effectively denied the existence of intermarriage between French settlers and native peoples, which has permitted geneticists to claim that frontier Quebec society was racially pure in biological terms.[17] These physical materials—produced in part through gendered and racialized intimate relations like sex or marriage and through scientific gathering and declarations—provide the basis upon which genetic, familial, racial, and national claims are made, delineating the boundaries of legal or legitimate families, racial formation, and the nation-state.[18] Thus, gender molds the symbolic meaning of these materials and the significance of the relations from which they arise. Gendered ideals and racial claims lie at the heart of how individual family members, nationalists, and geneticists collect, interpret, and narrate such materials for familial, racial, and nationalist questions and claims.

Lastly, the emphasis on family in immigration policymaking is inherently conservative, because it limits the meaning of responsibility and rights to paternalistic relations between state and subject. The parent-child relationship demands that the former provide for the latter and obligates the latter to behave in exchange for benefits. By talking about immigration rights in familial terms, immigration stakeholders reduce the complex process of migration to one in which the nation-state confers special rights on individuals and families who act responsibly and are deemed appropriate. In this sense, migration and the right to move across national borders to reunite with families becomes less a human right and more a state-sanctioned privilege for a select group.[19]

Given these limits and challenges with an immigration policy and policymaking rooted in family ideation, what would an immigration reform that addresses the interrelated issues of legal and unauthorized immigration look like?[20] Despite renewed political interest, realistic reform remains a difficult challenge. However, a fundamental question endures: as Senator Sessions asked, "What basis do we use to decide who gets to come?" Answers to this question—on which the possibility of any future reform proposal may depend—are quite likely to focus on the meaning and role of family and family reunification. Given the fact that family reunification is a dominant feature of unauthorized and legal immigration, including work-related immigration, lawmakers and other immigration stakeholders must agree on how significant they want family-related migration to be in American immigration policy. If lawmakers compromise on a solution, previous experience suggests that family ideation may indeed provide crucial gains for many of these immigrants, including a pathway to citizenship for unauthorized immigrants. However, family ideation could also lead us to declare that unauthorized immigrants and "distant" family members are not quite "like one of the family." Thus, if immigration policymaking revolves around family—regardless of the outcome—the inherently conservative narrative structure of family will limit the meaning of the rights and privileges of immigration to proper ties and natural substance.

Appendix: Data and Methods

This book examines the centrality of meanings of family and family reunification to American immigration policy and traces how ideas about family, race, and nation have permeated the development of immigration policy. Because I am concerned with how ideas influence policy, I focus on the construction and deployment of meaning by the actors who have been critical in creating and shaping immigration policy. These actors have varied from period to period but include politicians, leading intellectuals, social and moral reformers, labor organizers and unions, business leaders, immigrant activist groups, and religious and ethnic organizations.

To investigate their disseminated ideas, I spent a dozen years researching private and government archives, published government documents, and newspapers in over six cities and examined more than 20,000 pages of materials in addition to published secondary sources. These archives and published documents are listed in the references section.

After tracing the legislative and social history of immigration policy from the mid-1800s to the present day, I did close readings of primary materials and conducted content analysis, which forms the basis of the research for the book. Because of the particularly crucial role played by lawmakers and the legislative setting in immigration policymaking, I analyzed congressional debates, reports, documents, and hearings at length. To identify the major themes and discursive arguments used in legislative action, I analyzed lawmakers' arguments in support of or opposition to major immigration bills. Using HeinOnline (my search terms were the bill numbers and titles that became the immigration acts, during the years when they were passed), I located congressional debates and selected one day of debates for the House and Senate each for 1882, 1924, 1952, 1965, 1986, 1996, and 2006. I chose ten speakers from the House and Senate who made substantive arguments or provided a rationale for their position on the proposed bill and/or immigration, for a total of 140 unique speakers. I noted the position and explanation for each speaker and eventually categorized all of their utterances. These position statements and themes helped to identify the major categories of analysis to be found in the close reading and content analysis of the archival materials, House and Senate reports, and legislative hearings.

The analysis of the 140 unique speakers suggested the importance of themes of purity (chapter 3); urgency, humanity, merit, and national interest (chapter 4); and diversity, cultural pluralism, and responsibility (chapter 5) in relation to family and immigration. When conducting content analysis of the archival and legislative materials for each time period, I traced the introduction, types, and context of utterances and the related stories told or framing conducted using these themes as guidance.

Notes

CHAPTER 1

1. "Japanese Rice Growers in Texas," RG 85, box 13, Entry 9, File 51835/6, Box 13, entry 9, "Japanese Rice Growers in Texas," The National Archives and Records Administration, U.S. Bureau of Immigration, Washington, D.C.
2. In Takao Ozawa v. United States, the Supreme Court concluded that the plaintiff, Takao Ozawa, was not a "Caucasian" and instead a member of the "Mongoloid race," which meant that he was not white and therefore was ineligible for naturalization. In United States v. Bhagat Singh Thind, the Supreme Court agreed that the plaintiff, Bhagat Singh Thind, was indeed a member of the "Caucasoid" race, but was not "white," which meant that he too was ineligible for citizenship. Although the Supreme Court relied upon the science of race to refute Ozawa's claim to naturalization rights, it referred to everyday folk understandings of race to argue that Thind was also not entitled to naturalize. Takao Ozawa v. United States, 260 U.S. 178 (1922), and United States v. Bhagat Singh Thind, 261 U.S. 204 (1923); see also Haney López (1996, ch. 4).
3. Rachel L. Swarns, "DNA Tests Offer Immigrants Hope or Despair," *New York Times,* April 10, 2007.
4. "Senate Conference on Immigration" (CQ transcripts wire), *Washington Post,* May 17, 2007.
5. Between 2001 and 2010, 6,760,621 immigrants were admitted as immediate family members or based on the family preference system. In 2010, of the 148,343 immigrants who entered under the employer-based preference category, an estimated 81,354 of them were admitted as spouses or children (U.S. Department of Homeland Security 2010, "Table 6: Persons Obtaining Legal Permanent Resident Status by Type and Major Class of Admission: Fiscal Years 2001 to 2010"). Also available is the diversity lottery, which gives permanent residency to many immigrants from countries with traditionally (recently) low immigration to the United States.
6. African immigrants entered the United States using diversity visas, refugee provisions, and family sponsorship. In 2011, 48,123 Africans arrived through family sponsorship (7,940) or as immediate relatives (40,183) of U.S. citizens, out of a total 100,374 immigrants, representing nearly half of all legal entrants.
7. U.S. Department of Homeland Security, *Yearbook of Immigration Statistics 2011,* "Table 10: Persons Obtaining Legal Permanent Resident Status by Broad Class of Admission and Region and Country of Birth: Fiscal Year 2011."

8. On April 18, 2013, a bi-partisan group of eight senators proposed an immigration reform bill that would, among other features, provide a pathway to citizenship for the estimated 11 million unauthorized immigrants who were in the United States by December 31, 2011. Senate proposal available at: http://www.rubio.senate.gov/public/?a=Files.Serve&File_id=adefad85-7f5c-4f3e-a4dc-366a1b71ad38 (accessed May 21, 2013). Even a more modest reform policy, for example, passage of the DREAM Act, which would offer legal status and pathway to citizenship to an estimated 1.7 to 2.1 million minors and young adults, who were brought to the United States without authorization as children, could lead to increased family-sponsored immigration.

   On the Development, Relief, and Education for Alien Minors (DREAM) Act (H.R. 5281, December 8, 2010, U.S. House of Representatives), see David M. Herszenhorn, "Senate Blocks Bill for Young Illegal Immigrants," *New York Times,* December 18, 2010. According to a Migration Policy Institute (MPI) report (Batalova and McHugh 2010), slightly more than 2.1 million unauthorized individuals would have become eligible for legalization had the bill passed. The Obama administration's deferral program of June 15, 2012, would make as many as 1.7 million immigrants eligible for a kind of temporary permission to stay in the United States called *deferred action.* Millions of children and young adults who were recently given a suspension of deportation orders for being in the country without authorization could become eligible for a pathway to permanent resident or citizenship status if some form of the DREAM Act passes (Julia Preston, "Illegal Immigrants Line Up by Thousands for Deportation Deferrals," *New York Times,* August 15, 2012; Secretary of Homeland Security Janet Napolitano, "Exercising Prosecutorial Discretion with Respect to Individuals Who Came to the United States as Children" (memorandum), June 15, 2012, available at: http://www.dhs.gov/xlibrary/assets/s1-exercising-prosecutorial-discretion-individuals-who-came-to-us-as-children.pdf (accessed November 13, 2012).
9. On naturalization laws and whiteness, see Haney López 1996. On European immigrants' achievement of whiteness, see Ignatiev 1995; Roediger 1991; Jacobson 1998.
10. However, the growing and diverse Latino immigration is further complicating the meaning of the color line. Tomás Jiménez (2010) suggests that some Mexican Americans, the largest Latino group in the United States, may be increasingly embracing a white racial identity with each successive generation in this country. See also Foner 2005, ch. 1, and Lee and Bean 2010.
11. Abu El-Haj 2012; Hinterberger 2012a; Kohli-Laven 2012.
12. Hacking 1999; Hobsbawm and Ranger 1983.
13. On U.S. civic values, see Smith 1997.
14. Collins 1998, 2001.
15. Borjas 1990; Gonzalez 2006; Ness 2011; Sjaastad 1962; Todaro 1969, 1989; To-

daro and Maruszko 1987. For a critique of this perspective and an argument for a political economy approach, see Massey 1990, 2009; Massey et al. 1998; Massey, Goldring, and Durand 1994; Piore 1979; Sassen 1988; Stark 1991; and Todaro 1976.

16. Daniels 1988; Gutiérrez 1995; King 2000; Erika Lee 2003.
17. Ngai 2004; Smith 1997; Takaki 1979; Tichenor 2002; Zolberg 2006.
18. Brubaker 2004; Brubaker, Loveman, and Stamatov 2004.
19. Ngai 2004; Calavita 2007; Jacobson 1998.
20. Tichenor 2002, 1.
21. Gal and Kligman 2000b.
22. Zerubavel 2012.
23. Wailoo, Nelson, and Lee 2012; Zerubavel 2012.
24. Schneider 1977, 1980.
25. More specifically for Schneider, blood and genes are simply natural substance. Furthermore, he differentiates between relationship as substance and relationship as code for conduct (Schneider 1980). I argue that ties (however defined) and the putatively real, natural substance are both codes for conduct. This formulation partly addresses the critique that Schneider's formulations make unproblematic distinctions between nature and law. See Carsten 2002.
26. Zerubavel 2012; Wailoo et al. 2012; Abu El-Haj 2012.
27. Anderson 1991, 7.
28. Kligman 1998.
29. Barstow 2000; Meznaric 1994.
30. Mosse 1985; Mostov 1996; Douglas 2002.
31. Gardner 2005; Meznaric 1994; Mostov 1996.
32. Gal and Kligman 2000a; Nagel 1998; Pateman 1988.
33. Almaguer 1994.
34. Campbell 2002, 2004; Edelman 1964; Skrentny 2006; Steensland 2006.
35. For example, Weber 1958.
36. DiMaggio 1997; Zerubavel 1997.
37. Swidler 1986.
38. Stone 1989.
39. See also Birkland 1997.
40. Chavez 2004, 2008; Newton 2008; Huang 2008.
41. Edelman 1964; Ingram and Schneider 1993.
42. Gyory 1998.
43. Calavita 1992; Mize and Swords 2010.
44. Tichenor 2002.
45. Tichenor 2002, ch. 8; Skrentny 2002, ch. 3.
46. On minority groups, see Skrentny 2006. On Mexican immigrants, see Newton 2008; Chavez 2008.

47. On meaning and politics, see Stone 2002. On stories and narratives, see Frank 2010 and Polletta 2006.
48. On frame analysis, see Gamson 1992.
49. Ewick and Silbey 1995; Franzosi 1998; Ingram and Schneider 2005; Jasper 1997; Lakoff 2004; Newton 2008; Stone 1989. For an excellent discussion of narrative analysis and the importance of understanding storytelling in politics, see Polletta 2006.
50. Polletta 2006, 167.

CHAPTER 2

1. Rep. Victor L. Berger, *Congressional Record,* 68th Cong., 1st sess. (April 11, 1924): 6135.
2. This opportunity was made available to permanent residents after 1928 within the national origins quota system.
3. Sen. Kent Conrad, speaking in opposition to S. 358, *Congressional Record,* 101st Cong., 1st sess. (July 12, 1989): 14295.
4. In 2011, 688,089 immigrants entered using family provisions of the immigration law (as family-sponsored preferences and immediate relatives of U.S. citizens) (U.S. Department of Homeland Security, *Yearbook of Immigration Statistics 2011,* "Table 10. Persons Obtaining Legal Permanent Resident Status by Broad Class of Admission and Region and Country of Birth: Fiscal Year 2011").
5. As of 2011, there were 3,385,775 temporary workers and families (temporary workers and trainees; intracompany transferees; treaty traders and investors; and representatives of foreign information media) in the United States (U.S. Department of Homeland Security, *Yearbook of Immigration Statistics 2011,* "Table 25. Nonimmigrant Admissions by Class of Admission: Fiscal Years 2002 to 2011").
6. Rumbaut 1997, 6.
7. For an example of family planning, see Popenoe 1926. On "fitter families," "race betterment," and eugenics, see Kline 2001. On race, family, and eugenics, see Lovett 2007; Ordover 2002; Roberts 1997, chap. 2.
8. Bock and Thane 1991; Gal and Kligman 2000a; Gordon 1994; Koven and Michel 1993; Pateman 1988; Quadagno 1994.
9. Cott 2000; Lovett 2007; Stacey 1997.
10. Coontz 1992.
11. Gordon 2007, 86–104; Popenoe 1993, 1998.
12. Stacey 1990.
13. Stacey 1990; Stacey and Biblarz 2001; Weeks, Heaphy, and Donovan 2001; Weston 1991.
14. Bailey and Boyle 2001.
15. Stacey 2011.

16. Collins 1998; Zinn and Eitzen 1990.
17. Rodriguez 2009.
18. Moore 2011.
19. Collins 2001.
20. Donato et al. 2011; Donato et al. 2006; Gabaccia 1994; Kofman 2004; Moch 2005.
21. Bianchi 1997; Nauck and Settles 2001; Waters 1997.
22. Fix 2009; Park and Park 2005.
23. Bracalenti and Benini 2005; Grillo 2009.
24. Hein 1995; Jasso and Rosenzweig 1986, 1989, 1990, 1995; Meissner et al. 1993.
25. Alvarez 1987; Bashi 2007; Foner 1997; Massey and Parrado 1994; Portes and Rumbaut 1996.
26. Bryceson and Vuorela 2002; Hondagneu-Sotelo 1994; Settles, Hanks, and Sussman, 1993; Vasquez 2011.
27. King, Thomson, Fielding, and Warnes 2006.
28. Hondagneu-Sotelo 1994.
29. Yoshikawa 2011.
30. Fujiwara 2008; Park and Park 2005.
31. Park 2011, 6.
32. Sugarman 2008.
33. Strach 2007, 5.
34. Wisensale 2001.
35. An earlier version of the law originally capped each national quota at 2 percent of the total population of foreign-born persons of each nationality recorded in the 1890 census, with a minimum of 100. Western Hemisphere countries were exempted from national origin quotas (see Immigration Act of 1924, P.L. 68-139, 43 Stat. 153).
36. *Proclamation by the President of the United States,* Washington, D.C., March 22, 1929.
37. See chapter 1, note 2.
38. The Act of May 29, 1928 (45 Stat. 1009) gave preference to unmarried children under twenty-one years of age and wives of alien residents lawfully admitted for permanent residence.
39. Unmarried adult sons and daughters of U.S. citizens were moved up to the second preference category by the Act of September 22, 1959 (73 Stat. 644).
40. The 1959 act increased the maximum to 50 percent. "Sons and daughters" now referred to those who were married, regardless of age.
41. In 2011 immediate family members of U.S. citizens numbered 453,158—nearly half of all immigrants to the United States. See U.S. Department of Homeland Security, *Yearbook of Immigration Statistics 2011,* "Table 10. Persons Obtaining Legal Permanent Resident Status by Broad Class of Admission and Region and Country of Birth: Fiscal Year 2011").

42. U.S. Department of Homeland Security, *Yearbook of Immigration Statistics 2000,* "Table 4. Immigrants Admitted by Type and Selected Class of Admission: Fiscal Years 1986 to 2000."
43. U.S. Department of Homeland Security, *Yearbook of Immigration Statistics 2011,* "Table 7. Persons Obtaining Legal Permanent Resident Status by Type and Detailed Class of Admission: Fiscal Year 2011." This number does not include data withheld to limit disclosure.
44. For the last three decades, 5,752,701 people from Mexico have obtained legal permanent resident status, 1,693,507 from the Philippines, and 1,255,903 from China. In 2011, Mexico still led with 142,823 and China with 83,603, but India (66,331) outnumbered the Philippines (55,251) by about 11,000 (U.S. Department of Homeland Security, *Yearbook of Immigration Statistics 2011,* "Table 2. Persons Obtaining Legal Permanent Resident Status by Region and Selected Country of Last Residence: Fiscal Years 1820 to 2011").
45. Gabriel Chin (1996) argues otherwise. See also Reimers 1998, 65–70, Skrentny 2002, 331–32.
46. Bashi 2007; Jasso and Rosenzweig 1986; Yu 2008.
47. Jacobson 1996; Joppke 1998, 1999; Skrentny et al. 2007.
48. Gal and Kligman 2000a.
49. Cornelius, Martin, and Hollifield 1994; on Taiwan, see also Lan 2008.
50. Quoted in Lovett 2007, 1.

CHAPTER 3

1. Chew Hoy Quong v. White, 244 Fed. 749 (9th Cir. 1917); Chew Hoy Quong v. White, 249 Fed. 869 (9th Cir. 1918). For detailed descriptions of Quok Shee and her detention, see McClain 1994a; Bardes 2008; and Lee and Yung 2010.
2. "Kiyo Urakawa," RG 85, Box 00763, case file 13137/01204, National Archives and Records Administration, San Bruno, Calif.
3. Although the law denied entry to any subject coming from "China, Japan, or any oriental country," the real target was Chinese women (Peffer 1999; Chan 1991). See Rep. Horace Page's speech in introducing his bill, *Appendix to the Congressional Record,* 43d Cong., 2d sess. (February 10, 1875): 40–45.
4. Congress made the act permanent in 1902, but repealed it in 1943 when China allied with the United States in its war against Japan (Erika Lee 2003; Riggs 1950).
5. The Naturalization Act of 1870 had clearly specified that only whites and blacks were eligible for citizenship and explicitly did not mention Chinese immigrants (McClain 1994b). Following the Supreme Court decisions in Takao Ozawa v. United States and United States v. Bhagat Singh Thind, Asian immigrants were declared ineligible for citizenship (Haney López 1998). Yet Asian veterans ultimately succeeded in their fight for citizenship

when they secured the passage of the Nye-Lea Act in 1935, with the vital support of the American Legion (Salyer 2004).

6. For a lengthier discussion of gendered and racialized logics, see Catherine Lee 2003, 2010. Portions of this discussion appear in Catherine Lee 2010.
7. Daniels 1988; Lyman 1974.
8. Hirata 1979.
9. The Chinese male to female ratio was 27-to-1 in 1890 (male: 103,607, female: 3,868), 19-to-1 in 1900 (male: 85,341, female: 4,522), 14-to-1 in 1910 (male: 66,856, female: 4,675), and 7-to-1 in 1920 (male: 53,891, female: 7,748) (Glenn 1983; see also U.S. Bureau of the Census 2000). For discussion of the role of women in the early history of Chinese immigration in facilitating Chinese migration by helping to artificially cheapen Chinese men's labor, see Hirata 1979 and Espiritu 1997.
10. Peffer 1999.
11. Chan 1991; Gee 2003.
12. Stevens 2002; Shah 2001; Ting 1995.
13. On Chinese merchant men's efforts to unify their families, see Stevens 2002. On Chinese bachelor societies in the United States, see Shah 2001, introduction; Ting 1995. As an exception, some Filipino men married white women. For Filipino men and their relationships with white American women, see Ngai (2004, ch. 3). The Tydings-McDuffie Act of 1934 (P.L. 73-127, 48 Stat. 456) cut the Filipino immigration quota by placing Filipino immigrants under the general immigration laws. It defined Filipinos living in the United States who arrived before May 1, 1934, as "aliens not deportable," but they were subject to deportation for deportable acts committed after May 1, 1934. Along with repatriation measures targeting Filipinos in the United States, this act effectively excluded Filipinos from the United States. On bachelor society, see Courtwright 1996. On anti-miscegenation, see Leonard 2010; Moran 2001; Nash 1999; Pascoe 1996, 2009; Spickard 1989.
14. Calavita 1984; Gyory 1998; Higham 2002; Miller 1969; Mink 1986; Saxton 1971; Tichenor 2002.
15. California Legislature 1878, 50–77.
16. Stevens 2002, 297.
17. Stevens 2002, 289.
18. McClain 1994a; Ngai 2004, 204.
19. William Jack Chow, an immigration attorney, guessed that at least half of all Chinese immigrants who entered during the exclusion era did so illegally, using fraudulent claims and documents (Ngai 2004, 204).
20. *Congressional Record,* 47th Cong., 1st sess. (March 3, 1882): 1584.
21. California Legislature 1878, 217.
22. Some Chinese women were indeed prostitutes, while some were victims of forced prostitution (see McClain 1994b; Pascoe 1990).
23. Peffer 1999, 76.

24. *Congressional Record,* 47th Cong., 1st sess. (March 14, 1882): 1903.
25. On science and germ theory, see Tomes 1990, 1999. See also Shah 2001.
26. Miller 1969, 165.
27. California Legislature 1878, 153.
28. Of course, those who employed large numbers of Chinese laborers extolled the virtues of their work ethic. Men like Charles Crocker, who introduced many Chinese workers into railroad construction (so much so that Chinese workers were called "Crocker's Pets"), argued instead that "the effect of Chinese labor upon white labor has an elevating instead of a degrading tendency" (Daniels 1988, 48).
29. Shah 2001, 74.
30. Senate documents, RG 46, 47A-H10.1, box 110, National Archives and Records Administration, Washington, D.C.
31. California Legislature 1878, 16.
32. *Congressional Record,* 45th Cong., 3d sess. (February 14, 1879): 1301.
33. Lorenzo Sawyer, letter to Hubert Howe Bancroft, September 22, 1886, 4–5, "Letters," in Hubert Howe Bancroft Collection, Bancroft Library, University of California–Berkeley. As a federal district judge, Sawyer actually ruled many times in favor of Chinese immigrants and was lambasted for being a *friend* of the Chinese (Salyer 1995).
34. See also Espiritu 1997 and Hirata 1979. For contemporary examples, see Chavez 2004 and Chang 2000. For similar debates in Germany, see Brubaker 1989, 1992 and Joppke 1998, 1999.
35. The reference to the "continental United States" was an important distinction. Japanese immigrants first migrated to the Hawaiian islands (which was a U.S. territory until its statehood in 1959), then made a second migratory move to the continental United States, often landing on the Pacific Coast. Following the Gentlemen's Agreement, Japanese immigrants could no longer use Hawaii as a stepping-stone.
36. As of 1920, there were 110,010 Japanese on the U.S. mainland and 109,274 in Hawaii (Rossiter, Thorp, and Beales 1922, 137, 174).
37. Glenn 1986; Lee 2010.
38. Ichioka 1988; O'Brien and Fugita 1991.
39. Daniels 1977, 3.
40. Daniels 1988; Hing 1993.
41. Chan 1986.
42. Some exclusionists decried these farming wives' entry as evidence of a loophole in the Gentlemen's Agreement that allowed additional laborers to enter.
43. Beisel 1998; Donovan 2006.
44. Such rhetoric was and is not specific to this period. Following the Supreme Court's decision in Brown v. Board of Education of Topeka, Kansas (347 U.S. 483) in 1954, Circuit court judge Thomas Brady of Mississippi emphatically

declared that the South would "fight and die for the principles of racial purity and white womanhood" rather than follow the Court's decision (see Davis 1991, 17).

45. Davis 1991; Moran 2001; Pascoe 2009.
46. Bederman 1995; Burstyn 1999.
47. Bederman 1995; Beisel 1998; Connelly 1980; Donovan 2006; Hobson 1987; Pascoe 1990; Rosen 1982.
48. Some couples found creative ways to skirt antimiscegenation laws. Goto and McElwain married aboard a ship off the coast of California.
49. "Manzo Goto," RG 85, Entry 9, Box 66, file 53770/113, National Archives and Records Administration, U.S. Bureau of Immigration, Washington, D.C.
50. Bederman 1995; Donovan 2006.
51. Rosen 1982.
52. Aoki 1998.
53. Daniels 1977, 59.
54. Sen. James Phelan, letter to Secretary of State Robert Lansing, July 24, 1919: 2, file 52424/13B, folder 1, record group 85, entry 9, National Archives and Records Administration, Washington, D.C.
55. Commentators referred to a government report that Japanese immigrant women's birth rate was three times that of native-born white women. However, they obfuscated, or rather ignored, the fact that Japanese immigrant women were mostly of childbearing age and in the first years of their marriage, whereas the comparative native-born white women were in varying years of marriage (Daniels 1988, 146).
56. U.S. Congress, Senate, Committee on Immigration (1924), 5–6.
57. The phrase was made popular by Jack London in his sensationalist articles written for the Hearst Newspapers (Métraux 2010; Wu 1982).
58. Ngai 1999.
59. Haney López 1996.
60. Ngai 2004, ch. 5.
61. I use National Origins Act and Immigration Act of 1924 interchangeably, although technically the former was part of the latter, which included other acts.
62. The ethnic associations urged congressional members of Northern urban districts to defend the clauses for "near relatives" (Fiorello LaGuardia, letter to Max Kohler, February 9, 1924, box 3, House of Representatives folder, Max James Kohler Papers, American Jewish Historical Society). See also Tichenor 2002, 46.
63. *Congressional Record,* 66th Cong., 3d sess. (February 26, 1921): 3970.
64. "Hebrew Aid Society Attacks Alien Bill," *New York Times,* February 14, 1921. According to the Society, "If the bill is adopted there should be included in its provisions such amendments as will make possible: '1. The reunion of families. 2. A more just attitude toward the minority peoples and toward the

new and enlarge countries,' as well as revisions on the per cent limit of immigrants to be admitted to the United States."

65. U.S. Congress, House, Committee on Immigration and Naturalization (1925); see also Hsu 2002, 96.
66. "Table Ad950-954: Immigrants Admitted Under the Quota System: 1925–1968," and "Table Ad1-2: U.S. Immigrants and Emigrants: 1820–1998," both in Carter et al. 2006.
67. Act of May 29, 1928 (45 Stat. 1009). The Act of July 11, 1932 (47 Stat. 656) exempted foreign husbands of U.S. citizens married before July 1, 1932.
68. Bredbenner 1998, 138. See also U.S. Congress, House, Committee on Immigration and Naturalization 1918, 39; U.S. Congress, House, Committee on Immigration and Naturalization 1926, 18.
69. For the history of women's derivative citizenship status, see Sapiro 1984, Cott 1988, and Bredbenner 1998.
70. 1984, 10.
71. Bredbenner 1998, 97.
72. U.S. Congress, House, Committee on Immigration and Naturalization (1917), 33.
73. Ibid., 17.
74. Sapiro 1984, 14.
75. Cott 1988, 1469.
76. Limoncelli 2010.
77. 1988, 1471.
78. The Supreme Court in Lem Moon Sing v. United States (158 U.S. 538 [1895]), limited judicial review in cases in which immigrants' right to enter on merchant status was denied.
79. Ngai 2004, 204–5.
80. Salyer 1995, 72.
81. Ngai 2004, 205, emphasis in original.
82. Lau 2006.
83. On wives left behind, see Hirata 1979; Peffer 1999.
84. Lau 2006, 140–41; Ngai 2004, 205–6.
85. Many family members themselves were unaware of the complicated and contested ties, which blended fact and fiction. See Ngai 2004, 221, and Lau 2006.

CHAPTER 4

1. "10,000 British War Brides Will Hire a Hall to Protest Delays in Rejoining Husbands," *New York Times,* October 9, 1945, 15; "Army and Navy—to Soldiers' Wives," *Time,* October 22, 1945; Friedman 2007, 99; Burk 2008, 557.
2. Houstoun et al. 1984, 920; Shukert and Scibetta 1988, 1, 2, 7, and appendix A, 265.

3. Congress provided the right of entry to Chinese wives married to U.S. citizens prior to May 26, 1924, in an act approved on June 13, 1930. The act was the result of successful lobbying by the Chinese community. Chinese Americans argued the act would not lead to an increase in the number of Chinese entering the country (Zhao 2002, 17–21). The repeal of the Chinese Exclusion Act in the Magnuson Act of 1943 afforded Chinese immigrants the opportunity to naturalize. Congress made Indians and Filipinos eligible for citizenship in the Act of July 2, 1946 (60 Stat. 417) (Hutchinson 1981, 273).
4. See section 13 of the Immigration Act of 1924. Japanese wives, even those of U.S. citizens, were not allowed to enter the United States because subdivisions (b), (d), and (e) of section 13 did not include wives or children of U.S. citizens. This was made clear by the opinion in the U.S. Supreme Court case Chang Chan v. Nagle (268 U.S 346), issued in 1925. However, under subdivision (d) of section 4, Japanese wives of ministers or professors could enter, and Japanese wives of trade treaty aliens, defined in section 3, were also allowed to enter the United States; see also U.S. Congress, House, Committee on Immigration and Naturalization (1925), 38; Congress cited *Ex parte Chiu Shee* to show uncertainties concerning the right of Japanese or Chinese wives married to U.S. citizens to enter or stay in America. See U.S. Congress, House, Committee on Immigration and Naturalization (1925).
5. Wolgin 2011.
6. Polletta 2006, 167.
7. Barkan 1992, 344–45.
8. Kevles 1985; Ordover 2002, ch. 1; Roberts 1997, ch. 2; Tucker 2002.
9. Ordover 2002, 159–78.
10. United States and Wilson 1947, 146–48.
11. Dudziak 2000; Skrentny 2002.
12. Tichenor 2002, 176.
13. Barkan 1992.
14. Chin 1996, 287; Skrentny 2002; Dudziak 2000.
15. During World War II, Americans were willing to build a permanent military alliance with China. According to the 1943 Gallup Poll, more than 55 percent of Americans agreed that the United States and China should come to each other's defense immediately if the other was attacked at any future time. Antagonism toward the Japanese also subsided over the years. In 1949 the Gallup Poll asked Americans about their feelings toward the people of Japan: 34 percent had "friendly" feelings, 30 percent were neutral, 29 percent had unfriendly feelings, and 7 percent answered that they were undecided. When the same question was presented in 1951, six years after the war, 51 percent said that they had friendly feelings toward the Japanese, while 25 percent had unfriendly feelings, 18 percent were neutral, and 6 percent had no opinion ("Postwar Alliances," October 8, 1943, in Gallup [1972, 1:411]; "Japanese People," April 18, 1949, in Gallup [1972, 2:806–7]; "Japan," September 14,

1951, in Gallup [1972, 2:1007–8]; Shah 2001, ch. 9; Wong 2005; "How Many Europeans to Let In," January 14, 1946, in Gallup 1972, 1:555.

16. Riggs 1950, 47.
17. Ed Lee Gossett, *Congressional Record,* 78th Cong., 1st sess. October 20, 1943: 8581.
18. Takaki 1989/1998, 378.
19. Hutchinson 1981, 264–65.
20. U.S. Congress, House, Committee on Immigration and Naturalization (1943), 72–73.
21. Ed Lee Gossett, *Congressional Record,* 78th Cong., 1st sess. (October 20, 1943): 8581.
22. Takaki 1989/1998, 378.
23. Hutchinson 1981, 264–73.
24. "Justice to Our Ally, India—Repeal Exclusion of Her Nationals," Extension of Remarks of Hon. Emanuel Celler of New York, Appendix to Congressional Record, 78th Cong., 2d sess. (April 17, 1944): A1834.
25. Tichenor 2002, 178.
26. U.S. Congress, House, Committee on Immigration and Naturalization (1945), 2; U.S. Congress, Senate, Committee on Immigration (1945), 2; *Congressional Record,* 79th Cong., 1st sess. (December 19, 1945): 12342.
27. *Congressional Record,* 79th Cong., 1st sess. (December 10, 1945): 11738.
28. P.L. 79-271, 59 Stat. 659.
29. See also Wolgin and Bloemraad 2010, 31, fn. 4.
30. For discussion of the war brides' experience, see Zeiger 2010 and Höhn 2002. Not only did men and women who met and wished to marry during and after World War II and the Korean War have to contend with unfavorable family reunification policies (sexist policies that favored the arrangement of American military men marrying women abroad) but also racism, both in the United States and abroad, which made efforts to unite difficult. Höhn writes that black soldiers stationed in West Germany in the 1950s endured segregated units, the importation of Jim Crow segregation into Germany, and racism from local Germans. German war brides who wished to marry black soldiers faced great obstacles. On racist attitudes toward black military servicemen in Korea following the Korean War, see Nadia Kim, *Imperial Citizens* (2008). Furthermore, racial discrimination existed not only in national origins policy but also in the antimiscegenation laws of many states, which made interracial unions illegal. The Supreme Court ruled these antimiscegenation laws unconstitutional in Loving v. Virginia, 388 U.S. 1 (1967). See Moran 2001.
31. U.S. Congress, House, Committee on the Judiciary (1949), 3.
32. The passage of the Act of June 13, 1930 (46 Stat. 581) allowed this. U.S. Congress, Senate, Committee on Immigration (1946), 2.
33. U.S. Congress, House, Committee on Immigration and Naturalization, "To

Facilitate the Admission to the United States of Husbands, Wives, and Children of United States Citizen Men and Women Who Have Served Honorably in the Armed Forces of the United States During the Present World War," unpublished hearing on H.R. 714, 79th Cong., 1st sess. (May 23, 1945).

34. *Congressional Record,* 79th Cong., 2d sess. (August 2, 1946): 10729.
35. Congress passed the Soldier Brides Act of July 22, 1947 (P.L. 80-213, 61 Stat. 401).
36. U.S. Congress, Senate, Committee on the Judiciary (1947); U.S. Congress, House, Committee on the Judiciary (1947).
37. U.S. Congress, House, Committee on the Judiciary (1949), 3. The 1949 *Annual Report of the Immigration and Naturalization Service* (hereafter *INS Annual Report*) stated that during the fiscal year ended June 30, 1949, under the Act of December 28, 1945, 2,254 husbands, wives, and children entered the United States from Asia (Table 10). The 1950 *INS Annual Report* stated that during the years ended June 30, 1946, to 1950, 7,717 husbands, wives, and children from Asia were admitted (Table 8). See note 31.
38. 1950 Act on Alien Spouses and Children (P.L. 717, 64 Stat. 464).
39. Wolgin and Bloemraad 2010, 42.
40. *INS Annual Report,* 1950, 20–21.
41. Majone 1989, 150; Strach 2007.
42. "Joint Statement by Sponsors of New Omnibus Immigration and Naturalization Bill—Senators Humphrey, Lehman, Benton, Langer, Kilgore, Douglas, McMahon, Green, Pastore, Murray, Kefauver, Morse, and Moody," *Congressional Record,* 82d Cong., 1st sess. (March 12, 1952): 2141.
43. The McCarran bill, S. 2550 with S. Rpt. 1137, was proposed on January 29, 1952, and the Walter bill, H.R. 5678 with H. Rpt. 1356, on February 14, 1952. The Walter bill was brought up in the House on April 23, 1952, and passed two days later. Consideration of the Senate bill by McCarran began on May 9, 1952.
44. *Congressional Record,* 82d Cong., 1st sess. (May 13, 1952): 5089.
45. Ibid., 5090; Senate bill S. 2550.
46. Statement of Mike M. Masaoka, National Legislative Director, Japanese American Citizens League Antidiscrimination Committee, Washington, D.C., in Committees on the Judiciary (1951), 61.
47. Secretary of State Dean Acheson, memorandum to President Harry Truman, April 14, 1952, in *Foreign Relations of the United States, 1952-1954,* vol. 1, part 2, "General: Economic and Political Matters," document 241, PSF–General file, Truman papers, Truman Library, Office of the Historian, U.S. Department of State, available at: http://history.state.gov/historicaldocuments/frus1952-54v01p2/d241 (accessed April 19, 2012).
48. Center for Migration Studies of New York, Inc. 1964, 35. Under the leadership of McCarran and Walter, a conference report, H. Rpt. 2096, June 9, 1952, was drafted and agreed to by both houses of Congress and sent to President Truman on June 16, 1952 (Hutchinson 1981, 303–7).

49. P.L. 82-414, 66 Stat. 163.
50. The national origins formula, which became effective after July 1, 1927, by the 1924 act, was "a number which bears the same ratio to 150,000 as the number of inhabitants in continental United States in 1920 having that national origin . . . bears to the number of inhabitants in continental United States in 1920" (quoted in Hutchinson 1981, 308, fn. 104).
51. The 1952 Immigration and Nationality Act defined the Asia–Pacific triangle under section 202 as "comprising all quota areas and all colonies and other dependent areas situate wholly east of the meridian sixty degrees east of Greenwich, wholly west of the meridian one hundred and sixty-five degrees west, and wholly north of the parallel twenty-five degrees south latitude."
52. As table 4.2 shows, the Act of September 22, 1959, changed some of the features of the preference category. It moved up unmarried sons and daughters of U.S. citizens (twenty-one years of age or older) from the fourth to the second preference category and added unmarried sons and daughters (twenty-one years of age or older) of permanent residents to the third preference category. Under the 1959 act, accompanying spouses and children of brothers, sisters, sons, and daughters of U.S. citizens were added to the fourth preference. Sons and daughters in the fourth preference category now referred to married sons and daughters, regardless of age. The 1959 act also increased the percentage for the fourth preference from the maximum of 25 percent to 50 percent.
53. Several congressmen, including Rep. Emanuel Celler (D-NY) and Rep. Louis B. Heller (D-NY), argued that the quota was set for the new countries of Jamaica, Trinidad, and Guadeloupe to restrict the entry of racially different people (referred to as "Negroes") (*Congressional Record,* 82d Cong., 1st sess. [April 23, 1952]: 4306, 4311; see also Ngai 2004, 256–58).
54. Tichenor 2002, 211–16.
55. Emanuel Celler, "Further Examples of How the National Origins Theory Prove Unworkable," undated typed note: 2–3, box 492, folder: "Immigration—General 1961–62, Folder #1," Emanuel Celler Papers, Library of Congress (hereafter Celler Papers).
56. Ibid., 3. Celler also showed that national origins policy was not working, explaining that in the fiscal year ended in 1960, quota immigrants accounted for 101,373 admissions—out of a possible 154,887, leaving unused 53,514. However, a total of 265,398 aliens, both quota and nonquota, were admitted. Of the 164,025 nonquota immigrants, 34,215 were spouses and children of U.S. citizens; 91,701 were natives of Western Hemisphere countries and their spouses and children; 485 were ministers with their families; and 30,906 came under special legislation.
57. Celler, "The National Origins System Does Not Work," undated typed note: 5, box 492, folder: "Immigration—General 1961–62, Folder #1," Celler Papers.

58. Celler, undated handwritten note, box 492, folder: "Immigration—General 1961–62, Folder #2," Celler Papers.
59. Between 1954 and 1955, 22,951 Asian immigrants entered the United States, and between 1956 and 1965, 214,997 were admitted. See "Table 14. Immigrants Admitted, by Country or Region of Birth, Years Ended June 30, 1951–1960," in *INS Annual Report,* 1960, and "Table 14. Immigrants Admitted, by Country or Region of Birth, Years Ended June 20, 1956–1965," in *INS Annual Report,* 1965.
60. Dwight D. Eisenhower, "Special Message to Congress on Immigration Matters, February 8, 1956," Office of the Federal Register 1960, 241.
61. Richard Nixon, letter to Rep. Alfred E. Santangelo, September 26, 1960, available at: http://www.jfklink.com/speeches/joint/app15_santangelo.html (accessed May 7, 2012).
62. John F. Kennedy, letter to Rep. Alfred E. Santangelo, October 8, 1960, available at: http://www.jfklink.com/speeches/joint/app15_santangelo.html (accessed May 7, 2012).
63. Tichenor 2002, 209.
64. "Laws Dealing with Immigration—Message from the President of the United States (H. Doc. No. 52)," *Congressional Record,* 89th Cong., 1st sess. (January 13, 1965): 639.
65. Attorney General Nicholas Katzenbach, statement before the Immigration and Nationality Subcommittee, House Judiciary Committee, *An Act to Amend the Immigration and Nationality Act: Hearing on H.R. 2580,* 89th Cong., 1st sess. (March 3, 1965), 1, 5.
66. *Congressional Record,* 89th Cong., 1st sess. (August 25, 1965): 21770.
67. *Congressional Record,* 89th Cong., 1st sess. (September 17, 1965): 24238–39.
68. Lyndon B. Johnson and Edward Kennedy, phone conversation, March 8, 1965, 9:10 pm, recorded on tape WH6503-04-7043, Presidential Recordings Program, Miller Center, University of Virginia, transcript available at: http://whitehousetapes.net/transcript/johnson/wh6503-04-7043 (accessed April 19, 2012).
69. John V. Lindsay, introducing a comprehensive revision of the immigration, naturalization, and refugee laws, *Congressional Record,* 88th Cong., 2d sess. (June 1, 1964): 12252.
70. In fact, the number of parents entering the United States as immediate relatives of U.S. citizens has been well over 110,000 annually since 2006 (U.S. Department of Homeland Security, *Yearbook of Immigration Statistics 2011,* "Table 6. Persons Obtaining Legal Permanent Resident Status by Type and Major Class of Admission: Fiscal Years 2002 to 2011").
71. Reimers 1983.
72. Feighan added later: "To meet the immediate needs reflected in the quoted statement made by President Johnson [at an immigration conference regarding immigrant families, where Johnson called for changes in the immigration policy], I have introduced a bill, H.R. 12305, which is now pending in Con-

gress. Enactment of that legislation would relieve the problem of separated families, provide for skills needed to stimulate our economy which are now in short supply, and remove the stigma of parole from the refugees we admit, over a 2-year trial period. This would provide a remedy for our most pressing problems while Congress hammers out a modern, all-inclusive immigration policy" (Hon. Michael A. Feighan, statement before Democratic Platform Committee in Support of a New, Fair, and Sound Immigration Bill, "Extension of Remarks," *Congressional Record,* 88th Cong., 2d sess. [August 20, 1964]: 20760.)

73. Hon. Michael A. Feighan, U.S. Representative, 20th Ohio District, "Some Insights on Immigration," address delivered at the Thirty-Sixth Annual Conference of the American Coalition of Patriotic Societies, Mayflower Hotel, Washington, D.C., February 4, 1965: 10, box 40, folder: "Cleveland Hearings on H.R. 2580," Michael A. Feighan Papers, Seeley G. Mudd Manuscript Library, Princeton University.
74. On the assimilation of southern and eastern European immigrants, see Brodkin 1998; Jacobson 1998; Waters 1990. In his interviews with lawmakers, Gabriel Chin (1996) found that many claimed to have expected the rise of Asian and Latin American immigration following the 1965 reform. However, these politicians may have been trying to take credit for an outcome that they never anticipated (but that has been supported by many) in an effort to court these new immigrant groups.
75. In particular, by 1962 Italy had a backlog of 136,858 applicants seeking to enter using the fourth preference (Wolgin 2011, 42).
76. *Congressional Record,* 89th Cong., 1st sess. (September 20, 1965): 24467.
77. The 1965 law limited immigration from Western Hemisphere countries to 120,000 (effective July 1, 1968) and thus initially depressed immigration from Latin American countries. The 1976 Immigration and Naturalization Act amendments applied the 20,000-per-country limit to the Western Hemisphere, and the 1978 law set a single worldwide ceiling of 290,000, into which the separate limits for the Eastern and Western Hemispheres were combined. Other major laws, such as the Cuban Refugees Adjustment Act, the Nicaraguan Adjustment and Central American Relief Act, the Immigration Reform and Control Act of 1986, and the Immigration Act of 1990 helped to increase Latin American immigration—particularly as these immigrants sponsored family members for entry (Ngai 2004; Reimers 1985; Skrentny 2002). In addition to Asian and Latin American immigration, as stated previously, African immigration has grown substantially.

CHAPTER 5

1. Hyman Bookbinder, letter to Rep. Peter Rodino, June 11, 1984, in *Congressional Record,* 98th Cong., 2d sess. (June 13, 1984): 16282.

2. Initially, the Immigration and Naturalization Service (INS) estimate was that up to four million undocumented immigrants were in the country under the regular program, and several hundred thousand as special agricultural workers (SAWs), but by the time application for IRCA legalization began, the estimate was reduced to two million under the regular program (Chiswick 1988, 110).
3. *Congressional Record,* 101st Cong., 1st sess. (July 12, 1989): 14295.
4. *Congressional Record,* 98th Cong., 1st sess. (April 28, 1983): 10189.
5. For studies on the multiplier effect of family chain migration, see Jasso and Rosenzweig 1986. Their 1989 findings based on the GAO study of the fiscal year 1985 cohort indicate that immigrants were more likely to sponsor new immigrants than native-born Americans and that immigrant sponsors petitioned for new immigrants as soon as they became legally eligible to do so (Jasso and Rosenzweig 1989, 887).
6. *Congressional Record,* 98th Cong., 2d sess. (June 13, 1984): 16279.
7. Daniels 1990, 338; Ngai 2004, 227.
8. Between 2001 and 2010, immediate relatives of U.S. citizens and immigrants under family-sponsored preferences were responsible for 64 percent of the immigrants admitted to the United States (U.S. Department of Homeland Security, *Yearbook of Immigration Statistics 2010,* "Table 6. Persons Obtaining Legal Permanent Resident Status by Type and Major Class of Admission: Fiscal Years 2001 to 2010").
9. Zolberg 2006, 363.
10. In April and June 2007, the Gallup Poll asked who should be given higher priority to legally stay in the United States: people who are highly educated and highly skilled workers, or people who have family members already living in the country. In April, 38 percent answered "highly educated/highly skilled," while 49 percent preferred those who have family members already in the United States. In June the percentages changed, with 43 percent favoring "highly educated/highly skilled" and 44 percent preferring family-based immigration. For more data on immigration, see the Gallup Poll at http://www.gallup.com/poll/1660/immigration.aspx#4 (accessed August 22, 2012).
11. Gabaccia 2010a, 2010b.
12. Harwood 1986; Simon 1987; Tichenor 2002, 352, fn. 1.
13. Gimpel and Edwards 1999, 136–41, 154–58; Tichenor 2002, 253–58.
14. U.S. Congress, Senate, Committee on the Judiciary (1982), 3–16. The second preference included all unmarried sons and daughters, regardless of age.
15. U.S. Department of State, "Annual Report of Immigrant Visa Applicants in the Family-Sponsored and Employment-Based Preferences Registered at the National Visa Center as of November 1, 2011," available at: http://www.travel.state.gov/pdf/WaitingListItem.pdf (accessed May 29, 2013). During fiscal year 2012, the total number of family-sponsored preference visa applicants on the waiting list was 4,501,066, although the issuance number was

limited to no more than 226,000 in the same category. Specifically, while the worldwide family first preference limit was 23,400, the number of family first preference visa applicants on the waiting list was 295,168 as of 2011. For the family second preference, the limit was set at 114,250, but the waiting list figure was 839,755. Heavier backlogs were expected for the family third-preference visas: the annual limit was set at 23,400, but the number of visa applicants on the waiting list was 846,520.

16. On February 27, 1981, Rev. Theodore M. Hesburgh stated in a press conference: "A better immigration system may help to reduce the pressures for illegal migration to some extent. A look at present U.S. Immigration statistics reveals one relatively small but important source of illegal migration. Of the more than one million persons now registered at consular offices waiting for visas, more than 700,000 are relatives of U.S. citizens or resident aliens, including spouses and minor children of resident aliens" (*Congressional Record,* 97th Cong., 1st sess. [February 27, 1981]: 3291). Guillermina Jasso and Mark Rosenzweig (1990, 171), citing the U.S. Selection Commission on Immigration and Refugee Policy of 1981, explained that as of January 1980 the total worldwide number waiting was 1,088,063 from 169 countries. "If we ignore the preference-category and country-ceiling effects on allocation, this means that the supply of numerically limited visas for the next four years was already 'mortgaged.' But demand across countries varies considerably, so that, while some countries (e.g. Benin) were not even on the list, two (Mexico and the Philippines) had backlogs in excess of 250,000" (Select Commission on Immigration and Refugee Policy 1981).
17. U.S. Congress, House, Committee on the Judiciary (1982), 216.
18. U.S. Congress, Senate, Committee on the Judiciary (1983), 151. Reverend Hesburgh represented the Citizens' Committee for Immigration Reform.
19. Ibid., 171 (emphasis in original).
20. Massey, Durand, and Malone 2002, ch. 4).
21. Ngai 2004, 266; Donato, Durand, and Massey 1992.
22. In particular, there was a strong lobbying effort to promote Irish immigration. In a Senate hearing, Sean Minhane, national chairman of the Irish Immigration Reform Movement, argued: "The independent immigrant category replicates the experience of earlier immigrants who came here on their own and who helped to build our country. While we believe in the family reunification system as the basic foundation of our immigration policy, we believe there should always be a category open to independents. . . . The Irish Immigration Reform Movement has always viewed the inclusion of an independent immigrant category as an additive process as it relates to the family preference system. We have no *per se* objection to the family preference system except to the extent that by reason of an historical accident we are locked out of that system. Further, we have no prospect of getting into the system

without Congressional intervention" (U.S. Congress, Senate, Committee on the Judiciary (1989), 135–36; see also Law 2002).

23. DeLaet 2000; Tichenor 2002, 267.
24. Strach 2007, 51; see also Hacker 2002; Majone 1989, 150.
25. *Congressional Record,* 110th Cong., 1st sess. (May 21, 2007): S6363.
26. Hoefer, Rytina, and Baker 2012; Wasem 2012. The number of families is based on 2008 data.
27. Taylor et al. 2011.
28. Fix and Zimmerman *1999;* Fujiwara 2008; Park and Park 2005; Yoshikawa 2011.
29. *Congressional Record,* 104th Cong., 1st sess. (March 21, 1995): 8525.
30. Ibid., 8552.
31. Sen. Christopher Dodd (D-CT), *Congressional Record,* 104th Cong., 2d sess. (August 1, 1996): 20952.
32. Title V, Subtitle C, Illegal Immigration Reform and Immigrant Responsibility Act of 1996 (IIRIRA, P.L. 104-208, 110 Stat. 3009-546). Some provisions of IIRIRA and PRWOA were reversed later. For example, there were changes in the affidavit of support process. In 1997 an interim rule (published on October 20, it became effective on December 19 of the same year) defined a sponsor's ongoing obligations under the affidavit of support and specified the procedures that federal, state, or local agencies or private entities had to follow to seek reimbursement from the sponsor for providing means-tested public benefits. Under this rule, three new public forms were created. On July 21, 2006, the final rule came into effect. The final rule adopted the interim rule of October 20, 1997, with several changes to make the affidavit of support process less burdensome and more efficient. The changes include reducing the required initial documentation, adopting two additional public use forms, deleting the affidavit from the support requirement in certain cases, allowing two joint sponsors per family unit, providing a more flexible definition of "household size," and reducing the amount of assets required to cover any income shortfalls. In addition, the final rule made clear that U.S. Citizenship and Immigration Services may disclose a sponsor's social security number, as well as the sponsor's last known address, to a benefit granting agency seeking to obtain reimbursement from the sponsor. See U.S. Department of Homeland Security, U.S. Citizenship and Immigration Services, "Affidavits of Support on Behalf of Immigrants (71 FR 35732) (FR 23-06)," June 21, 2006, available at: http://www.uscis.gov/ilink/docView/FR/HTML/FR/0-0-0-1/0-0-0-111373/0-0-0-119337/0-0-0-119363.html (accessed February 24, 2013); U.S. Citizenship and Immigration Services, "Fact Sheet: Final Rule Regarding Affidavits of Support," June 21, 2006, available at: http://www.uscis.gov/files/pressrelease/AffSupp_062106FS.pdf (accessed February 24, 2013). IIRIRA's retroactive definitions of criminality, which subjected immi-

grants to deportation for crimes committed any time in the past, also met challenges. In 2001 the U.S. Supreme Court reaffirmed the due process rights of immigrants by ruling against the retroactive application of the provision (INS v. St. Cyr, 533 U.S. 289, 121 S. Ct. 2271). As for PRWOA, in 1998, P.L. 105-185 restored food stamp eligibility for legal immigrants, who had lost it under PRWOA. For historical discussion on financial responsibility and efforts to regulate immigrants based on their "likely to become a public charge" (LPC) status, see Gardner 2005, ch. 5.

33. The Department of Homeland Security (DHS) was created in March 2003 with the passage of the Homeland Security Act in November 2002 (see U.S. Department of Homeland Security, "Creation of the Department of Homeland Security," available at: http://www.dhs.gov/creation-department-homeland-security [accessed April 19, 2012]). The DHS also assumed responsibility for the operational assets of the U.S. Immigration and Naturalization Service (INS), which was split into three new agencies: U.S. Customs and Border Protection (CBP), U.S. Immigration and Customs Enforcement (ICE), and U.S. Citizenship and Immigration Services (USCIS). For more information, see U.S. Department of Homeland Security, "Who Joined DHS?" available at: http://www.dhs.gov/who-joined-dhs (accessed April 19, 2012).
34. Newton 2008; Chavez 2008; Massey, and Sánchez 2010.
35. d'Appollonia 2012; see also Brotherton and Kretsedemas 2008; Kanstroom 2012.
36. Kanstroom 2007.
37. U.S. Immigration and Customs Enforcement, "Enforcement and Removal: Removal Statistics" (for fiscal year 2012), available at: http://www.ice.gov/removal-statistics (accessed February 20, 2013). Border control has toughened more under President Obama than under any previous president. Some researchers and politicians suggest that this aggressive stance may afford the administration more leeway in negotiations over immigration reform debates. See John Skrentny, "Obama's Immigration Reform: A Tough Sell for a Grand Bargain" in *Reaching for a New Deal: Ambitious Governance, Economic Meltdown, and Polarized Politics* in *Obama's First Two Years,* edited by Theda Skocpol and Lawrence Jacobs, (Russell Sage Foundation, 2011), 273–320. Also, statement by Sen. Patrick Leahy (D-VT), "How Comprehensive Immigration Reform Should Address the Needs of Women and Families," Senate Judiciary Committee, March 18, 2013, available at: http://www.judiciary.senate.gov/pdf/3-18-13LeahyStatement.pdf (accessed March 25, 2013).
38. Nina Berstein, "U.S. to Reform Policy on Detention for Immigrants," *New York Times,* August 6, 2009, A1.
39. Applied Research Center, "Shattered Families," November 2011, available at: http://www.arc.org/shatteredfamilies (accessed February 20, 2013); see also Golash-Boza 2011.

40. Rep. Ron Mazzoli submitted the report to accompany H.R. 3737; see U.S. Congress, House, Committee on the Judiciary (1986), 6. This estimate, however, was at best misleading and based on misinterpretation of preliminary survey data.
41. U.S. Congress, Senate, Committee on the Judiciary (1985), 3–4.
42. Michael L. Aytes, Associate Director, Domestic Operations, U.S. Citizenship and Immigration Services, U.S. Department of Homeland Security, memo to Field Leadership, "Genetic Relationship Testing; Suggesting DNA Tests Revisions to the Adjudicators Field Manual (AFM) Chapter 21," March 19, 2008, available at: http://www.uscis.gov/files/pressrelease/genetic_testing.pdf (accessed May 7, 2012).
43. Miriam Jordan, "Refugee Program Halted as DNA Tests Show Fraud," *Wall Street Journal,* August 20, 2008; U.S. Department of State, Bureau of Population, Refugees, and Migration, "Fraud in the Refugee Family Reunification (Priority Three) Program" (fact sheet), December 4, 2008, available at: http://2001-2009.state.gov/g/prm/refadm/rls/fs/2008/112760.htm (accessed May 7, 2012).
44. Tuan 1998.
45. "Asian Americans Seen Negatively," *San Francisco Chronicle,* April 27, 2001, (1)1.
46. Foner 2005; Lee and Bean 2010.
47. This unease can be said of the gains of the entire civil rights era—especially black civil rights. See, for example, Bonilla-Silva 2003 and Fobanjong 2001.
48. Kim 1999.
49. On Asian American political participation, see Wong et al. 2011 and Lien, Conway, and Wong 2004.
50. *Congressional Record,* 104th Cong., 1st sess. (March 23, 1995): 9002.
51. Abramovitz 1996; Neubeck and Cazenave 2001; Park 2011.
52. For critiques of the Asian American "model minority" myth, see Chou and Feagin 2008.
53. Wu 1995.
54. Jenny Anderson, "Admitted, but Left Out," *New York Times,* October 19, 2012; Kyle Spencer, "For Asians, School Tests Are Vital Steppingstones," *New York Times,* October 27, 2012; Ethan Bronner, "Asian-Americans in the Argument," *New York Times,* November 4, 2012; Carolyn Chen, "Asians: Too Smart for Their Own Good?" *New York Times,* December 19, 2012; Josh Gerstein, "Alito Speaks Up for Asian Americans," *Politico,* October 11, 2012, available at: http://www.politico.com/blogs/under-the-radar/2012/10/alito-speaks-up-for-asian-americans-138099.html (accessed November 3, 2012).
55. Julia Preston, "Tweak in Rule to Ease a Path to Green Card," *New York Times,* January 6, 2012; The White House, Office of the Press Secretary, "Remarks by the President on Immigration," June 15, 2012, available at: http://www.whitehouse.gov/the-press-office/2012/06/15/remarks-president-immigration (accessed November 3, 2013); Secretary of Homeland Security Janet Napolitano, "Exer-

cising Prosecutorial Discretion with Respect to Individuals Who Came to the United States as Children," June 15, 2012, available at: http://www.dhs.gov/xlibrary/assets/s1-exercising-prosecutorial-discretion-individuals-who-came-to-us-as-children.pdf (accessed November 3, 2012).

56. "Romney Calls Immigration Reform 'Moral Imperative,'" *Washington Times,* June 21, 2012.
57. Fifty-nine percent of whites voted for Romney, while 93 percent of black voters supported Obama; see "President Exit Polls: 2012," *New York Times,* available at: http://elections.nytimes.com/2012/results/president/exit-polls (accessed February 20, 2013).
58. Julia Preston, "Republicans' Immigration Bill Blocked by Senate Democrats," *New York Times,* December 5, 2012; Preston, "Immigration Change to Ease Family Separations, *New York Times,* January 2, 2013; Preston, "Senators Offer a Bipartisan Blueprint for Immigration," *New York Times,* January 28, 2013; Preston, "Skilled Science Workers at Focus of Second Senate Proposal on Immigration," *New York Times,* January 28, 2013; Ashley Parker, "Senators Call Their Bipartisan Immigration Plan a 'Breakthrough,'" *New York Times,* January 28, 2013; Mark Landler, "Obama Urges Speed on Immigration Plan, but Exposes Conflicts," *New York Times,* January 29, 2013; Ashley Parker, "House Group Works to Present Its Own Immigration Plan," *New York Times,* February 2, 2013. For the senate bill introduced by Sen. Marco Rubio (R-FL) and others on April 18, 2013, see the following, available at: http://www.rubio.senate.gov/public/?a=Files.Serve&File_id=adefad85-7f5c-4f3e-a4dc-366a1b71ad38 (accessed May 21, 2013).

CHAPTER 6

1. CIRA: S. 1348 (110th) introduced on May 9, 2007. Rep. King (R-IA) estimated that there were 12 to 20 Million unauthorized immigrants. See statement of Rep. Steve King (R-IA), U.S. Congress, House, Committee on the Judiciary (2007, 2). More reliable estimates put the number closer to 12 million in 2007. See Michael Hoeffer, Nancy Rytina, and Christopher Campbell, "Estimates of the Unauthorized Immigrant Population Residing in the United States: January 2006," Population Estimate, August 2007. Office of Immigration Statistics, Department of Homeland Security, available at: http://www.dhs.gov/xlibrary/assets/statistics/publications/ill_pe_2006.pdf (accessed April 22, 2013). Countries such as Australia and Canada have a point-based system. For a comparison of the development of the U.S. immigration system with Canada's, see Bloemraad 2006.
2. *Congressional Record,* 110th Cong., 1st sess. (June 11, 2007): S7445.
3. *Congressional Record,* 110th Cong., 1st sess. (May 21, 2007): S6375.
4. Statement available at http://www.judiciary.senate.gov/pdf/3-18-13LeahyStatement.pdf (accessed March 25, 2013). Senate proposal available at: http://

www.rubio.senate.gov/public/?a=Files.Serve&File_id=adefad85-7f5c-4f3e-a4dc-366a1b71ad38 (accessed May 21, 2013).

5. Fetner 2008; Warner 1999.
6. P.L. 104-199, 110 Stat. 2419. For legal challenges against DOMA, see John Schwartz, "U.S. Marriage Act Is Unfair to Gays, Court Panel Says," *New York Times,* October 18, 2012. Supporters of same-sex marriage were encouraged by President Obama's decision to direct the Justice Department to stop defending the law in court. See also Charlie Savage and Sheryl Gay Stolberg, "In Shift, U.S. Says Marriage Act Blocks Gay Rights," *New York Times,* February 23, 2011.
7. Julia Preston, "Noncitizens Sue over U.S. Gay Marriage Ban," *New York Times,* April 2, 2012.
8. Department of Justice, Office of Public Affairs, "Statement of Attorney General on Litigation Involving the Defense of Marriage Act," February 23, 2011, available at: http://www.justice.gov/opa/pr/2011/February/11-ag-222.html (accessed February 24, 2013). However, on February 22, 2013, the Obama administration filed a legal brief with the Justice Department and urged the Supreme Court to rethink DOMA. The brief argued that section 3 of DOMA, which defines marriage as a union between a man and a woman and therefore denies same-sex couples federal benefits, is unconstitutional. See Reuters, "Obama Administration Urges Justices to Overturn Anti-Gay Marriage Law," *New York Times,* February 22, 2013.
9. Julia Preston, "With No Shortcut to a Green Card, Gay Couples Leave U.S.," *New York Times,* February 17, 2013. However, there has been growing support for same-sex married couples and their rights.
10. Michael L. Aytes, Associate Director, Domestic Operations, U.S. Department of Homeland Security, U.S. Citizenship and Immigration Services, memo to Field Leadership, "Genetic Relationship Testing; Suggesting DNA Tests Revisions to the Adjudicators Field Manual (AFM) Chapter 21," March 19, 2008, available at: http://www.uscis.gov/files/pressrelease/genetic_testing.pdf (accessed May 7, 2012).
11. An earlier exploration of these ideas appears in Catherine Lee 2012.
12. Fassin 2011.
13. Abu El-Haj 2001. On myths and nation-building, see Gellner 1983; Hobsbawm and Ranger 1983.
14. On ancestral testing, see Nelson 2008, 2012.
15. For a discussion of how genes tell stories, see Wald 2012.
16. Hondagneu-Sotelo 1994; Hirata 1979.
17. Kohli-Laven 2012.
18. Hinterberger 2012a, 2012b.
19. Freeman 1998; Guiraudon 1998; Jacobson 1996; Morris 2003; Soysal 1995.
20. For a detailed proposal on what features a new policy should include, see Massey, Durand, and Malone 2002, ch. 7.

References

ARCHIVAL AND OTHER PRIMARY SOURCES

American Jewish Historical Society, New York, N.Y.: Max James Kholer Papers.

King County Library System, Washington: Special Library Collections

Library of Congress, Washington, D.C.: Emmanuel Celler Papers

Multnomah County Library, Oregon: John Wilson Special Collections

Princeton University, Princeton, N.J.: Michael A. Feighan Papers, Seeley G. Mudd Manuscript Library

University of California–Berkeley: Bancroft Library

University of California–Los Angeles: Asian American Studies Center Special Collections

University of Washington–Seattle: Special Collections

U.S. National Archives and Records Administration, College Park, Md.: U.S. Department of State, record group 59; U.S. Department of Treasury, record group 56; U.S. Immigration and Naturalization Service, record group 85

U.S. National Archives and Records Administration, San Bruno: Segregated Chinese Files, Pacific Region

U.S. National Archives and Records Administration, Washington, D.C.: U.S. Congress, House of Representatives, record group 233; U.S. Congress, Senate, record group 46; Subject Correspondence Files

NEWSPAPERS AND PERIODICALS

China Daily

New York Times

San Francisco Chronicle

Time magazine

Wall Street Journal

Washington Post

Washington Times

GOVERNMENT SERIAL PUBLICATIONS

Congressional Record

U.S. Department of Homeland Security. 1996–2001. *Yearbooks of Immigration Statistics.* Washington: U.S. Department of Homeland Security, Office of Immigration Statistics.

U.S. Department of Justice. Immigration and Naturalization Service. 2002. *Triennial Comprehensive Report on Immigration* (Washington: U.S. Government Printing Office).

U.S. Department of Commerce and Labor. Various years. *Annual Report of the Commissioner of Immigration to the Secretary of Commerce and Labor.* Washington: U.S. Department of Commerce and Labor.

U.S. Department of Labor. Various years. *Annual Report of the Commissioner General of Immigration to the Secretary of Labor.* Washington: U.S. Department of Labor.

PUBLISHED GOVERNMENT DOCUMENTS

California Legislature. Senate. Special Committee on Chinese Immigration. 1878. *Chinese Immigration: The Social, Moral, and Political Effect of Chinese Immigration. Policy and Means of Exclusion. Memorial of the Senate of California to the Congress of the United States, and an Address to the People of the United States.* Sacramento: State Printing Office.

Office of the Federal Register. 1960. *Public Papers of the Presidents of the United States: Dwight D. Eisenhower.* Washington: Office of the Federal Register, National Archives and Records Service, General Services Administration.

Rossiter, William Sidney, Willard Long Thorp, and LeVerne Beales. 1922. *Increase of Population in the United States, 1910–1920: A Study of Changes in the Population of Divisions, States, Counties, and Rural and Urban Areas, and in Sex, Color, and Nativity, at the Fourteenth Census.* Washington, D.C.: U.S. Government Printing Office.

Select Commission on Immigration and Refugee Policy. 1981. "U.S. Immigration Policy and the National Interest." Staff report. Washington: U.S. Government Printing Office (April 30).

U.S. Bureau of the Census. 2000. *Fourteenth Census of the United States Taken in the Year 1920.* New York: Norman Ross.

U.S. Congress. Committees on the Judiciary. 1951. *Revision of Immigration, Naturalization, and Nationality Laws: Joint Hearings on S. 716, H.R. 2379, and H.R. 2816.* 82d Cong., 1st sess. (March 6–April 9).

U.S. Congress. House of Representatives. Committee on Immigration and Naturalization. 1917. *Relative to Citizenship of American Women Married to Foreigners: Hearings Before the Committee on Immigration and Naturalization.* 65th Cong., 2d sess. (December 13–14).

U.S. Congress. House of Representatives. Committee on Immigration and Naturalization. 1918. *Relative to Citizenship of American Women Married to Foreigners: Hearings Before the Committee on Immigration and Naturalization.* 65th Cong., 2d sess.

——. 1925. *Japanese Exclusion: A Study of the Policy and the Law* by John B. Trevor, 68th Cong., 2d sess., H. Doc. 600 (January 8).

U.S. Congress. House of Representatives. Committee on Immigration and Naturalization. 1926. *Immigration and Citizenship of American-Born Women Married to Aliens: Hearings Before the Committee on Immigration and Natuturalization.* 69th Cong., 1st sess.

——. 1943. *Repeal of the Chinese Exclusion Acts: Hearings on H.R. 1882 and H.R. 2309.* 78th Cong., 1st sess. (May 9–June 3).

——. 1945. *Expediting the Admission to the United States of Alien Spouses and Alien Minor Children of Citizen Members of the United States Armed Forces.* 79th Cong., 1st sess. H. Rpt. 1320 (November 30).

——. Committee on the Judiciary. 1947. *Amending Act to Admit Alien Spouses of Members of Armed Forces so as to Admit Racially Inadmissible Spouses.* 80th Cong., 1st sess., H. Rpt. 478 (May 28).

——. 1949. *Admission into U.S. of Certain Alien Fiancés and Fiancées of Members or Former Members of Armed Forces.* 81st Cong., 1st sess., H. Rpt. 150 (February 21).

——. 1965. *An Act to Amend the Immigration and Nationality Act: Hearing on H.R. 2580.* 89th Cong., 1st sess.

——. 1982. *Immigration Reform and Control Act of 1982.* 97th Cong., 2d Sess., H. Rpt. 890 (September 28).

——. 1986. *Immigration and Marriage Fraud Amendments of 1986.* 99th Cong., 2d sess., H. Rpt. 906 (September 26).

——. 2007. *Comprehensive Immigration Reform: Government Perspectives on Immigration Statistics (Continued): Hearing Before the Subcommittee on Immigration, Citizenship, Refugees, Border Security, and International Law.* 110th Cong., 1st sess., H. Hrg. 43 (June 19).

U.S. Congress. Senate. Committee on Immigration. 1924. *Japanese Immigration Legislation: Hearings Before the Committee on Immigration.* 68th Cong., 1st sess.

——. 1945. *Expediting the Admission to the United States of Alien Spouses and Alien Minor Children of Citizen Members of the United States Armed Forces.* 79th Cong., 1st sess. S. Rpt. 860 (December 18).

——. 1946. *Placing Chinese Wives of American Citizens on a Nonquota Basis.* 79th Cong., 2d sess., S. Rpt. 1927 (August 1).

——. Committee on the Judiciary. 1947. *Amending Act to Admit Alien Spouses of Members of Armed Forces so as to Admit Racially Inadmissible Spouses.* 80th Cong., 1st sess., S. Rpt. 501 (July 11).

——. 1982. *Immigration Reform and Control.* 97th Cong., 2d sess., S. Rpt. 485 (June 30).

——. 1983. *Immigration Reform and Control Act: Hearing Before the Subcommittee on Immigration and Refugee Policy.* 98th Cong., 1st Sess., S. Hrg. 198 (February 24, 25, and 28 and March 7).

——. 1985. *Immigration Marriage Fraud: Hearing Before the Subcommittee on Immigration and Refugee Policy.* 99th Cong., 1st Sess., S. Hrg. 325 (July 26).

——. 1989. *Hearing Before the Subcommittee on Immigration and Refugee Affairs.* 101st Cong., 1st sess. S. Hrg. 607 (March 3).

PUBLISHED BOOKS AND ARTICLES

Abramovitz, Mimi. 1996. *Under Attack, Fighting Back: Women and Welfare in the United States.* New York: Monthly Review Press.

Abu El-Haj, Nadia. 2001. *Facts on the Ground: Archaeological Practice and Territorial Self-Fashioning in Israeli Society.* Chicago: University of Chicago Press.

——. 2012. *The Genealogical Science: The Search for Jewish Origins and the Politics of Epistemology.* Chicago: University of Chicago Press.

Almaguer, Tomás. 1994. *Racial Fault Lines: The Historical Origins of White Supremacy in California.* Berkeley: University of California Press.

Alvarez, Robert R. 1987. *Familia Migration and Adaptation in Baja and Alta California, 1800–1975.* Berkeley: University of California Press.

Anderson, Benedict. 1991. *Imagined Communities: Reflections on the Origin and Spread of Nationalism.* London: Verso.

Aoki, Keith. 1998. "The Early Twentieth-Century 'Alien Land Law' as a Prelude to Internment." *Boston College Law Review* 40: 37–72.

Bailey, Adrian J., and Paul Boyle. 2001. "Untying and Retying Family Migration in the New Europe." *Journal of Ethnic and Migration Studies* 30(2): 229–42.

Bardes, Robert. 2008. *Immigration at the Golden Gate: Passenger Ships, Exclusion, and Angel Island.* Westport, Conn.: Praeger.

Barkan, Elazar. 1992. *The Retreat of Scientific Racism: Changing Concepts of Race in Britain and the United States Between the World Wars.* Cambridge: Cambridge University Press.

Barstow, Anne Llewellyn. 2000. "Introduction." In *War's Dirty Secret: Rape, Prostitution, and Other Crimes Against Women,* edited by Anne Llewellyn Barstow. Cleveland: Pilgrim.

Bashi, Vilna. 2007. *Survival of the Knitted: Immigrant Social Networks in a Stratified World.* Stanford, Calif.: Stanford University Press.

Batalova, Jeanne, and Margie McHugh. 2010. "DREAM vs. Reality: An Analysis of Potential DREAM Act Beneficiaries." Washington, D.C.: Migration Policy Institute, National Center on Immigrant Integration Policy (July). Available at: http://www.migrationpolicy.org/pubs/DREAM-Insight-July2010.pdf (accessed April 19, 2012).

Bederman, Gail. 1995. *Manliness and Civilization: A Cultural History of Gender and Race in the United States, 1880–1917.* Chicago: University of Chicago Press.

Beisel, Nicola Kay. 1998. *Imperiled Innocents: Anthony Comstock and Family Reproduction in Victorian America.* Princeton, N.J.: Princeton University Press.

Bianchi, Suzanne M. 1997. "Whither the 1950s? The Family and Macroeconomic Context of Immigration and Welfare Reform in the 1990s." In *Immigration and the Family: Research and Policy on U.S. Immigrants,* edited by Alan Booth, Ann C. Crouter, and Nancy Landale. Mahwah, N.J.: Lawrence Erlbaum Associates.

Birkland, Thomas A. 1997. *After Disaster: Agenda Setting, Public Policy, and Focusing Events.* Washington, D.C.: Georgetown University Press.

Bloemraad, Irene. 2006. *Becoming a Citizen: Incorporating Immigrants and Refugees in the United States and Canada.* Berkeley: University of California Press.

Bock, Gisela, and Pat Thane, eds. 1991. *Maternity and Gender Policies: Women and the Rise of the European Welfare States, 1880s–1950s.* London: Routledge.

Bonilla-Silva, Eduardo. 2003. *Racism Without Racists: Color-Blind Racism and the Persistence of Racial Inequality in the United States.* Lanham, Md.: Rowman & Littlefield.

Borjas, George. 1990. *Friends or Strangers: The Impact of Immigrants on the U.S. Economy.* New York: Basic Books.

Bracalenti, Raffaele, and Moreno Benini. 2005. "The Role of Families in the Migrant Integration Process." In *Migration and the Family in the European Union,* edited by Johannes Pflegerl and Sylvia Trnka. Vienna: Austrian Institute for Family Studies.

Bredbenner, Candice Lewis. 1998. *A Nationality of Her Own: Women, Marriage, and the Law of Citizenship.* Berkeley: University of California Press.

Brodkin, Karen. 1998. *How Jews Became White Folks and What That Says About Race in America.* New Brunswick, N.J.: Rutgers University Press.

Brotherton, David, and Philip Kretsedemas. 2008. *Keeping Out the Other: A Critical Introduction to Immigration Enforcement Today.* New York: Columbia University Press.

Brubaker, Rogers. 1989. "Membership Without Citizenship: The Economic and Social Rights of Noncitizens." In *Immigration and the Politics of Citizenship in Europe and North America,* edited by Rogers Brubaker. Lanham: University Press of America.

———. 1992. *Citizenship and Nationhood in France and Germany.* Cambridge, Mass.: Harvard University Press.

———. 2004. *Ethnicity Without Groups.* Cambridge, Mass.: Harvard University Press.

Brubaker, Rogers, Mara Loveman, and Peter Stamatov. 2004. "Ethnicity as Cognition." *Theory and Society* 33(1): 31–64.

Bryceson, Deborah Fahy, and Ulla Vuorela. 2002. *The Transnational Family: New European Frontiers and Global Networks.* Oxford: Berg.

Burk, Kathleen. 2008. *Old World, New World: Great Britain and America.* New York: Atlantic Monthly Press.

Burstyn, Varda. 1999. *The Rites of Men: Manhood, Politics, and the Culture of Sport.* Toronto: University of Toronto Press.

Calavita, Kitty. 1984. *U.S. Immigration Law and the Control of Labor, 1820–1924.* London: Academic Press.

———. 1992. *Inside the State: The Bracero Program, Immigration, and the INS.* New York: Routledge.

———. 2007. *Law, Immigration, and Exclusion in Italy and Spain.* Barcelona: Universitat Autònoma de Barcelona, Department of Sociology.

Campbell, John L. 2002. "Ideas, Politics, and Public Policy." *Annual Review of Sociology* 28: 21–38.

———. 2004. *Institutional Change and Globalization.* Princeton, N.J.: Princeton University Press.

Carsten, Janet. 2002. "Substantivism, Antisubstantivism, and Anti-antisubstantivism." In *Relative Values: Reconfiguring Kinship Studies,* edited by Sarah Franklin, and Susan McKinnon. Durham, N.C.: Duke University Press.

Carter, Susan B., Scott Sigmund Gartner, Michael R. Haines, Alan L. Olmstead, Richard Sutch, and Gavin Wright, eds. 2006. *Historical Statistics of the United States: Millennial Edition Online.* New York: Cambridge University Press.

Center for Migration Studies of New York, Inc. 1964. "The Immigration and Nationality Act of 1952 as Amended Through 1961." *International Migration Digest* 1(1, Spring): 34–46.

Chan, Sucheng. 1986. *This Bittersweet Soil: The Chinese in California Agriculture, 1860–1910.* Berkeley: University of California Press.

———. 1991. "The Exclusion of Chinese Women, 1870–1943." In *Entry Denied: Exclusion and the Chinese Community in America, 1882–1943,* edited by Sucheng Chan. Philadelphia: Temple University Press.

Chang, Grace. 2000. *Disposable Domestics: Immigrant Women Workers in the Global Economy.* Cambridge, Mass.: South End Press.

Chavez, Leo R. 2004. "A Glass Half Empty: Latina Reproduction and Public Discourse." *Human Organization* 63(2): 173–88.

———. 2008. *The Latino Threat: Constructing Immigrants, Citizens, and the Nation.* Stanford, Calif.: Stanford University Press.

Chin, Gabriel J. 1996. "The Civil Rights Revolution Comes to Immigration Law: A New Look at the Immigration and Nationality Act of 1965." *North Carolina Law Review* 75: 273–345.

Chiswick, Barry R. 1988. "Illegal Immigration and Immigration Control." *Journal of Economic Perspectives* 2(3, Summer): 101–15.

Chou, Rosalind, and Joe R. Feagin. 2008. *The Myth of the Model Minority: Asian Americans Facing Racism.* Boulder, Colo.: Paradigm Publishers.

Collins, Patricia Hill. 1998. "It's All in the Family: Intersections of Gender, Race, and Nation." *Hypatia* ("Border Crossings: Multicultural and Postcolonial Feminist Challenges to Philosophy") 13(3, pt. 2, Summer): 62–82.

———. 2001. "'Like One of the Family': Race, Ethnicity, and the Paradox of U.S. National Identity." *Ethnic and Racial Studies* 24(1, January): 3–28.

Connelly, Mark Thomas. 1980. *The Response to Prostitution in the Progressive Era.* Chapel Hill: University of North Carolina Press.

Coontz, Stephanie. 1992. *The Way We Never Were: American Families and the Nostalgia Trap.* New York: Basic Books.

Cornelius, Wayne A., Philip L. Martin, and James Frank Hollifield. 1994. *Controlling Immigration: A Global Perspective.* Stanford, Calif.: Stanford University Press.

Cott, Nancy F. 1988. "Marriage and Women's Citizenship in the United States, 1830–1934." *American Historical Review* 103(5): 1440–74.

——. 2000. *Public Vows: A History of Marriage and the Nation.* Cambridge, Mass.: Harvard University Press.

Courtwright, David T. 1996. *Violent Land: Single Men and Social Disorder from the Frontier to the Inner City.* Cambridge, Mass.: Harvard University Press.

Coutin, Susan Bibler. 2007. *Nations of Emigrants: Shifting Boundaries of Citizenship in El Salvador and the United States.* Ithaca, N.Y.: Cornell University Press.

Daniels, Roger. 1977. *The Politics of Prejudice: The Anti-Japanese Movement in California and the Struggle for Japanese Exclusion.* Berkeley: University of California Press.

——. 1988. *Asian America: Chinese and Japanese in the United States Since 1850.* Seattle: University of Washington Press.

——. 1990. *Coming to America: A History of Immigration and Ethnicity in American Life.* New York: HarperCollins.

D'Appollonia, Ariane Chebel. 2012. *Frontiers of Fear: Immigration and Insecurity in the United States and Europe.* Ithaca, N.Y.: Cornell University Press.

Davis, F. James. 1991. *Who Is Black? One Nation's Definition.* University Park: Pennsylvania State University Press.

DeLaet, Debra L. 2000. *U.S. Immigration Policy in an Age of Rights.* Westport, Conn.: Praeger.

DIANE Publishing Co. 1995. *Immigration and Nationality Act (1995).* Prepared for the use of the Committee on the Judiciary of the House of Representatives, 104th Cong., 1st sess. Darby, Penn.: DIANE Publishing Co.

DiMaggio, Paul. 1997. "Culture and Cognition." *Annual Review of Sociology* 23: 263–87.

Donato, Katharine M., J. Trent Alexander, Donna R. Gabaccia, and Johanna Leinonen. 2011. "Variations in the Gender Composition of Immigrant Populations: How and Why They Matter." *International Migration Review* 45(3): 295–526.

Donato, Katharine M., Jorge Durand, and Douglas S. Massey. 1992. "Stemming the Tide? Assessing the Deterrent Effects of the Immigration Reform and Control Act." *Demography* 29(2): 139–57.

Donato, Katharine M., Donna R. Gabaccia, Jennifer Holdaway, Martin Manalansan IV, and Patricia R. Pessar. 2006. "A Glass Half Full? Gender in Migration Studies." *International Migration Review* 40(1): 3–26.

Donovan, Brian. 2006. *White Slave Crusaders: Race, Gender, and Anti-Vice Activism, 1887–1917.* Urbana: University of Illinois Press.

Douglas, Mary. 2002. *Purity and Danger: An Analysis of Concept of Pollution and Taboo.* London: Routledge.

Dudziak, Mary L. 2000. *Cold War Civil Rights: Race and the Image of American Democracy.* Princeton, N.J.: Princeton University Press.

Edelman, Murray J. 1964. *The Symbolic Uses of Politics.* Urbana: University of Illinois Press.

Espiritu, Yen Le. 1997. *Asian American Women and Men: Labor, Laws, and Love.* Thousand Oaks, Calif.: Sage Publications.

Ewick, Patricia, and Susan S. Silbey. 1995. "Subversive Stories and Hegemonic Tales: Toward a Sociology of Narrative." *Law and Society Review* 29: 197–226.

Fassin, Didier. 2011. "The Mystery Child and the Politics of Reproduction: Between National Imaginaries and Transnational Confrontations." In *Reproduction, Globalization, and the State: New Theoretical and Ethnographic Perspectives,* edited by Carole H. Browner and Carolyn Fishel Sargent. Durham, N.C.: Duke University Press.

Fetner, Tina. 2008. *How the Religious Right Shaped Lesbian and Gay Activism.* Minneapolis: University of Minnesota Press.

Fix, Michael E., ed. 2009. *Immigrants and Welfare: The Impact of Welfare Reform on America's Newcomers.* New York: Russell Sage Foundation.

Fix, Michael, and Wendy Zimmerman. 1999. *All Under One Roof: Mixed-Status Families in an Era of Reform.* Washington, D.C.: Urban Institute.

Fobanjong, John. 2001. *Understanding the Backlash Against Affirmative Action.* Huntington, N.Y.: Nova Science Publishers.

Foner, Nancy. 1997. "The Immigrant Family: Cultural Legacies and Cultural Changes." *International Migration Review* 31(4): 961–74.

———. 2005. *In a New Land: A Comparative View of Immigration.* New York: New York University Press.

Frank, Arthur W. 2010. *Letting Stories Breathe: A Socio-Narratology.* Chicago: University of Chicago Press.

Franzosi, Roberto. 1998. "Narrative Analysis—or Why (and How) Sociologists Should Be Interested in Narrative." *Annual Review of Sociology* 24: 517–54.

Freeman, Gary. 1998. "The Decline of Sovereignty: Politics and Immigration Restriction in Liberal States." In *Challenge to the Nation-State: Immigration to Western Europe and the United States,* edited by Christian Joppke. Oxford: Oxford University Press.

Friedman, Barbara G. 2007. *From the Battlefront to the Bridal Suite: Media Coverage of British War Brides, 1921–1946.* Columbia: University of Missouri Press.

Fujiwara, Lynn. 2008. *Mothers Without Citizenship: Asian Immigrant Families and the Consequences of Welfare Reform.* Minneapolis: University of Minnesota Press.

Gabaccia, Donna R. 1994. *From the Other Side: Women, Gender, and Immigrant Life in the United States, 1820–1990.* Bloomington: Indiana University Press.

———. 2010a. "Nations of Immigrants: Do Words Matter?" *The Pluralist* 5(3, Fall): 5–31.

———. 2010b. "Response to Marilyn Fischer, Jose Jorge Mendoza, and Celia Bardwell-Jones." *The Pluralist* 5(3, Fall): 56–62.

Gal, Susan, and Gail Kligman. 2000a. *Reproducing Gender: Politics, Publics, and Everyday Life After Socialism.* Princeton, N.J.: Princeton University Press.

———. 2000b. *The Politics of Gender After Socialism: A Comparative-Historical Essay.* Princeton, N.J.: Princeton University Press.

Gallup, George H. 1972. *The Gallup Poll: Public Opinion, 1935–1972.* New York: Random House.

Gamson, William A. 1992. *Talking Politics.* Cambridge: Cambridge University Press.

Gardner, Martha. 2005. *The Qualities of a Citizen: Women, Immigration, and Citizenship, 1870–1965.* Princeton, N.J.: Princeton University Press.

Gee, Jennifer. 2003. "Housewives, Men's Villages, and Sexual Respectability: Gender and the Interrogation of Asian Women at the Angel Island Immigration Station." In *Asian/Pacific Islander American Women: A Historical Anthology,* edited by Shirley Hune and Gail Nomura. New York: New York University Press.

Gellner, Ernest. 1983. *Nations and Nationalism.* Ithaca, N.Y.: Cornell University Press.

Gimpel, James G., and James R. Edwards Jr. 1999. *The Congressional Politics of Immigration Reform, 1982–1994.* Boston: Allyn and Bacon.

Glenn, Evelyn Nakano. 1983. "Split Household, Small Producer, and Dual Wage Earner: An Analysis of Chinese-American Family Strategies." *Journal of Marriage and the Family* 45(1): 35–46.

———. 1986. *Issei, Nisei, War Bride: Three Generations of Japanese American Women in Domestic Service.* Philadelphia: Temple University Press.

Golash-Boza, Tanya Maria. 2011. *Immigration Nation: Raids, Detentions, and Deportations in Post-9/11 America.* Boulder, Colo.: Paradigm Publishers.

Gonzalez, Gilbert G. 2006. *Guest Workers or Colonized Labor? Mexican Labor Migration to the United States.* Boulder, Colo.: Paradigm Publishers.

Gordon, Linda. 1994. *Pitied but Not Entitled: Single Mothers and the History of Welfare, 1890–1935.* New York: Free Press.

———. 2007. *The Moral Property of Women: A History of Birth Control Politics in America.* Urbana: University of Illinois Press.

Grillo, Ralph. 2009. *The Family in Question: Immigrant and Ethnic Minorities in Multicultural Europe.* Amsterdam: Amsterdam University Press.

Guiraudon, Virginie. 1998. "Citizenship Rights for Noncitizens: France, Germany, and the Netherlands." In *Challenge to the Nation-State: Immigration to Western Europe and the United States,* edited by Christian Joppke. Oxford: Oxford University Press.

Gutiérrez, David Gregory. 1995. *Walls and Mirrors: Mexican Americans, Mexican Immigrants, and the Politics of Ethnicity.* Berkeley: University of California Press.

Gyory, Andrew. 1998. *Closing the Gate: Race, Politics, and the Chinese Exclusion Act.* Chapel Hill: University of North Carolina Press.

Hacker, Jacob S. 2002. *The Divided Welfare State: The Battle over Public and Private Social Benefits in the United States.* New York: Cambridge University Press.

Hacking, Ian. 1999. *The Social Construction of What?* Cambridge, Mass.: Harvard University Press.

Haney López, Ian. 1996. *White by Law: The Legal Construction of Race.* New York: New York University Press.

Harwood, Edwin. 1986. "American Public Opinion and U.S. Immigration Policy." *Annals of the American Academy of Political and Social Science* 287: 201–12.

Hein, Jeremy. 1995. *From Vietnam, Laos, and Cambodia: A Refugee Experience in the United States.* New York: Twayne Publishers.

Higham, John. 2002. *Strangers in the Land: Patterns of American Nativism, 1860–1925.* New Brunswick, N.J.: Rutgers University Press.

Hing, Bill Ong. 1993. *Making and Remaking Asian America Through Immigration Policy, 1850–1990.* Stanford, Calif.: Stanford University Press.

Hinterberger, Amy. 2012a. "Categorization, Census, and Multiculturalism: Molecular Politics and the Material of Nation." In *Genetics and the Unsettled Past: The Collision of DNA, Race, and History,* edited by Keith Wailoo, Alondra Nelson, and Catherine Lee. New Brunswick, N.J.: Rutgers University Press.

———. 2012b. "Investing in Life, Investing in Difference: Nations, Populations, and Genomes." *Theory, Culture, and Society* 29(3, May): 72–93.

Hirata, Lucie Cheng. 1979. "Free, Indentured, Enslaved: Chinese Prostitutes in Nineteenth-Century America." *Signs* 5(1, Autumn): 3–29.

Hobsbawm, Eric J., and Terence O. Ranger. 1983. *The Invention of Tradition.* Cambridge: Cambridge University Press.

Hobson, Barbara Meil. 1987. *Uneasy Virtue: The Politics of Prostitution and the American Reform Tradition.* New York: Basic Books.

Hoefer, Michael, Nancy Rytina, and Bryan Baker. 2012. "Estimates of the Unauthorized Immigrant Population Residing in the United States: January 2011." *Population Estimates* (March): 1–7. Available at: http://www.dhs.gov/xlibrary/assets/statistics/publications/ois_ill_pe_2011.pdf (accessed February 24, 2013).

Höhn, Maria. 2002. *GIs and Fräuleins: The German-American Encounter in 1950s West Germany.* Chapel Hill: University of North Carolina Press.

Hondagneu-Sotelo, Pierrette. 1994. *Gendered Transitions: Mexican Experiences of Immigration.* Berkeley: University of California Press.

Houstoun, Marion F., et al. 1984. "Female Predominance in Immigration to the United States Since 1930: A First Look." *International Migration Review* (special issue: "Women in Migration") 18(4, Winter): 908–63.

Hsu, Madeline Y. 2002. *Dreaming of Gold, Dreaming of Home: Transnationalism and Migration Between the United States and South China, 1882–1943.* Stanford, Calif.: Stanford University Press.

Huang, Priscilla. 2008. "Anchor Babies, Over-Breeders, and the Population Bomb: The Reemergence of Nativism and Population Control in Anti-Immigration Policies." *Harvard Law and Policy Review* 2(2): 385–406.

Hutchinson, Edward P. 1981. *Legislative History of American Immigration Policy, 1798–1965.* Philadelphia: University of Pennsylvania Press.

Ichioka, Yuji. 1988. *The Issei: The World of the First-Generation Japanese Immigrants, 1885–1924.* New York: Free Press.

Ignatiev, Noel. 1995. *How the Irish Became White.* New York: Routledge.

Ingram, Helen M., and Anne L. Schneider. 1993. "Social Construction of Target Populations." *American Political Science Review* 87(2): 334–47.

———. 2005. "Public Policy and the Social Construction of Deservedness." In *Deserving and Entitled: Social Constructions and Public Policy,* edited by Anne L. Schneider and Helen M. Ingram. Albany: State University of New York Press.

Jacobson, David. 1996. *Rights Across Borders: Immigration and the Decline of Citizenship.* Baltimore: Johns Hopkins University Press.

Jacobson, Matthew Frye. 1998. *Whiteness of a Different Color: European Immigrants and the Alchemy of Race.* Cambridge, Mass.: Harvard University Press.

Jasper, James M. 1997. *The Art of Moral Protest: Culture, Biography, and Creativity in Social Movements.* Chicago: University of Chicago Press.

Jasso, Guillermina, and Mark R. Rosenzweig. 1986. "Family Reunification and the Immigration Multiplier: U.S. Immigration Law, Origin-Country Conditions, and the Reproduction of Immigrants." *Demography* 23(3): 291–311.

——. 1989. "Sponsors, Sponsorship Rates, and the Immigration Multiplier." *International Migration Review* 23(4): 856–88.

——. 1990. *The New Chosen People: Immigrants in the United States.* New York: Russell Sage Foundation.

——. 1995. "Do Immigrants Screened for Skills Do Better Than Family Reunification Immigrants?" *International Migration Review* 29(1): 85–111.

Jiménez, Tomás R. 2010. *Replenished Ethnicity: Mexican Americans, Immigration, and Identity.* Berkeley: University of California Press.

Joppke, Christian, ed. 1998. *Challenge to the Nation-State: Immigration in Western Europe and the United States.* Oxford: Oxford University Press.

——. 1999. *Immigration and the Nation-State: The United States, Germany, and Great Britain.* Oxford: Oxford University Press.

Kanstroom, Dan. 2007. *Deportation Nation: Outsiders in American History.* Cambridge, Mass.: Harvard University Press.

——. 2012. *Aftermath: Deportation Law and the New American Diaspora.* Oxford: Oxford University Press.

Keely, Charles B. 1975. "Immigration Composition and Population Policy." In *Population: Dynamics, Ethics, and Policy,* edited by Priscilla Reining and Irene Tinker. Washington, D.C.: American Association for the Advancement of Science.

Kevles, Daniel J. 1985. *In the Name of Eugenics: Genetics and the Uses of Human Heredity.* New York: Knopf.

Kim, Claire Jean. 1999. "The Racial Triangulation of Asian Americans." *Politics and Society* 27(1): 105–38.

Kim, Nadia. 2008. *Imperial Citizens: Koreans and Race from Seoul to LA.* Palo Alto, Calif.: Stanford University Press.

King, Desmond S. 2000. *Making Americans: Immigration, Race, and the Origins of the Diverse Democracy.* Cambridge, Mass.: Harvard University Press.

King, Russell, Mark Thomson, Tony Fielding, and Tony Warnes. 2006. "Time, Generations, and Gender in Migration and Settlement." In *The Dynamics of International Migration and Settlement in Europe: A State of the Art,* edited by Rinus Penninx, Maria Berger, and Karen Kraal. Amsterdam: Amsterdam University Press.

Kligman, Gail. 1998. *The Politics of Duplicity: Controlling Reproduction in Ceausescu's Romania.* Berkeley: University of California Press.

Kline, Wendy. 2001. *Building a Better Race: Gender, Sexuality, and Eugenics from the Turn of the Century to the Baby Boom.* Berkeley: University of California Press.

Kofman, Eleonore. 2004. "Family-Related Migration: A Critical Review of European Studies." *Journal of Ethnic and Migration Studies* 30(2): 243–62.

Kohli-Laven, Nina. 2012. "French Families, Paper Facts: Genetics, Nation, and Explanation." In *Genetics and the Unsettled Past: The Collision of DNA, Race, and History,* edited by Keith Wailoo, Alondra Nelson, and Catherine Lee. New Brunswick, N.J.: Rutgers University Press.

Koven, Seth, and Sonya Michel. 1993. *Mothers of a New World: Maternalist Politics and the Origins of Welfare States.* New York: Routledge.

Kraler, Albert. 2010. "Civic Stratification, Gender, and Family Migration Policies in Europe." New Orientations for Democracy in Europe (NODE) Final Report. Vienna: International Centre for Migration Policy Development (ICMPD) (May). Available at: http://research.icmpd.org/fileadmin/Research-Website/Project_material/NODE/FINAL_Report_Family_Migration_Policies_Online_FINAL.pdf (accessed November 3, 2012)

Lakoff, George. 2004. *Don't Think of an Elephant: Know Your Values and Frame the Debate.* White River Junction, Vt.: Chelsea Green Publishing.

Lan, Pei Chai. 2008. "Migrant Women's Bodies as Boundary Markers: Reproductive Crisis and Sexual Control in the Ethnic Frontier of Taiwan." *Signs* 33(4): 833–62.

Lau, Estelle T. 2006. *Paper Families: Identity, Immigration Administration, and Chinese Exclusion.* Durham, N.C.: Duke University Press.

Law, Anna O. 2002. "The Diversity Visa Lottery: A Cycle of Unintended Consequences in United States Immigration Policy." *Journal of American Ethnic History* 21(4, Summer): 3–29.

Leahy, Sen. Patrick (D-VT). 2013, March 18. "How Comprehensive Immigration Reform Should Address the Needs of Women and Families." Senate Judiciary Committee, March 18, 2013. Available at: http://www.judiciary.senate.gov/pdf/3-18-13LeahyStatement.pdf (accessed March 25, 2013).

Lee, Catherine. 2003. "Settling the Nation: Race, Gender, and Chinese and Japanese Immigration to the United States, 1870–1924." PhD diss., University of California, Los Angeles.

———. 2010. "'Where the Danger Lies': Race, Gender, and Chinese and Japanese Exclusion in the United States, 1870–1924." *Sociological Forum* 25(2, June): 248–71.

———. 2012. "The Unspoken Significance of Gender in Constructing Kinship, Race, and Nation." In *Genetics and the Unsettled Past: The Collision of DNA, Race, and History,* edited by Keith Wailoo, Alondra Nelson, and Catherine Lee. New Brunswick, N.J.: Rutgers University Press.

Lee, Erika. 2003. *At America's Gates: Chinese Immigration During the Exclusion Era, 1882–1943.* Chapel Hill: University of North Carolina Press.

Lee, Erika, and Judy Yung. 2010. *Angel Island: Immigrant Gateway to America.* Oxford: Oxford University Press.

Lee, Jennifer, and Frank D. Bean. 2010. *The Diversity Paradox: Immigration and the Color Line in Twenty-First-Century America.* New York: Russell Sage Foundation.

Leonard, Karen. 2010. *Making Ethnic Choices: California's Punjabi Mexican Americans.* Philadelphia: Temple University Press.

Lien, Pei-te, M. Margaret Conway, and Janelle Wong. 2004. *The Politics of Asian America: Diversity and Community.* New York: Routledge.

Limoncelli, Stephanie A. 2010. *The Politics of Trafficking: The First International Movement to Combat the Sexual Exploitation of Women.* Stanford, Calif.: Stanford University Press.

Lin, Ji-Ping. 2012. "Tradition and Progress: Taiwan's Evolving Migration Policy." *Migration Information Source* (January). Available at: http://www.migrationinformation.org/Profiles/print.cfm?ID=877 (accessed November 3, 2012).

——. 1998. "Race and Erasure: The Salience of Race to Latinos/as." In *The Latino/a Condition: A Critical Reader,* edited by Richard Delgado and Jean Stefancic. New York: New York University Press.

Lovett, Laura L. 2007. *Conceiving the Future: Pronatalism, Reproduction, and the Family in the United States, 1890–1938.* Chapel Hill: University of North Carolina Press.

Lyman, Stanford M. 1974. *Chinese Americans.* New York: Random House.

Majone, Giandomenico. 1989. *Evidence, Argument, and Persuasion in the Policy Process.* New Haven, Conn.: Yale University Press.

Massey, Douglas S. 1990. "Social Structure, Household Strategies, and the Cumulative Causation of Migration." *Population Index* 56(1): 3–26.

——. 2009. "The Political Economy of Migration in an Era of Globalization." In *International Migration and Human Rights: The Global Repercussions of U.S. Policy,* edited by Samuel Martinez. Berkeley: University of California Press.

Massey, Douglas S., Joaquin Arango, Graeme Hugo, Ali Kouaouci, Adela Pellegrino, and J. Edward Taylor. 1998. *Worlds in Motion: Understanding International Migration at the End of the Millennium.* Oxford: Clarendon Press.

Massey, Douglas S. Jorge Durand, and Nolan J. Malone. 2002. *Beyond Smoke and Mirrors: Mexican Immigration in an Era of Economic Integration.* New York: Russell Sage Foundation.

Massey, Douglas S., Luin Goldring, and Jorge Durand. 1994. "Continuities in Transnational Migration: An Analysis of Nineteen Mexican Communities." *American Journal of Sociology* 99(6): 1492–1533.

Massey, Douglas S., and Emilio Parrado. 1994. "Migradollars: The Remittances and Savings of Mexican Migrants to the USA." *Population Research and Policy Review* 13: 3–30.

Massey, Douglas S., and Magaly Sánchez. 2010. *Brokered Boundaries: Creating Immigrant Identity in Anti-Immigrant Times.* New York: Russell Sage Foundation.

McClain, Charles J. 1994a. *Chinese Immigrants and American Law.* New York: Garland Publishing.

——. 1994b. *In Search of Equality: The Chinese Struggle Against Discrimination in Nineteenth-Century America.* Berkeley: University of California Press.

Meissner, Doris M., Robert D. Hormats, Antonio Garrigues Walker, and Shijuro Ogata. 1993. *International Migration Challenges in a New Era: Policy Perspectives and Priorities for Europe, Japan, North America, and the International Community.* New York: Trilateral Commission.

Métraux, Daniel A. 2010. "Jack London: The Adventurer-Writer Who Chronicled Asian Wars, Confronted Racism—and Saw the Future." *Asia-Pacific Journal* 4(3, January 25).

Meznaric, Silva. 1994. "Gender as an Ethno-Marker: Rape, War, and Identity Politics in the Former Yugoslavia." In *Identity Politics and Women: Cultural Reassertions and Feminisms in International Perspective,* edited by Valentine M. Moghadam. Boulder, Colo.: Westview.

Miller, Stuart Creighton. 1969. *The Unwelcome Immigrant: The American Image of the Chinese, 1785–1882.* Berkeley: University of California Press.

Mink, Gwendolyn. 1986. *Old Labor and New Immigrants in American Political Development: Union, Party, and State, 1875–1920.* Ithaca, N.Y.: Cornell University Press.

Mitchell, Christopher. 1992. "Introduction: Immigration and U.S. Foreign Policy Toward the Caribbean, Central America, and Mexico." In *Western Hemisphere Immigration and United States Foreign Policy,* edited by Christopher Mitchell. University Park: Pennsylvania State University Press.

Mize, Ronald L., and Allicia C. S. Swords. 2010. *Consuming Mexican Labor: From the Bracero Program to NAFTA.* Toronto: University of Toronto Press.

Moch, Leslie Page. 2005. "Gender and Migration Research." In *International Migration Research: Constructions, Omissions, and the Promises of Interdisciplinarity,* edited by Michael Bommes and Ewa Morawska. Aldershot, U.K.: Ashgate.

Moore, Mignon R. 2011. *Invisible Families: Gay Identities, Relationships, and Motherhood Among Black Women.* Berkeley: University of California Press.

Moran, Rachel F. 2001. *Interracial Intimacy: The Regulation of Race and Romance.* Chicago: University of Chicago Press.

Morris, Lydia. 2003. "Managing Contradiction: Civic Stratification and Migrants' Rights." *International Migration Review* 37(1): 74–100.

Mosse, George L. 1985. *Nationalism and Sexuality: Respectability and Abnormal Sexuality in Modern Europe.* New York: Howard Fertig.

Mostov, Julie. 1996. "Endangered Citizenship." In *Russia and Eastern Europe After Communism,* edited by Michael Kraus and Ronald D. Liebowitz. New York: Westview.

Nagel, Joanne. 1998. "Masculinity and Nationalism: Gender and Sexuality in the Making of Nations." *Ethnic and Racial Studies* 21(2, March): 242–69.

Napolitano, Janet. 2012. "Exercising Prosecutorial Discretion with Respect to Individuals Who Came to the United States as Children" (memorandum), June 15. Available at: http://www.dhs.gov/xlibrary/assets/s1-exercising-prosecutorial-discretion-individuals-who-came-to-us-as-children.pdf (accessed November 3, 2012).

Nash, Gary B. 1999. "The Hidden History of Mestizo America." In *Sex, Love, Race:*

Crossing Boundaries in North American History, edited by Martha Hodes. New York: New York University Press.

Nauck, Bernhard, and Barbara H. Settles. 2001. "Immigrant and Ethnic Minority Families: An Introduction." *Journal of Comparative Family Studies* 32(4): 461–63.

Nelson, Alonda. 2008. "Bio Science: Genetic Genealogy Testing and the Pursuit of African Ancestry." *Social Studies of Science* 38(5, October): 759–83.

———. 2012. "Reconciliation Projects: From Kinship to Justice." In *Genetics and the Unsettled Past: The Collision of DNA, Race, and History*, edited by Keith Wailoo, Alondra Nelson, and Catherine Lee. New Brunswick, N.J.: Rutgers University Press.

Ness, Immanuel. 2011. *Guest Workers and Resistance to U.S. Corporate Despotism.* Urbana: University of Illinois Press.

Neubeck, Kenneth J., and Noel A. Cazenave. 2001. *Welfare Racism: Playing the Race Card Against America's Poor.* New York: Routledge.

Newton, Lina. 2008. *Illegal, Alien, or Immigrant: The Politics of Immigration Reform.* New York: New York University Press.

Ngai, Mae M. 1999. "The Architecture of Race in American Immigration Law: A Reexamination of the Immigration Act of 1924." *Journal of American History* 86(1): 67–92.

———. 2004. *Impossible Subjects: Illegal Aliens and the Making of Modern America.* Princeton, N.J.: Princeton University Press.

O'Brien, David J., and Stephen Fugita. 1991. *The Japanese American Experience.* Bloomington: Indiana University Press.

Ordover, Nancy. 2002. *American Eugenics: Race, Queer Anatomy, and the Science of Nationalism.* Minneapolis: University of Minnesota Press.

Organization for Economic Cooperation and Development. 2001. *Trends in International Migration 2001: Continuing Reporting System on Migration.* Paris: OECD Publishing.

———. 2012. *International Migration Outlook 2012: Trends in International Migration Flows and in the Immigrant Population.* Paris: OECD Publishing.

Park, Edward J., and John S. Park. 2005. *Probationary Americans: Contemporary Immigration Policies and the Shaping of Asian American Communities.* New York: Routledge.

Park, Lisa Sun-Hee. 2011. *Entitled to Nothing: The Struggle for Immigrant Health Care in the Age of Welfare Reform.* New York: New York University Press.

Pascoe, Peggy. 1990. *Relations of Rescue: The Search for Female Moral Authority in the American West, 1874–1939.* New York: Oxford University Press.

———. 1996. "Miscegenation Law, Court Cases, and Ideologies of 'Race' in Twentieth-Century America." *Journal of American History* 83(1, June): 44–69.

———. 2009. *What Comes Naturally: Miscegenation Law and the Making of Race in America.* New York: Oxford University Press.

Pateman, Carole. 1988. *The Sexual Contract.* Stanford, Calif.: Stanford University Press.

Peffer, George Anthony. 1999. *If They Don't Bring Their Women Here: Chinese Female Immigration Before Exclusion.* Urbana: University of Illinois Press.

Piore, Michael J. 1979. *Birds of Passage: Migrant Labor and Industrial Societies.* Cambridge: Cambridge University Press.

Polletta, Francesca. 2006. *It Was Like a Fever: Storytelling in Protest and Politics.* Chicago: University of Chicago Press.

Popenoe, David. 1993. *The Fatherhood Problem.* New York: Institute for American Values.

——. 1998. *Disturbing the Nest: Family Change and Decline in Modern Societies.* Hawthorne: Aldine de Gruyter.

Popenoe, Paul Bowman. 1926. *The Conservation of the Family.* Baltimore: Williams & Wilkins Co.

Portes, Alejandro, and Rubén G. Rumbaut. 1996. *Immigrant America: A Portrait.* Berkeley: University of California Press.

Quadagno, Jill S. 1994. *The Color of Welfare: How Racism Undermined the War on Poverty.* New York: Oxford University Press.

Reimers, David M. 1983. "An Unintended Reform: The 1965 Immigration Act and Third World Immigration to the United States." *Journal of American Ethnic History* 3(1, Fall): 9–28.

——. 1985. *Still the Golden Door: The Third World Comes to America.* New York: Columbia University Press.

——. 1998. *Unwelcome Strangers: American Identity and the Turn Against Immigration.* New York: Columbia University Press.

Riggs, Fred Warren. 1950. *Pressures on Congress: A Study of the Repeal of Chinese Exclusion.* New York: King's Crown Press.

Roberts, Dorothy E. 1997. *Killing the Black Body: Race, Reproduction, and the Meaning of Liberty.* New York: Pantheon Books.

Rodriguez, Richard T. 2009. *Next of Kin: The Family in Chicano/a Cultural Politics.* Durham, N.C.: Duke University Press.

Roediger, David R. 1991. *The Wages of Whiteness: Race and the Making of the American Working Class.* London: Verso.

Rosen, Ruth. 1982. *The Lost Sisterhood: Prostitution in America, 1900–1918.* Baltimore: Johns Hopkins University Press.

Rosenberg, Charles. 1987. *The Case of Strangers: The Rise of America's Hospital System.* New York: Basic Books.

Rumbaut, Rubén. 1997. "Ties That Bind: Immigration and Immigrant Families in the United States." In *Immigration and the Family: Research and Policy on U.S. Immigrants,* edited by Alan Booth, Ann C. Crouter, and Nancy Landale. Mahwah, N.J.: Lawrence Erlbaum Associates.

Salyer, Lucy E. 1995. *Laws Harsh as Tigers: Chinese Immigrants and the Shaping of Modern Immigration Law.* Chapel Hill: University of North Carolina Press.

——. 2004. "Baptism by Fire: Race, Military Service, and U.S. Citizenship Policy, 1918–1935." *Journal of American History* 91(3, December): 847–76.

Sapiro, Virginia. 1984. "Women, Citizenship, and Nationality: Immigration and Naturalization Policies in the United States." *Politics and Society* 13: 1–26.

Sassen, Saskia. 1988. *The Mobility of Labor and Capital: A Study in International Investment and Labor Flow.* Cambridge: Cambridge University Press.

Saxton, Alexander. 1971. *The Indispensable Enemy: Labor and the Anti-Chinese Movement in California.* Berkeley: University of California Press.

Schneider, David M. 1977. "Kinship, Nationality, and Religion in American Culture: Towards a Definition of Kinship." In *Symbolic Anthropology: A Reader in the Study of Symbols and Meanings,* edited by Janet L. Dolgin, D. S. Kemnitzer, and David M. Schneider. New York: Columbia University Press.

——. 1980. *American Kinship: A Cultural Account.* Chicago: University of Chicago Press.

"Senate Conference on Immigration." CQ Transcripts Wire, *Washington Post,* May 17, 2007.

Settles, Barbara H., Daniel E. Hanks, and Marvin B. Sussman. 1993. *Families on the Move: Migration, Immigration, Emigration, and Mobility.* New York: Haworth Press.

Shah, Nayan. 2001. *Contagious Divides: Epidemics and Race in San Francisco's Chinatown.* Berkeley: University of California Press.

Shukert, Elfrieda, and Barbara Scibetta. 1988. *War Brides of World War II.* Novato, Calif.: Presidio Press.

Simon, Rita. 1987. "Immigration and American Attitudes." *Public Opinion* 10(2): 47–50.

Sjaastad, Larry A. 1962. "The Costs and Returns of Human Migration." *Journal of Political Economy* 70S: 80–93.

Skrentny, John D. 2002. *The Minority Rights Revolution.* Cambridge, Mass.: Belknap Press of Harvard University Press.

——. 2006. "Policy-Elite Perceptions and Social Movement Success: Understanding Variations in Group Inclusion in Affirmative Action." *American Journal of Sociology* 111(6): 1762–1815.

——. 2011. "Obama's Immigration Reform: A Tough Sell for a Grand Bargain." In *Reaching for a New Deal: Ambitious Governance, Economic Meltdown, and Polarized Politics in Obama's First Two Years,* edited by Theda Skocpol and Lawrence Jacobs. New York: Russell Sage Foundation.

Skrentny, John D., Stephanie Chan, Jon Fox, and Denis Kim. 2007. "Defining Nations in Asia and Europe: A Comparative Analysis of Ethnic Return Migration Policy." *International Migration Review* 41(4, Winter): 793–825.

Smith, Rogers M. 1997. *Civic Ideals: Conflicting Visions of Citizenship in U.S. History.* New Haven, Conn.: Yale University Press.

Soysal, Yasemin. 1995. *Limits of Citizenship: Migrants and Postnational Membership in Europe.* Chicago: University of Chicago Press.

Spickard, Paul R. 1989. *Mixed Blood: Intermarriage and Ethnic Identity in Twentieth-Century America.* Madison: University of Wisconsin Press.

Stacey, Judith. 1990. *Brave New Families: Stories of Domestic Upheaval in Late Twentieth-Century America.* New York: Basic Books.

———. 1997. *In the Name of the Family: Rethinking Family Values in the Postmodern Age.* Boston: Beacon Press.

———. 2011. *Unhitched: Love, Marriage, and Family Values from West Hollywood to Western China.* New York: New York University Press.

Stacey, Judith, and Timothy J. Biblarz. 2001. "(How) Does the Sexual Orientation of Parents Matter?" *American Sociological Review* 66(2): 159–83.

Stark, Oded. 1991. *The Migration of Labor.* Cambridge, Mass.: Basil Blackwell.

Steensland, Brian. 2006. "Cultural Categories and the American Welfare State: The Case of Guaranteed Income Policy." *American Journal of Sociology* 111(5): 1273–1326.

Stevens, Todd. 2002. "Tender Ties: Husbands' Rights and Racial Exclusion in Chinese Marriage Cases, 1882–1924." *Law and Social Inquiry* 27(2): 271–305.

Stone, Deborah. 1989. "Causal Stories and the Formation of Policy Agendas." *Political Science Quarterly* 104: 281–300.

———. 2002. *Policy Paradox: The Art of Political Decision Making.* New York: Norton.

Strach, Patricia. 2007. *All in the Family: The Private Roots of American Public Policy.* Stanford, Calif.: Stanford University Press.

Sugarman, Stephen D. 2008. "What Is a 'Family'? Conflicting Messages from Our Public Programs." *Family Law Quarterly* 42(2): 231–61.

Swarns, Rachel L. "DNA Tests Offer Immigrants Hope or Despair." *New York Times,* April 10, 2007.

Swidler, Ann. 1986. "Culture in Action: Symbols and Strategies." *American Sociological Review* 51(2): 273–86.

Takaki, Ronald T. 1998. *Strangers from a Different Shore: A History of Asian Americans.* Updated and revised edition. Boston: Little, Brown. (Originally published in 1989.)

———. 1998. *Iron Cages: Race and Culture in Nineteenth-Century America.* New York: Knopf.

Taylor, Paul, Mark Hugo Lopez, Jeffrey Passel, and Seth Motel. 2011. "Unauthorized Immigrants: Length of Residency, Patterns of Parenthood." Washington, D.C.: Pew Research Hispanic Center (December 1). Available at: http://www.pewhispanic.org/2011/12/01/unauthorized-immigrants-length-of-residency-patterns-of-parenthood/#fn-9726-3 (accessed May 21, 2013).

Tichenor, Daniel J. 2002. *Dividing Lines: The Politics of Immigration Control in America.* Princeton, N.J.: Princeton University Press.

Ting, Jennifer. 1995. "Bachelor Society: Deviant Heterosexuality and Asian American Historiography." In *Privileging Positions: The Sites of Asian American Studies,* edited by Gary Okihiro et al. Pullman: Washington State University Press.

Todaro, Michael P. 1969. "A Model of Labor Migration and Urban Unemployment in Less-Developed Countries." *American Economic Review* 59: 138–48.

———. 1976. *Internal Migration in Developing Countries.* Geneva: International Labor Office.

——. 1989. *Economic Development in the Third World*. New York: Longman.

Todaro, Michael P., and Lydia Maruszko. 1987. "Illegal Migration and U.S. Immigration Reform: A Conceptual Framework." *Population and Development Review* 13: 101–14.

Tomes, Nancy. 1990. "The Private Side of Public Health: Sanitary Science, Domestic Hygiene,m and the Germ Theory, 1870–1900." *Bulletin of the History of Medicine* 64: 509–39.

———. 1999. *Gospel of Germs: Men, Women, and the Microbe in American Life*. Cambridge, Mass.: Harvard University Press.

Tsuda, Takeyuki. 2008. "Local Citizenship and Foreign Workers in Japan." *Asia-Pacific Journal: Japan Focus,* May 26. Available at: http://japanfocus.org/-Takeyuki-Tsuda/2762 (accessed November 3, 2012).

Tuan, Mia. 1998. *Forever Foreigners or Honorary Whites? The Asian Ethnic Experience Today*. New Brunswick, N.J.: Rutgers University Press.

Tucker, William H. 2002. *The Funding of Scientific Racism: Wickliffe Draper and the Pioneer Fund*. Urbana: University of Illinois Press.

United States and William P. Dillingham. 1993. *Reports of the Immigration Commission, 1907–1910*. Wilmington, Del.: Scholarly Resources.

United States and Charles Erwin Wilson. 1947. *To Secure These Rights: The Report of the President's Committee on Civil Rights*. New York: Simon & Schuster.

U.S. Department of Justice. Various years. *Annual Report of the Immigration and Naturalization Service*. Washington: U.S. Department of Justice.

Vasquez, Jessica M. 2011. *Mexican Americans Across Generations: Immigrant Families, Racial Realities*. New York: New York University Press.

Wailoo, Keith, Alondra Nelson, and Catherine Lee, eds. 2012. *Genetics and the Unsettled Past: The Collision of DNA, Race, and History*. New Brunswick, N.J.: Rutgers University Press.

Wald, Priscilla. 2012. "Cells, Genes, and Stories: HeLa's Journey from Labs to Literature." In *Genetics and the Unsettled Past: The Collision of DNA, Race, and History,* edited by Keith Wailoo, Alondra Nelson, and Catherine Lee. New Brunswick, N.J.: Rutgers University Press.

Warner, Michael. 1999. *The Trouble with Normal: Sex, Politics, and the Ethics of Queer Life*. New York: Free Press.

Wasem, Ruth Ellen. 2012. "Unauthorized Aliens' Access to Federal Benefits: Policy and Issues." *Congressional Research Service* RL34500 (September 17). Available at: http://www.fas.org/sgp/crs/homesec/RL34500.pdf (accessed February 24, 2013).

Waters, Mary C. 1990. *Ethnic Options: Choosing Identities in America*. Berkeley: University of California Press.

——. 1997. "Immigrant Families at Risk: Factors That Undermine Chances for Success." In *Immigration and the Family: Research and Policy on U.S. Immigrants,* edited by Alan Booth, Ann C. Crouter, and Nancy Landale. Mahwah, N.J.: Lawrence Erlbaum Associates.

Weber, Max. 1958. *The Protestant Ethic and the Spirit of Capitalism*. New York: Scribner.

Weeks, Jeffrey, Brian Heaphy, and Catherine Donovan. 2001. *Same-Sex Intimacies: Families of Choice and Other Life Experiments.* London: Routledge.

Weston, Kath. 1991. *Families We Choose: Lesbians, Gays, Kinship.* New York: Columbia University Press.

Wisensale, Steven K. 2001. *Family Leave Policy: The Political Economy of Work and Family in America.* Armonk, N.Y.: M. E. Sharpe.

Wolgin, Philip. 2011. "Beyond National Origins: The Development of Modern Immigration Policymaking, 1948–1968." PhD diss., University of California–Berkeley.

Wolgin, Philip E., and Irene Bloemraad. 2010. "'Our Gratitude to Our Soldiers': Military Spouses, Family Reunification, and Postwar Immigration Reform." *Journal of Interdisciplinary History* 41(1): 27–60.

Wong, Janelle S., Karthick Ramakrishnan, Taeku Lee, and Jane Junn. 2011. *Asian American Political Participation: Emerging Constituents and Their Political Identities.* New York: Russell Sage Foundation.

Wong, K. Scott. 2005. *Americans First: Chinese Americans and the Second World War.* Cambridge, Mass.: Harvard University Press.

Wu, Frank H. 1995. "Neither Black nor White: Asian Americans and Affirmative Action." *Boston College Third World Law Journal* 15(2): 225–84. Available at: http://lawdigitalcommons.bc.edu/twlj/vol15/iss2/1 (accessed November 3, 2012).

Wu, William F. 1982. *The Yellow Peril: Chinese-Americans in American Fiction, 1850–1940.* Hamden, Conn.: Archon Books.

Yoshikawa, Hirokazu. 2011. *Immigrants Raising Citizens: Undocumented Parents and Their Young Children.* New York: Russell Sage Foundation.

Yu, Bin. 2008. *Chain Migration Explained: The Power of the Immigration Multiplier.* New York: LFB Scholarly Publishing.

Zeiger, Susan. 2010. *Entangling Alliances: Foreign War Brides and American Soldiers in the Twentieth Century.* New York: New York University Press.

Zerubavel, Eviatar. 1997. *Social Mindscapes: An Invitation to Cognitive Sociology.* Cambridge, Mass.: Harvard University Press.

———. 2012. *Ancestors and Relatives: Genealogy, Identity, and Community.* Oxford: Oxford University Press.

Zhao, Xiaojian. 2002. *Remaking Chinese America: Immigration, Family, and Community, 1940–1965.* New Brunswick, N.J.: Rutgers University Press.

Zinn, Maxine Baca, and D. Stanley Eitzen. 1990. *Diversity in Families.* New York: Harper & Row.

Zolberg, Aristide R. 2006. *A Nation by Design: Immigration Policy in the Fashioning of America.* New York: Russell Sage Foundation/Harvard University Press.

Index

Boldface numbers refer to figures and tables.